"*Family: The Compact Among Generations* is fundamentally a book of deep, translational wisdom based on Jay Hughes's remarkable reading of philosophy, religion, and psychology as they apply to the complex journey of family life. The book is based on Hughes's lifetime of service and counsel to families of great wealth, but as I read the book and began to understand its central metaphor—"shirtsleeves to shirtsleeves in three generations"—words other than *family* kept coming to mind, words like *community*, *society*, and *citizenship*. Hughes may not have intended the metaphor to apply to the journey of the human race, but in a world precariously balanced between disastrous decline and the potential for the resolution of major social dilemmas, it is the investment in human capital and the awakening of the citizen within that will tell the difference.

"This book is a gift. Read it. And when you do, consider its wisdom from your individual and family persona and your public persona."

—PETER KAROFF
Founder and Chairman, The Philanthropic Initiative
Author of *The World We Want: New Dimensions in Philanthropy and Social Change* (AltaMira Press)

"Chapter after chapter, I marveled at how this most gifted counselor to families wove together his heart, intellect, and soul into a tapestry of discovery and profound learning on families. This book helps the rest of us—first to see the whole, then to grasp the wonder of so many interwoven threads of family business, leadership, and communications. Just glancing at the bibliography of *Family* reveals the depth and breadth of the journey in store for the reader. What a gift for those within a family, for those who advise families, and for all of us who are pilgrims on both journeys!"

—CHARLOTTE B. BEYER
Founder and CEO, Institute for Private Investors

"In the world of wealthy families, James Hughes is a seer. The knowledge presented in this book extends to any family concerned about future generations. Wisdom is scarce nowadays, but Hughes delivers an abundance of useful packets blended with insights from history and philosophy."

—JOHN O'NEIL
President, The Center for Leadership Renewal

"*Family* takes us straight to the heart of Jay Hughes's lifework, with intelligence, humility, and great insight. By inviting us *inside* his personal journey from lawyer to leader of the discipline of wealth consultation, which he helped found, *Family* tells the reader what is necessary in order to truly become a *personne de confiance*. Strategies for multigenerational family leadership, family governance, and family unity are offered in the context of Jay's personal evolution—he offers guidance on the developmental changes needed *within oneself* in order to fully understand and be effective in working with families. Even more, he brilliantly brings together key ideas from philosophy, social sciences, and religion to inform and inspire the reader's personal journey. *Family* is among the precious few books that effectively interweave high-level thinking with the emotion of a personal journey, wisdom from the heart with tactical advice. It is a book to be read and enjoyed not only by those in the field of wealth consulting/counseling but by all of us whose work and personal identity are found in the role of confidant, adviser, counselor, or coach—guided by, as *Family* prescribes, the importance of placing high value on trust, integrity, deep understanding, and humble, effective leadership."

—DR. STEPHEN GOLDBART AND JOAN DIFURIA
Codirectors, Money, Meaning & Choices Institute

"Once again, Jay has authored a timeless, essential guide on the challenges faced by generations of family wealth. *Family: The Compact Among Generations* is a must-read for everyone in the wealth-management industry and a valuable tool for patriarchs and matriarchs who must ultimately contend with the "shirt sleeves to shirt sleeves in three generations" phenomenon. Jay's new philosophical viewpoints are as relevant today as they were a thousand years ago: *The sleep of the laborer is sweet, whether he eats little or much, but the abundance of a rich man permits him no sleep.*" — *Ecclesiastes* 5.12

—PETER E. "TONY" GUERNSEY JR.
President, Wilmington Trust FSB New York

"Another groundbreaking book from Jay Hughes. He provides a broad perspective on how to challenge families to thrive over multiple generations."

—CHARLES W. COLLIER
Senior Philanthropic Adviser, Harvard University

"Mr. Hughes brings important new concepts to the forefront—the role of 'affinity' in family enterprises as a force that forms an inclusive rather than exclusive system. He also articulates the role of the second generation as it has never before been addressed, pointing out the dual mission forced on all wealth inheritors, the critical issue of trusting others, and the impact of regressing to the mean. This book must be read by all owners who find themselves inheriting wealth!"

—SARA S. HAMILTON
Founder and CEO, Family Office Exchange

"Our journey of learning continues! Jay has extended his seminal work on preserving family wealth with this tapestry of thought—weaving concepts from fields as disparate as physics and philosophy into the experiences he has amassed during his life of service to families—to create an extraordinary treatise."

—MARY K. DUKE
Managing Director, Head of HSBC Private Bank's Global Family Wealth Initiative

"Jay Hughes's prescription for the family of affinity combines the wisdom of the ages with the compassionate pragmatism of an experienced professional. For families wanting to stay together and prosper in every sense of the word, Jay's book is *the* book."

—PETER WHITE
Vice Chairman, U.S. Trust Company

Family

The Compact Among Generations

Also by James E. Hughes Jr.

Family Wealth—Keeping It in the Family:
How Family Members and Their Advisers Preserve Human,
Intellectual, and Financial Assets for Generations

Also available from
BLOOMBERG PRESS

The Dilemmas of Family Wealth:
Insights on Succession, Cohesion, and Legacy
by Judy Martel

———————————

A complete list of our titles is available at
www.bloomberg.com/books

Family

The Compact Among Generations

James E. Hughes Jr.

BLOOMBERG PRESS

NEW YORK

First Edition published 2007
1 3 5 7 9 10 8 6 4 2

Library of Congress Cataloging-in-Publication Data

Hughes, James E. Jr.
    Family : the compact among generations / James E. Hughes, Jr. -- 1st ed.
        p. cm.
    Summary: "A resource for families and professionals, expanding on the principles presented in Family Wealth, explaining the author's insights on what makes families flourish, and laying out his comprehensive vision for family governance"--Provided by publisher.
    Includes bibliographical references and index.
    ISBN-13: 978-1-57660-024-5
    ISBN-10: 1-57660-024-6
  1. Family. 2. Generations. 3. Success. 4. Human capital. 5. Financial security. I. Title.

HG734.H9166 2007
646.7'8--dc22   2007010743

Acquired by Jared Kieling

Edited by Mary Ann McGuigan

*This book is dedicated to the pilgrims
past, present, and future on their journey to
serve families, who, like the pilgrims in
The Canterbury Tales, walk along together,
telling each other their stories.*

Contents

Part Four—Family Leadership

Part Five—Tools and Pathfinders

PREFACE

The journey is the reward.

—Proverb

WELCOME TO THOSE who have been on the pilgrimage, wearing your round hats and your scallop shells and carrying your staffs. I hope the journey that we began together in *Family Wealth* has brought you closer to the goal of growing great families. Welcome also to all new pilgrims beginning the same journey.

In *Family Wealth* I offered the view of a family governance system of joint decision making, founded on the idea that a family can preserve itself for more than three generations. To do so, the family as a whole—gently assisted by its financial capital—must nurture the human and intellectual capital of each family member.

When I wrote *Family Wealth*, I felt I had some insights to share on the entropic effects of the proverb "From shirtsleeves to shirtsleeves in three generations"—which predicts a family's growth, stagnation, and dissipation—and on the philosophical, governance, vision, mission, benchmarking, and relationship practices a family could use to retard them. I am happy to say that many of those practices are now being used by families all over the world, and they seem to be making a difference. I am even happier to report that many of those families do not possess great financial wealth, so the practices are filtering down to benefit larger segments of society. What's more, a growing number of practitioners are now using the vocabulary I introduced to explain the practices, particularly the concepts surrounding growing and enhancing a family's human and intellectual capital. The increasing popularity of this approach means that many more families will have a chance to consider and employ these practices in their journeys toward happiness.

In the ten years since the first publication of *Family Wealth* and the three years since its republication by Bloomberg Press in 2004, friends, peers, and clients of all income levels have asked me repeatedly to explain the philosophy that underlies my work and to chart how the ideas were developed. I was concerned, however, that it would appear hubristic to attempt to assert these ideas as a philosophy and to offer that philosophy as a set of practices a family could use as it seeks to avoid the fate of the shirtsleeves proverb. Ultimately, however, I decided that the potential benefits to families outweigh that risk and the even greater risk that I might be flat wrong and could do harm to those I most wish to help.

Family: The Compact Among Generations was born of that decision. It is a book of ideas and its intent is to explain to families and to the professionals who serve them the ideas that helped shape the philosophy and the practices that I've learned can help a family combat the entropic fate of the proverb. Indeed, these ideas can help a family avoid indefinitely the outcome the proverb predicts.

No proverb as culturally universal and ancient as this one can truly be overcome. But can its fulfillment be delayed? My answer is yes, provided we as family members and professionals are prepared for the lifelong journey of finding useful answers to the many questions that will confront us. In *Family*, I ask readers to consider what some of those questions will be. It is in the questions we ask and in the experiential searches we undertake to find our answers that our deepest learning occurs. Stick with the questions and the answers will ultimately emerge. There is, however, one overriding provision: *hasten slowly*. Find the best answer, not the one nearest by.

Please know that there are no answers I can offer that will definitely cancel the proverb's entropic dictate. Indeed, providing answers would not only be hubristic but likely cause the harm that acting irresponsibly always does. A family has two hundred years or more to reach its fifth generation and to go on from there to flourish. This is the span of the journey toward greatness. Only those families who take the long view—adopting the tortoise's view of time—will make this journey successfully. After all, it is not for lack of understanding of the human condition that the Chinese, with the oldest continuously recorded history of any culture, chose the tortoise as their symbol of longevity. The two tortoises I keep as fetishes on my desk remind me that time is a very useful ally for families on their journeys, provided they and those who serve them don't waste it.

It has long been my hope to share my journey of learning with others and, by doing so, to honor my mentors, my teachers, and the families I've served, who have taught me with infinite patience all I know about the question of growing a great family. My goal is to honor them by sharing my understanding of their teachings in a way that will reduce the human suffering expressed in the proverb. I hope to offer families and the professionals who serve them a way to imagine how they can dynamically preserve a family and help them see a path they can follow on the journey to achieving that goal. To all who might be considering this journey, I hope in some small way to offer encouragement that it can be made successfully, albeit with many pitfalls, twists, turns, and canyons.

We have much territory to cover. And what is my starting point for a voyage of such magnitude? I believe that any journey undertaken to help others must begin by asking with humility, Will I do harm before I do good? If I can satisfy myself that I will not do harm, then I can ask, How can I help?

ACKNOWLEDGMENTS

FIRST AND FOREMOST I wish to acknowledge my clients, the hundreds of families around the world who honored me by asking for my service and my help and, most important, who taught me so much of what I know. I honor them most by honoring their privacy.

I also wish to honor

• the extraordinary contribution to this book and to my life of my mentor and dear friend, Richard Bakal, whose life work has been to find and teach excellence in how to grow a great family. Dick is a man for whom only the noble truth of reality is acceptable. His constant questioning, pushing, and prodding have made me far more than I otherwise would be. Thank you, Dick.

• the work of my daughter, Ellen Berry Hughes Webster, who copyedited every chapter of my manuscript. Thank you, Bee.

• the help of my life partner, Jacqueline Merrill, and of my twenty-one-year partner in the service of our clients, Anne D'Andrea, for their deep caring and love for me for each of their editorial contributions. Thank you, Jacquie and Anne.

• the work of Mary Ann McGuigan, executive developmental editor at Bloomberg. It is Mary Ann's work you're experiencing in its excellence. Thank you, Mary Ann.

• my father, James E. Hughes Sr., and my mother, Elizabeth B. Hughes, for the creation of our Buermann Hughes family of affinity. Thank you, Mom and Dad.

I'm grateful also to Ann Cassella and Rose Casella, who typed every page of my manuscript from my atrocious handwriting.

I also wish to honor and thank the following readers of my manuscript for their help and willingness to persevere: Patricia Angus,

Kristin Armstrong, Dick Bakal, Tim Belber, Charlotte Beyer, Marna Broida, Joanie Bronfman, Ulrich Burkhard, Martin Bury, Paul Cameron, David Cohn, Charles Collier, Mary Duke, Bryan Dunn, Peter Evans, Jesse Fink, Kathryn Fulton, Dan Garvey, Robert H. Gibson Jr., Ed Granski, Lisa Gray, Sara Hamilton, Anne Hargrave, George Harris, Katherine Heath, Robert Y. C. Ho, Will Hughes, Dennis Jaffe, Nicola Jones, Peter Karoff, Don Kozusko, Bill Lyons, Valerie Maxwell, Kathryn McCarthy, Stanley D. Neeleman, Bill O'Brien, John O'Neil, Ed Orazem, Ellen Perry, Ken Polk, Robert Rikoon, Ned Rollhaus, Hill Snellings, Bente Strong, John Trask, Frank Wallis, John Warnick, Chester Weber, John Webster, Ellen Webster, Keith Whitaker, and Peter White.

Next, I honor and thank the men and women with whom I have been lucky enough to share this journey. Each of you is a dear friend and colleague whose work every day reduces suffering and increases human happiness: David Altshuler, Alec Anderson, Christopher and Judy Armstrong, Agnes Auyeung, Brett Barth, Ed Bastian, Nan-b de Gaspe Beaubien, Louis Begley, Renata Bernhoeft, Art Black, David Bork, Alice Bowers, Olivia Boyce-Abel, Joseph Breiteneicher, Laura Brevetti, William Bricker, Jean Brunel, Matthew Burton, Nathalie Rollhaus Burton, John Campbell, Paul Caron, Jon Carroll, Carol Carruthers, Marty Carter, Richard Caruso, Mark Casella, Michael Casey, Jim Chandler, Gail Cohen, Chalan Colby, Paul Comstock, Simon Cox, Greg Curtis, John Dadakis, Victor D'Andrea, Serge D'Araujo, Peter Davis, Francois de Visscher, William Dietel, Joan diFuria, Amy Domini, Emilo A. Dominianni, Rob Drucker Jr., John Duncan, Gerald Dunworth, Horst Duseberg, Robert Elliott, Jim Ellis, John Enteman, Martin Escher, Virginia Esposito, Simon Evans, George Farnham, Kate Fering, Joseph A. Field, Betsy Fink, Michael Fisher, Jennifer Fletcher, Rick Fogg, Biff Folberth, Arthur Frank, M.E. Freeman, James Frye, David Gage, Heidi Steiger Gallo, Christine Galloway, David Garcia, Claire Gaudiani, Barry Geller, Kelin Gersick, Barbara Hughes Gibson, Robert H. Gibson, Barbara Gill, Joline Godfrey, Stephan Goldbart, James Goldschmidt, Hartley Goldstone, Jim Goodfellow, Joe Goodman, Martyn Goossen, Davidson T. Gordon, Jody Green, Herbert Grossman, Richard Grossman,

James Grubman, Tony Guernsey, Jamie Gutteridge, Karen Harris, Barbara Hauser, Tim Hawkins, Richard Hay, Alan Heath, Fredda Herz-Brown, Patrick Ho, Steve Hoch, David Horn, Alan Houghton, Jack J.T. Huang, Alyssa Johl Hughes, Nancy R. Hughes, Peter Hughes, Neen Hunt, Mimi Hutton, Norman Inkster, Nancy Jacobs, Dan Jaech, Jamie Johnson, Stephen Johnson, Alan Jones, Jim Jones, Gerard F. Joyce, Dirk Junge, Werner Kaech, Wendy Kane, Kenneth Kaye, John F. King, Katie Kinsey, Christopher Knowdell, Nancy Elizabeth Knowdell, Adele Kozusko, Ellen Kratzer, William Kreisel, Kaycee Krysty, Maria-Elena Lagomasino, John and Jill Lahey, Nancy Lamb, Ivan Lansberg, Raquel Laredo, Barbara Lawrence, Robert Lawrence, Jim Lawson, John de Lande Long, David MacDonald, Juan Carlos Marino, Marilyn Mason, Elizabeth Mathieu, Bernice McCarthy, Richard McCune, Brian McNally, William Mears, Robert Meijes, Drew Mendoza, Juan and Virginia Meyer, Leon M. and Joan Meyers, William J. Miller, Sam Minzberg, Raymond Moore, Todd Morgan, Frank Mutch, Diane Neiman, Stephen Nelson, Walter Noel, Mark O'Connell, Mary Adams O'Connell, Galen Oelkers, Pat O'Neil, Jessie O'Neill, Michael Orr, Richard Pease, Judith S. Peck, Jennifer Pendergast, Michael Peretz, Hap Perry, Michael Pfeiffer, Ken Polk, Florence Pratt, Karen Putnam, Tom Ragan, Rick Reibesell, Ellen Remmer, Ralph Rittenour, Tom Rogerson, Catherine Rollhaus, Brian Rose, Evan Roth, Jane Gregory Rubin, Mark Rubin, Jim Ruddy, Roberta Ruddy, Eric Ryan, Roy Ryan, Lal Sani, Suresh Sani, Peter Scaturro, Carolyn Schuham, Joachim Schwass, Paul Setlakwe, Michael Smith, Peter Sperling, Peter Steingless, David Steinman, Howard Stephenson, Christian Stewart, Eric Stoeckli, Tim Taylor, Elisabeth Hughes Templeton, Rob Templeton, Michael Thompson, Nick Thomson, Richard Tinervan, Terrence Todman, Debra Treyz, Lorraine Tzavaris, Ernst van den Biggelaar, Maarten Van Hengel Jr., Charles Vaughn-Johnson, Steve Vetter, Philip Vineberg, Jan Von Haeften, Andreas von Planta, Eugene Wadsworth, John Ward, Rashad Wareh, Ron Weiss, G. Warren Whitaker, Thayer Willis, Hunter Wilson, Kathy Wiseman, Vincent Worms, Ralph Wyman, Kana Yamada, Ken Yamashita, Shoya Zichy, Henry Ziegler, Andy Zmuda.

INTRODUCTION

From shirtsleeves to shirtsleeves in three generations.
—AMERICAN VERSION OF ANCIENT CHINESE PROVERB

SINCE 1993, I have been running, like Forrest Gump, down every road I could find to try to discover an antidote to the tragedy inherent in the proverb "From shirtsleeves to shirtsleeves in three generations," which predicts a family's growth, stagnation, and dissipation. I've searched for ideas and practices that might give me the courage to believe that I could alter the outcome. Although reading has been my primary method of learning on this journey, the depth of insight I have gained comes from my Virgils—the mentors and elders who asked me the questions that told me where to look next. As Dante's *Divine Comedy* teaches us, if our mentors—our Virgils and Beatrices—do not appear, we remain forever in the "dark wood" of our unconscious, trapped there by our fears and desires. Only through the love of our elders and mentors and the questions they present can we find the courage we need to emerge, grow, and continue our journeys. It has been my privilege to honor my elders and mentors by offering help to families and by stepping into the role of mentor.

Family Wealth: Laying the Foundation

Only a decade has passed since *Family Wealth*'s 1997 publication. Clearly, ten years isn't long enough to measure the effectiveness of ideas or the practices they spawn, especially considering that assessing a family's progress vis-à-vis the proverb takes about one hundred years, which is the length of time needed for a third generation to be born and die. As I pointed out in *Family Wealth*, planting a tree like the copper beech tree is an act of faith because the gardener will never live to see the tree grow to more than one-third of its size. However, the gardener does see whether the tree is thriving and likely to mature or is failing and in need of healing intervention. Like the gardener, I can see families beginning to thrive by using these practices, and sadly I can see many more that could benefit from them.

The practices described in *Family Wealth* are not something I came up with on my own; they are the synthesis of what my journey has produced and the products of observing the hundreds of families who have honored me by asking me to serve them. These sources seem to inspire new practices every year, which I try to bring to the attention of families everywhere through a series of essays I call *Reflections*. Some are now a part of the revised edition of *Family Wealth*; the balance can be found at www.jamesehughes.com.

The Seven Fundamental Principles

Chapter 1 of *Family Wealth* presents the basic tenets of the philosophy of preserving family wealth as follows:

1) Long-term preservation of family wealth is a question of human behavior.

2) The preservation of family wealth is a dynamic process of group activity, or governance, which must be successfully reenergized in each successive generation to overcome the ever-present threat of entropy.

3) The assets of a family are its individual members.

4) a) The wealth of a family consists of the human and intellectual capital of its members.

b) A family's financial capital is a tool to support the growth of the family's human and intellectual capital.

5) To successfully preserve a family's wealth, individual family members must form a social compact reflecting their shared values. Each successive generation must reaffirm and readopt that social compact.

6) To successfully preserve its wealth, a family must agree to create a system of representative governance through which to actively practice its values. Each successive generation must reaffirm its participation in that system of governance.

7) The vision and mission underlying a system of family governance must be to preserve the family's wealth—that is, its human, intellectual, and financial capital—over the long term and to achieve that preservation by enhancing the pursuit of happiness of each individual family member as part of the enhancement of the family as a whole.

A Family of Affinity

In *Family: The Compact Among Generations*, I want to restate my belief in that philosophy of family preservation and explain the ideas that underlie these seven principles and the view they represent. I believe that a family can preserve itself for many more than five generations if it adopts these ideas and actively practices the seven fundamental principles. Indeed, it is through a family's embrace of these principles and the practices they suggest that it becomes a "family of affinity"—a family that sees itself as linked by affinity and a common mission rather than simply by genetic lineage—and eventually expresses its uniqueness, or "differentness." I prefer the word "differentness" because I doubt that any family is truly unique and because I worry that uniqueness can be a slippery slope toward "better than" and the intemperance that follows.

No proverb so deeply ingrained in the fabric of human behavior can be overcome indefinitely. For a family to imagine that it can do so amounts to hubris, which, as the Greeks taught, is to see oneself as God.[1] All hubris can do is offer the illusion that we can somehow overcome the natural order that governs human behavior. Such a path, as I know from studying the histories of many families who disappeared just as the proverb predicted, leads only to the unraveling of family bonds and the disintegration of the family fabric. In light of the proverb's prediction about human behavior, far better to build a family foundation with humility and to hope that the family can, over many generations, hold the proverb at bay by never failing to acknowledge its existence and the risk it foretells.

Drawing From the World's Wisdom

To develop my ideas into a philosophy and practice, I've tapped into many bodies of learning. I undertook a personal journey of discovery into each of these disciplines in hopes of uncovering the mysteries and wisdom that could offer insights into how to wrestle with the proverb and to find the integrity in this work I continue to seek.[2] Each discipline and the knowledge I've gained from it offer real hope to a family seeking to discover and create ways to enhance the growth of the human and intellectual capital of each of its members as it seeks to dynamically preserve itself. What's more, every one of these disciplines can reward its students with wonderful insights, happy digressions, and extraordinary and enlightening experiences.

Most important, however, my studies have reinforced my deep belief that families of affinity can succeed in this work. As I was preparing to write *Family*, I was struck by how many of the bodies of knowledge I had studied were born in the eighteenth and nineteenth centuries but were truly developed in the twentieth century. Indeed, *Homo faber*, man the toolmaker, outdid himself in the twentieth century in making use of the arts and sciences to improve the quality of his existence. Families today have so many more tools at their disposal than did families in earlier times. This change strengthens my belief that families of affinity can succeed in avoiding the proverb's impact, and I am greatly encouraged in that belief by what I've learned about these tools.

The Key Disciplines

When I was developing the ideas that formed the concepts presented in *Family Wealth*, I was struck by the fact that they were influenced significantly and in equal measure by three disciplines:

1) Ancient wisdom and history. Ancient wisdom shows us how to live a life that's in touch with a philosophical and spiritual dimension; history demonstrates the progress of our species and the cultures and civilizations it spawned. I place particular emphasis on the evolution of thought within these two bodies of knowledge—the set of ideas, stories, practices, and tools used in their development as represented in the accumulated heritage of our species.

2) Modern psychology. Modern psychology is basically a set of twentieth-century ideas, although its teachings influence our daily lives as if these ideas and the practices had been a part of human beings' toolboxes throughout all of our history. Freud, Jung, James, Maslow, Piaget, Erikson, Bowen, Levinson, Johnson, Hillman, and Csikszentmihalyi spent all or the largest part of their lives in the twentieth century. These are the voices in this field whose messages we treat today as fundamental to understanding our emotional lives and to achieving success in our most treasured relationships. Indeed, today's widely accepted understanding that most people follow clearly demarcated developmental stages in their maturation was known only to the academic world less than fifty years ago. Widely recognized as these voices may be, we are just beginning to understand the tools they offer for a successful life. Had families in previous centuries had the benefit of the wisdom of the great minds who shaped this body of knowledge, I have no doubt that we would have many more stories of families who successfully overcame the proverb. Equally, had families had the benefit of Murray Bowen's family systems theory, much unhappiness could have been avoided. Going forward, however, we can use their voices and the tools they helped bring into existence.

3) Modern organizational and management science. These disciplines were extremely valuable in my exploration of leadership practices and how management differs from ownership. My discoveries in these areas were the most surprising. In *Family Wealth*, the practices I suggested for families have four building blocks:

a) Capital, that is, human and intellectual assets assisted by financial capital

b) Time

c) Vision

d) Governance

A business entrepreneur requires the very same building blocks. Rarely, however, does a book about business science mention that the skills and practices involved apply to the family. Yet in every society on earth, family enterprises represent far more commerce than any other form of business organization. As I began to read more widely in this discipline, I discovered author after author whose ideas could be applied to families without any modification. In fact, the more I study this area, the more I realize that my idea of dynamic preservation is founded on the principle of families being enterprising and acting as an organization in the same way that businesses do to direct and complete their work. Families also interact with the outside world in the same enterprising ways as businesses do with customers and suppliers. Successful families, like successful businesses at their best, are successful enterprises.

Of course, not every business practice is applicable to families. But ask successful CEOs what the most important asset of their business is, and they will say "our people" and "what they know and can learn." Their answer will never be "the financial capital we have in the bank." A family's critical assets, like those of every enterprise, are the human beings who make up the organization; their human capital; and the knowledge these individuals have, can learn, and can integrate into the family's bank of knowledge. That collective knowledge is the family's intellectual capital, which it uses to dynamically preserve itself.

Other Disciplines

Although these three areas of study—history, psychology, and organizational management—offer the greatest possibilities for fruitful inquiry into the wisdom available to families seeking to dynamically preserve themselves, there are others that lead to valuable insights. Interestingly, all but one are fundamentally twentieth-century sciences. Political science, the exception, finds its roots in Aristotle's *Politics*, written in the fourth century BC. Other areas include the study of fusion and avoiding entropy; cultural anthropology, including archaeology and sociology; demography; and modern educational theory. These disciplines, which I also refer to in this book, offer insights into the nature of our species; how we learn; and how we form groups, especially how families become clans and tribes.

Because these humanities and sciences have been seen as outside the range of the relevant disciplines, families have been deprived for far too long of the knowledge of themselves that they offer. My experience mentoring and counseling families has shown me not only that they can benefit immediately from the ideas in these disciplines but also that the lack of this knowledge reduces the possibilities for their success. I hope this book will dispel this misprision and open these bodies of knowledge to much wider applications.

The Personne de Confiance

Families are unlikely on their own to find their way to the guidance these disciplines can provide. Who can families of affinity look to, to bring this knowledge into their sphere of learning and help them access the wisdom available? The answer lies in the men and women in the helping professions whose high calling is to serve such families. The title *personne de confiance* describes the person called to this work. Members of the helping professions—whether medicine, including psychology and social work; law; ministry; teaching; or fee-only financial advice—all seek to help families connect to the world's wisdom. These professionals, the people of confidence whom families trust, often offer the only window through which the privacy-conscious families can see out to the larger world.

I hope that in this new century these men and women will see that the most fulfilling aspect of their professions is to become catalysts for the development of the human and intellectual capacities of the families and the individuals they serve. In these many disciplines lies the knowledge families need, but without the translators, that knowledge remains inaccessible to them. Prompted by these serving professionals, families can embrace this knowledge in their quests to understand themselves and their behaviors, their differentness. The Rosetta Stone sat for many years until the French scholar Jean-Francois Champollion saw that it offered a means to reach into the wisdom hidden within ancient languages, which until then had been untranslatable. The great personnes de confiance—men like my father, James Elliott Hughes Sr.—are the people who willingly take on the role of translator. We can never have enough of them, but without them families cannot hope to alleviate the continued suffering from the effects of the proverb.

Essential Questions for the Family of Affinity

I hope that the exploration I began out of the dark night of my own spirit has managed to channel some inspiration from all the unrelated voices I've listened to in laying the foundation for the tools families need to battle the proverb. I don't have a definitive answer to the proverb's challenge, but I believe I have uncovered the essential questions arising out of each of these disciplines that can be posed to a family. These questions offer a family ways to understand and organize its behavior and its governance, ways that point to answers that can shape its effort to retard the effects of the proverb. May the spirit that has been awakened in me by my teachers offer light to those families willing to do the work required to create families of affinity that achieve their fifth generations and evolve from there.

Here are the questions I ask the families I serve. (Note that italicized terms are discussed in later chapters):

1) As a family of affinity, is the family community founded on the virtues of fusion, altruism, beauty as harmony, and love expressed as joy? Are family members connected in all their relationships to the principle of seeking to enhance each other's happiness, and are they prepared to embrace the proverb as a friend, as a mantra? Are they prepared to ask themselves today and every day during the lives of current family members how they're doing as a family and as individuals in avoiding the prediction? What positive steps are members taking to help one another flourish and to flourish as a family? Is the family seeking to establish a process that helps each future generation ask itself the same questions?

2) Is the family seeking to grow dynamically the human and intellectual capital of each member, today and every day? Is it seeking to instill in the family a process of enhancement that will achieve this same goal for the next five generations? Is it committed to the goal of each family member achieving the highest order of happiness, that is, the highest level of self-awareness and the freedom of self that grows from it? Does the family appreciate that this is the process most likely to lead to the dynamic preservation of a family as a whole for the next five generations and the one most likely to help it become a tribe that can ward off the proverb?

3) Do family members understand that by assisting in the individuation and differentiation of each member of the second generation and by helping each of them discover and fulfill an individual dream, they make it possible for that entire generation to learn to become dynamic steward-conservators of the dreams of the previous generation? Does the family understand that this is the critical journey each member of each succeeding generation must take, so that all members are forever part of a virtual second generation—meaning a dynamic generation? In this way, the family will never face the plateau and stasis of energy in its second generation that leads to the dissipation of energy in the third, as ordained in the proverb.

4) Does the family encourage all members to become excellent steward-conservators of all of the financial assets they inherit and to learn to be stakeholder-owners of all forms of family enterprise? Do family members recognize that this responsibility is secondary to their responsibility to discover the work they're called to do individually? Their task as an apprentice in that work is to find the mentors and teachers necessary to master it. In this process of mastering work, does the family actively encourage family virtues of individual discovery, creativity, curiosity, and seeking fulfillment of the spirit?

5) Does the family understand that a family system in which one generation tells the succeeding generation, "Do this for us and we might do something for you" represents enslavement and is therefore profoundly unfree and unattractive to potential new members? Saying instead, "How can I help you without *and* before seeking anything from you?" represents a free system, one that positively attracts members. In this process, a family acknowledges altruism as one of its virtues and practices it in all of its dealings inside and outside the family. This choice increases the family's store of social capital, so that it has larger amounts of it to share with everyone with whom it interacts.

6) Does the family embrace the principle of *fusion* in all of

the interconnected multiple relationships that make up the family systems of affinity, with a goal of gently evolving and growing the sphere of energy that encompasses the family? Does it seek to avoid the *fission* leading to *entropy* and *inertia* in those relationships, which will cause them to fail? Does the family understand that the family's best hope for success lies in the principle of affinity and the positive connections it represents and fosters?

7) Does the family recognize that its future depends on successfully managing multiple long-term *transitions* in a family of affinity's evolution? Does the family recognize that no short-term *transaction* will make a difference to the success of the journey unless that transaction can be successfully integrated into and positively enhance the successful completion of these transitions?

8) Does the family recognize that its family systems are webs of multiple interconnected relationships of incredible *complexity*, which for the family's well-being must constantly organically evolve toward higher orders of complexity? And does the family understand that if those relationships are not promoting this process of growth, the family is likely to be in entropy, leading to its demise?

9) Does the family recognize that the practice of a family of affinity's system of *governance, its system of joint decision making*, is fundamental to its well-being and that each joint decision it positively engenders is a fundamental step in achieving its *long-term dynamic preservation*?

10) Does the family seek to encourage great elders who will act to *mediate* its disputes; remind the family of its history by telling its *stories*; *intermediate* toward the family's spiritual well-being, especially in helping members successfully navigate the *stages of their lives*; and exercise the authority the family grants them to choose its leaders, especially leaders for peace, *leaders from behind*?

11) Does the family hold as a virtue the practice of *beauty as harmony*? Such beauty does not require the dimming of individual energies but rather grows from individuals' evolving to higher orders of happiness. Each member flourishes as an individual tile in a more and more beautiful mosaic composed of the tiles of all those who've gone before and those living now amid virtual space for those to come.

12) Does the family cultivate a *beginner's mind* leavened with *seventh-generation* thinking as the needed practices for long-term successful family survival and flourishing?

The Journey Begins

No list of this kind is ever complete. New learning surfaces about every subject as we evolve to appreciate it. This list is especially incomplete because it calls on each reader to add, subtract, and amend it as life experiences dictate. I hope that this list will suggest the threads that lead to the possibilities inherent in a flourishing family of affinity. I hope too that it will awaken possibilities in the hearts of *personnes de confiance* and in the minds of *personnes d'affaires* that will help each find the questions especially needed for the families they serve.

Many of the italicized terms in these questions may seem new. Each one will be defined in a chapter to come. Although I could have defined the terms here, I believe that meeting them as friends in the context I've chosen will be much more useful to understanding them. Perhaps by the end of the book, they won't be new acquaintances but familiar and valued companions. The questions are intended to provide families and the professionals who serve them with a new vocabulary that will facilitate the dialogue about the best processes for achieving a fifth generation and for moving on from there as a flourishing family of affinity.

Families are complex systems evolving toward ever more complex systems as they become clans—that is, clusters of families joined in one system—and tribes. If all goes well, they may become tribes like the Lebanese, the Maya, the Hakka, or the Jews whose existences can span two-plus millennia. Families who achieve such longevity will be those who seek out the kernels of knowledge in every academic discipline that can help them understand themselves. They will be families at the play of curiosity and creativity—*familiae ludens*—the families who will find the consiliences relevant to the improvement of their conditions and will, as *familiae faber*, build the tools they need to use this knowledge toward their dynamic preservation, connection, linkage, and affinity. They may indeed put the proverb into long-term suspended animation while keeping a place for its admonition and prophecy in the family psyche.

Chapter Notes

1. The Greek pantheon of gods includes a minor female god called Hubris. Hubris possessed an overwhelming ego, esteemed herself as equal to or greater than all the other gods, and was characterized by insolence, lack of restraint, and acting on instinct rather than reason.

2. Although I am sure there are other disciplines to be mined for their insights, I continue to feel that these form the core of the multidisciplinary approach needed for a family to do battle with the proverb.

Family

The Compact Among Generations

PART ONE

Families of Affinity
Their Nature and
Practices

Chapter One

A Family of Affinity

By its dominant voices, its most unforgettable faces, and its chief acts of bravery does a generation recognize itself and history mark it.

—ERIC SEVAREID, American journalist

WHAT IS THIS thing we call "family" and what are its characteristics? I define a family as two or more people who by either genetic lineage or bonds of affinity consider themselves related to each other. The core of my philosophy is my belief that a family that sees itself as linked not only by blood but by affinity and acts from that philosophical base has the greatest chance of successfully enhancing the individual development and growth of its members and thus of dynamically preserving the family as a whole for at least five generations. Families who see themselves principally as linked by genetic lineage, or by blood, rarely if ever, in my experience, overcome the proverb.

Paradoxically, most families define themselves by blood alone and not also by affinity. Regardless of popular sentiment for such a definition, I have repeatedly found that a family that defines itself in this way closes its systems to new members from outside the family. These outsiders represent the new energy the family needs to overcome what it will lose by natural attrition. A family of affinity maintains open systems that welcome new members, giving the family a better chance of survival.

The Family and Its Functions

The function of the family is closely tied to the traits that characterize the human species. What characteristics capture how the human species is different from all others? First, we are defined by our gregariousness, our desire to be with others of our kind; second, as Dutch historian Johan Huizinga said, by our desire to play, our curiosity (*Homo ludens*); and third, by our desire to make tools (*Homo faber*). How are these characteristics manifested in a family?

Family is where our sense of gregariousness begins and is first worked out. Play within family is how we first learn and in many cases how we discover and define ourselves for the rest of our lives. Family is often the place we must leave in order to learn to individuate but to which we most want to return to tell the stories of our lives to those most willing to hear them. The parable of the prodigal son comes to mind. Our ability to make tools that manipulate our environment has led to our ability to survive and prosper within it. Family is often the place that spawns our creativity and offers us a laboratory for trying out new tools. It's the place we find responses to new questions.

This definition of family puts the issues of the affinity of altruism and the selfishness of blood in direct opposition. It creates a dynamic competition of ideas between the sciences and the humanities, which can influence the family's journey. That competition of ideas is between

a) the possibility that we are simply individual biological life forms, bundles of evolved genes, seeking selfishly to replicate ourselves, consciously or unconsciously, and

b) individuals of spirit, or consciousness, who seek to know ourselves through our interactions with other individuals likewise seeking to know themselves, all toward an enlightened self.

I believe that we are altruistic and that insofar as success as a family is concerned, altruism—the act of truly caring for another and acting generously toward that other—is likely to be a far more successful behavioral trait than is selfish genetic combat to survive.

In my view, family founders who believe that their family's differentness is worth preserving cannot begin with any view other than that altruism toward the spirit of each of their descendants and of all other sentient beings must govern all actions. Betting on a selfish goal of individual survival or, worse, on the biologically fallacious belief that one family's DNA is superior to another's will cause the family to lose the preservation race before it is very far along.

Defining Affinity

What are the connotations of the word *affinity* that make it so useful in my model description of a successful family? The *Oxford English Dictionary* offers many usages for this word. Let's consider the definitions of this word that offer insight into its power in helping to define successful families.

1) Relationship by marriage as opposed to consanguinity, hence, collectively, relations by marriage. In these few words, we find the reality of family. Every family begins with two people, as all creation myths inform us. Certainly, in all general discussions of family, we link the concept to two people whom we see as its founders. Until very recently in human social history, these two people were always linked by some sort of marriage ritual, either a religious ceremony or the act of living together as a recognized couple for an extended period. Because such relationships are still the norm throughout the different cultures of the world, this is the form of family I will be describing throughout this book. Often today, even in single-sex families, two or more individuals who see themselves as founders seek a ritual to validate their union.

2) The spiritual relationship between sponsors and their godchild or between the sponsors themselves. In this definition, *affinity* can extend beyond blood or consanguinity and beyond relations by marriage. Bonds of emotion—defined as affinities—form between a sponsor and a child, and those affinities need not come from any genetic link. This form of affinity underlies the connections in successful tribes. Its powerful force of attraction and the tribe's system of "seventh-generation thinking" reinforce this way of defining family relationships (see chapter 2).

3) Relationship or kinship generally between individuals or races; collectively, relations, kindred. This definition of *affinity* picks up where the second leaves off. *Affinity* describes relationships that we define as "kin." These relations can be as broad as our relations with the races with whom we feel an affinity or as narrow as third cousins whom we rarely see.

4) Structural resemblance between different animals, plants, or minerals, suggesting modifications of one or (in the case of the two former) gradual differentiation from a common stock. This definition, taken from natural history, describes *affinity* in terms of our evolution as animals through the modification of our primary type. We have affinities as *Homo sapiens* to our original ancestors—the earliest members of the genus *Homo*—and to their ancestors from whom we split some 6 to 7 million years ago and to the evolving life form of our current species as it will inevitably evolve far into the future. All families as they evolve through their many successor generations reflect their affinity to their originators. When family members lose these links and their affinities cannot be traced, they are no longer families but rather only individual genetic realities.

5) Causal relationship or connection (as flowing the one from the other or having a common source) or such agreement or similarity of nature or character as might result from such relationship if it existed; family likeness. This definition captures the importance I attach to stories as the glue that creates a family's affinity. Genetics can, through DNA testing, show to whom we are related. For most of us, our genetic lines are hidden. The telling of our oral histories, however, is the visible and auditory means by which we learn and experience in the present what links us by affinity to our past. Family stories are how we define the specific ideas as well as the values and practices flowing from them that characterize our sense of family, our differentness. We seek the connections and the sense of common family nature these stories offer. In them, we find our shared sense of our connections and the relationships they reflect and engender. These common sources help us to know our family's differentness and recognize its affinity.

6) Voluntary social relationships, companionship, alliance, association. The word voluntary in this definition is a critical element in defining the concept of a family of affinity. Individual family members are linked as parts of a family system. All of these linkages to family, however, are in my view based on voluntary acts we make of conscious will or intuitive spirit to join in the social relationships of companionship, alliance, and association called family. These relationships are the social compacts that underlie the entities we call families. Members perceive that here, in a family where openness to the growth of the individual is reflected in its voluntary social compacts, they will receive the sustenance needed to achieve that growth. If members experience family life as a prison, then any hope for the growth of human and intellectual capital or for enlightenment is severely reduced.

The choice of where we seek community in which to do our life's work of development of self is of extraordinary importance to the outcome. Seeking and finding communities of affinity is one of our greatest challenges. Families of affinity are defined by their openness to fostering individual dreams and growth; in so doing, they offer fertile possibilities for the successful undertaking of each family member's most important work. That work is to find a calling and to achieve the greatest self-awareness and the full flourishing of spirit that follows. A family practicing affinity through fostering generative social compacts does work that is deeply beneficial to its preservation. Such a family enables exactly the kinds of enhancing relationships human beings seek and therefore it is more likely to gain and retain the members it needs for a successful long-term family journey.

7) A natural friendliness, liking, attractiveness, or an attraction drawing to anything. Here, affinity represents a positive attraction. The word offers the possibility of a system providing positive feedback for our endeavors. A "liking" is positive; it connotes feelings that are enjoyable. It suggests relations of profound joy and humor, virtues that encourage participation. A family that expresses friendliness to its members is "attractive;" it draws them in. The family serves as a place of community, where each individual's journey can be accommodated. Perhaps a family can even become a place where members can express gratitude for others' gifts to them; in this way, a member learns another side of altruism and experiences the comfortable giving up of self to help others that is so essential to the development of self. This positive feedback loop of giving self to gain self is the most essential process we can engage in to develop ourselves.

8) *Chemical attraction: the tendency which certain elementary substances of compounds have to unite with other elements and form new compounds.* Where can we find a better vision of a successful family dynamically preserving itself than in this definition? Elementary substances (individual family members) unite with other elements (all other members of a family of affinity) to form new compounds (forms of community that are new and "different"). In this definition, we discover the ecology of families: the hidden building blocks of family life organically combining from individual substances to form the new compounds needed for higher orders of family life. No individual disappears in a family of affinity but rather each contributes to the compound of community. Fortunately, even as the family expresses its common process, it also expresses its differentness.

Equally fascinating in the life of a family is to imagine the life forms to come that will grow out of the next set of "chemical attractions" as new members enter the process. Whether new members are born into the family or marry in or join by mutual attraction, each will contribute unique substances to that family. To recognize the necessity of welcoming those new substances into the energetic body of the family is to recognize the truth of how families meet new challenges to their essences, their affinities. Families that recognize through their rituals the positive energy they gain by accretion do well. Families that create out-laws out of their in-laws perform less well. No family attempting to evolve to the next level of complexity, and thus a higher order of existence, can do so successfully by relying only on the assets of those born into the family. After all, a family begins with two unique genetic signatures deciding to mate and, as with every evolving form of life, it needs all the positive energetic additions it can attract to find the necessary combinations of substances needed to successfully evolve to a higher order of itself.

As with all evolution, the addition of a new substance can lead to a mutation of the original substance that can kill it, so we cannot say that all evolved change through adaptation to new members will be positive for family growth. It won't be. The strongest life forms succeed because they are better at defending themselves against such intruders than their competitors are. I believe that families of affinity, because of their characteristics as seekers of new connections and their awareness of the riches and rewards of those connections, carry within themselves the capacity to better adapt to the mutations caused by new life forms joining them and indeed can benefit from them.

9) *A physical or spiritual attraction believed by some sects to exist between persons; sometimes applied concretely to the subjects or objects of the affinity.* In this definition, the word *affinity* captures the family of man and its members' attraction to each other. It defines that attraction in terms of the conscious, curious, playful *Homo ludens* we are. Affinity is associated with the longest-lived of all families: the religious, or spiritual, bodies we know as animism, Hinduism, Confucianism, Taoism, Buddhism, Stoicism, Shintoism, Judaism, Jainism, Zoroastrianism, Christianity, Islam, Sikhism, and secular humanism. Affinity, here, represents attraction based on physical and biochemical links that could describe the link the secular humanist feels to the species as a whole. In spiritual terms, affinity describes attractions based on common sets of beliefs leading to faith in a higher power. Likewise, it links those who believe that reason and intellect guide our actions to those who believe intuition and emotion guide those same actions (I am in the latter camp). What's more, if we are willing, we can accept the teaching of modern physics that we are, as is the universe of which we are a part, pure energy. We may be linked physically and spiritually, but, most important, we are linked energetically as well.

As applied to a family, this definition takes affinity to its highest order. A family of affinity and its individual members can be seen as bits of energy linked by affinity to each other and to all other bits of energy in the universe. As I once heard Sri Swami Satchidananda, the founder of Integral Yoga, say, "All rivers [religions] lead to the same common ocean, so, I say, do all single elements of energy flow to the ocean of light to make up the energy of the universe." A family that knows its members are all part of the common family of light encourages its members to see the innumerable number of linkages they share within the vastness of the universe and reminds them, whenever their egos need it, of how very small they are in the scheme of things. Ideally, it also encourages them in their search for self to seek out the wisdom of the philosophers, the sages, the prophets, the divines, the aesthetic voices of the arts, and the voices of reason in science to help them reach an enlightened understanding of how all families came to be and how they are evolving within the larger energetic realms of which they are a part.

"Seek, and ye shall find": Ask the questions about the affinities that lead to the next generation of affinity. Seek the psychic, spiritual, and energetic linkages that come from paradox—what doesn't seem to be, but is—to find out where the true affinities lie. Families of affinity are always asking questions, always creating, always discovering, always seeking to find the linkages between their past and present that provide hints to the secrets of their future. Families of affinity challenge the conventional while preserving their unique order, their differentness.

—∽—

MY OWN DEFINITION of *affinity* relates it most closely to fusion. Fusion is the principle in physics that describes the connection between two energetic bodies, whereby the energy that each contributes leads to greater energy flowing from the whole. Indeed, the whole is more than the sum of its parts. For a family, the fusion that arises out of positive affinities—members' positive relationships with each other—is the holy grail of family life. The image of affinity as fusion is at the heart of a successful family vision and at the heart of its mission and of the practices that foster positive relationships that enhance the lives of each of its members and thereby preserve the family. Affinity as fusion offers a family an image of possibility that is the most profound I have yet experienced toward my goal of helping families see how to avoid the proverb's suffering.

Chapter Two

Defying a Proverb

The generations of living things pass in a short time and, like runners, hand on the torch of life.

—LUCRETIUS, Roman philosopher

T HE YEAR IS 1974, and I am sitting contentedly at my desk in the New York office of Coudert Brothers, an international law firm, when a partner enters and advises me that a client of his in Singapore has asked me to come and talk to him. "Why me?" I ask. "Never mind why," I'm quickly instructed. "Just go." Still, I wonder aloud what the client wants to talk to me about. The partner doesn't know, but the man is a good client and I am to go and find out. The next thing I know I'm flying twenty-six hours to Singapore. Only much later do I realize that the first leg of my long journey in the study of families of affinity has begun.

From Shirtsleeves to Shirtsleeves in Three Generations

The day of my arrival in Singapore, I had dinner with members of the client's family and asked them why their father had summoned me. They didn't know, although they did tell me that this was not his customary mode of operation. The following morning I arrived at the address I'd been given, found the office, and was advised by the receptionist that I was expected and may go right in. I soon found myself in a huge office; at the far end of it sat the client behind his desk, which was raised on a platform. In front of his desk was a small chair, and it was clear that I was to take the long walk across the room and be seated. Somehow, despite the butterflies inhabiting my stomach, I got to the other side of the room, sat down in the chair, and introduced myself.

I was face-to-face with a very distinguished Chinese gentleman. The client suggested we have tea. I accepted, and in the moments that followed, we shared our thoughts on the world's problems. Finally, the gentleman said to me, "Perhaps, Mr. Hughes, you are wondering why I asked that you come halfway around the world to see me?" I confirmed that I was. "Well, we Chinese have a proverb," he told me, and it occurred to me that they indeed have hundreds of them, so I remained in the dark about where this could be leading. "From shirtsleeves to shirtsleeves in three generations," he said finally. "I want you to tell me all of the ways families in the West avoid the prediction of this proverb so that my family can avoid it too."

With this question, my life changed because my life's work became clear. My first response to this delightful gentleman was to tell him that we had experienced the fate described in this proverb in my family as well, my grandfather having lost his inheritance in the Great Depression. I admitted that I could not yet give him a satisfactory answer but that I would study his question and report back to him.

During the ensuing thirty-three years, I encountered this proverb among many families as I traveled the globe. Sometimes the wording was "clogs to clogs," sometimes "rags to rags," and sometimes "rice paddy to rice paddy," which is the idiom I prefer. In fact, the proverb is culturally universal. Somehow, when a family amasses financial wealth, that wealth will disappear within three generations of its accumulation. The pattern is common to all: the first generation, a man and wife, come together as a unit and together create a financial fortune. Normally, they do not greatly change their way of life, often remaining in the same village or region where they began married life. They are fully sustained by the values and practices with which they began their lives together. The second generation obtains a quality education, moves to a city, manages large enterprises, adopts an extravagant lifestyle, and funds and leads philanthropies. The third generation, having no experience of work and no understanding of work as a calling, consumes the fortune. The fourth generation finds itself back in the "rice paddy," pulling rice. In these thirty-three years, I have yet to find a family with significant financial capital that isn't familiar with this proverb and isn't deeply afraid that it too will experience the fate of the proverb.

The question, of course, is can the fate of the proverb be avoided for a long period of time? Yes, it can, provided we, whether as family members or as the professionals who serve them, are prepared for a lifelong journey to find useful answers to the multiple questions families will face as they strive to achieve lasting happiness.

Escaping the Fate of the Proverb

The journey pits us against a formidable force. After all, this proverb describes the universe's process for the birth of matter from pure energy and the application of the law of entropy, which causes all such matter to return to pure energy. At its birth, a family comprises the energies of two people. As the next two generations plateau, decay, and dissipate, entropy is at work, until the family completely disintegrates and its material self changes back into energy. Families who fail to understand this process are doomed to repeat the pattern. *In the first generation, material reality will be created in the form of financial capital; in the second generation, the growth of its financial capital will be static; and in the third generation, the financial capital will be consumed and that which was material will disappear.*

If a family adopts a program of dynamic preservation through the active enhancement, growth, and development of its human assets and uses its financial capital as a tool in that work, it has a chance to defy the odds. Its work must focus on assisting each of its members in achieving the highest level of happiness. In turn, the family hopes for a reciprocal commitment from each family member to the parallel dynamic preservation of the family as a whole. Ultimately, individual self-interest lies at the heart of everything we do in this life, and if a family is to do well, vis-à-vis the proverb, it must understand and act on that reality.

The family must also begin with a deep commitment of its heart rather than its mind if it is to form the belief—bordering on faith— that its highest calling is to enhance the journey of happiness of its individual members to ensure the family's dynamic preservation. The family's decision must embrace the idea that dynamic preservation of itself is a worthy cause to which individual family members can ascribe and that they may do so without any diminution of their individual spiritual beliefs. Without such a commitment of spirit and deep belief in the worthiness of the endeavor, the proverb will become reality.

Dynamic Preservation

For a family to overcome the fate described in the proverb, it must constantly bring new life-generating energy into its process. To do that, it must act dynamically. Preservation alone represents merely stasis, or death, just as formaldehyde preserves a corpse. Eros, as a life force, or energy, must be present in sufficient quantity, an amount that leads not to chaos but to the generation of life. As theoretical biologist Stuart Kauffman points out in *At Home in the Universe: The Search for the Laws of Self-Organization and Complexity*, life begins and can be sustained energetically *only* just beyond the point at which it evolves out of pure order, but never so far into chaos that it is blown away. The word *dynamic*, as I use it throughout this book, stands for the never-ending creative energy and life at Kauffman's inflection point. It is that "sweet spot" of creation, where life begins and thrives.

The birth of a family's spirit begins at this inflection point—just above order and barely into chaos—with all the generativity such a process foretells. The dynamic preservation of the energy that forms that spirit, if leavened with humility, offers the greatest likelihood that the forecast of the proverb can be delayed for an extended period. It offers a controlled dynamic process of generativity in which the spirits of the individual family members and of the family as a whole have the greatest possibility of achieving the family's highest calling, the happiness of each individual member and thus the happiness and preservation of the whole.

Beginner's Mind

To achieve this outcome, a family must seek at all times to have a "beginner's mind," balanced with the capacity for "seventh-generation thinking" and enhanced with a commitment to discovery, creativity, and seeking. Early in my journey, I came upon a book by the Japanese Zen master Shunryu Suzuki called *Zen Mind, Beginner's Mind*. In this volume, Suzuki seeks to explain Zen to the Western mind and heart. While it is impossible to try to explain here the depth of the insights of Zen on the question of how to live a fulfilled life (and certainly I am in no way qualified to do so), aspects of the process Suzuki describes are essential to a family's goal of preservation.

Paramount is the need for a beginner's mind. To paraphrase Suzuki, this is the mind of the newborn, of the apprentice, of the artist at his or her creative "aha" moment. Isn't it immensely joyful to remember those moments in our lives when we gave ourselves permission to be true beginners? Those moments when not knowing it all was all right? When the journey of learning and discovery was simply so exciting that we could begin without worrying about the outcome? When a question troubled us in such a profound way that we could imagine starting life all over again in a profoundly different direction? These are the moments when we can begin our most important work, graced by the real possibility that our open-mindedness will lead to deep insight into who we are and where we are meant to travel. For a family, these are the fertile and pregnant moments when a beginner's mind offers limitless possibilities to grow its human and intellectual capital. Perhaps, as Suzuki says, these are the moments when we, as individuals and as families, are "awake."

How might a family cultivate beginner's mind? To be useful to an individual's self-development, all work must follow the ancient route from apprentice to journeyman to master. We give ourselves the privilege of being apprentices by finding a master at whose feet we're prepared to sit and learn. When we choose a master, as we listen to what he says and watch what he does, we absorb and integrate those words and movements into ourselves so they become part of us. What happens when we decide that the apprentice period will take too much time and we jump into the journeyman phase directly? We discover that having a toolbox full of a journeyman's tools but no skills in using them leads to one failure after another. When we seek to learn a new skill, we need to fill the empty toolbox of the apprentice with each tool as we become skilled in using it. Eventually, we have a toolbox full of useful tools with which we can practice and hone our skills. Only through this slow accretion of competence can we hope to eventually acquire the skills to achieve mastery.

A family, as well as its individual members, can achieve a higher order of skills if it will give itself the privilege of being an apprentice as it begins any work. A family that skips the apprentice step and jumps into an endeavor as a journeyman is just as likely as any one of its individual members to fail to learn the skills needed for mastery. Empty toolboxes are not signs of failure; rather they are opportunities for families, as apprentices, to fill them up with the tools and skills needed to become journeymen.

When a family and the individuals within it joyfully participate in the possibilities of new learning offered by adopting a beginner's mind and apprenticeship, they experience the excitement of creativity, in which everything is new. This is the fertile state where everything is possible. However, without a great master/elder acting as a crucible to hold the family's temperature at its most efficacious point for learning, the learning experience can become chaotic. As the Cheshire cat told Alice, "If you do not know where you are going, you are guaranteed to get there." True masters/elders in families offer a safety valve for the underlying chaos of the undirected beginner's mind by helping family members proceed along paths that will help them find their callings and their individual happiness. For the individual, these paths lead to deeper self-awareness; for the family, they lead to a greater likelihood of achieving the dynamic preservation of itself.

Seventh-Generation Thinking

Tribes that survive the longest ensure their preservation by practicing what's called "seventh-generation thinking." I believe this type of thinking is essential to the success of a family. I define that success as reaching the fifth generation with its bonds of affinity intact, not just its genealogy, and going on from there to become a tribe. Cultural anthropology explains this evolutionary process: a tribe is no more than an original family of two persons of affinity, which has evolved five or six generations later into an extended human system. But why does success require six generations? Why not four? Simply because reaching the fourth generation may be a matter of luck. But if a family successfully reaches its fifth generation, as a family of affinity, I believe it constitutes a system with real possibilities for long-term success. Luck, while always useful, is no longer likely to be its chief engine for growth.

To understand the essence of seventh-generation thinking, consider the statement used by the senior Iroquois elder at the beginning of each meeting of the tribe convened in solemn council. I paraphrase: "As we begin our sacred work of tribal decision making, let us hope that our decisions today as well as the care, deliberation, and wisdom we use in making those decisions will be honored by and truly beneficial to the members of our tribe seven generations from today, as we today honor the decisions made by our ancestors seven generations ago." Such thinking assures the existence of the tribe far into the future and far beyond the lifetime of any living member of the tribe. The elder's words remind us that building a family for long-term success requires vision far beyond any individual's lifetime and far beyond the imagination of any one person. The elder calls on the collective imagination. The elder imagines what the tribe's members will think seven generations from now about the decisions the tribe will make today and asks each tribal member individually to exercise his or her imagination in the same way. The elder gently reminds the tribal family to think back seven generations and to consider how blessed they are by the decisions their forebears made all those years ago, which permit them to be assembled together so many years later.

Hidden in the elder's wisdom is an admonition that my father, as the elder of our family tribe, frequently offered as we began our work: "Hasten slowly." The tribe practicing seventh-generation thinking understands that without action, entropy and stasis will cause the tribe to disappear as its energy dissipates. But unchecked action that results in chaos will lead just as certainly to the death of the tribe from a surfeit of energy it cannot absorb. Hastening slowly offers the means to use time as a friend, to find time to be a beginner, to be an apprentice, to move on to journeyman, and then to refine the skills for mastery.

To develop and survive, a family, like a tribe, needs to enhance the growth of its members' human and intellectual capital to its highest capacity. Without such enhancement, the family will not have the human assets required to take advantage of the new opportunities the future will offer and to combat the new threats it will pose. Fostering beginner's mind in combination with seventh-generation thinking affords a family a process and practice that lets its talents and gifts emerge through the increased self-awareness and happiness of its members. It balances the youthful joy and chaos such a process reflects with the elders' ordered sense of the wisdom of time as a friend. The elder helps leaven the enthusiasm of the beginner's mind with the patience of seventh-generation thinking. Hastening slowly is the path of deliberate, gradual accretion of skills that leads the apprentice to eventual mastery. This is the tried-and-true process of a family's development and enhancement that works best for achieving its successful evolution from family to tribe.

Chapter Three

Obstacles to Affinity
The Seven Paradoxes

Man is often heedless of what's going on on each side of him. This poor perspective often produces wonderful and pathetic paradoxes.

—NEAL A. MAXWELL, author and ordained apostle of the
Church of Jesus Christ of Latter-day Saints

THE SHIRTSLEEVES-TO-shirtsleeves proverb continues to work its will among families all over the world. This unfortunate fate is almost invariably the culmination of self-defeating behavior patterns, and I've observed them in many families. These patterns reveal the inability of many families to understand certain paradoxes inherent in the choices they face about how to govern themselves. Understanding these paradoxes can propel a family to success; ignoring them can stand in the way of achieving it.

The Seven Paradoxes

1) A Family of Affinity Versus a Family of Blood. Families think of themselves as being related through blood. The paradox is that no family ever begins with blood relations. All families begin by an affinity of two people who seek to begin a common journey. As soon as a family begins to think of itself as related by blood, it has actually abandoned its dual heritage and based its idea of family on a fallacy. What's more, when a family thinks of itself as connected by blood as opposed to affinity, it becomes a closed system. To be part of that system, all members must be of the same blood. Modern physics tells us that if a family system isn't open, it can't get the energy—the fusion of elements—in each generation that's needed to replenish the energy it inevitably loses.

When a family thinks of itself as a family of affinity, it is defining itself as an open system. It is a family system that declares that anyone who loves its stories and embraces its value system is welcome to join. Such a family knows that for its own well-being, each generation must bring in more energy than it loses. It also recognizes that some members related by blood will not care to join in its journey.

2) *The Art of Ownership Versus the Science of Management.* Of the many families I've observed over the years who owned enterprises that failed, and sadly there have been many, most failed because they spent 80 percent of their time together on management issues and on questions of who within the family would enter management and less than 20 percent on matters of ownership and teaching their members how to be great owners. The paradox is that the ratio should be reversed.

All family members, whether born, adopted, or married into a family of affinity—whether the family has an active business or manages a large financial fortune—become owners of that fortune the day they enter the family. That ownership has nothing to do with whether the person ever owns one share of stock or one dollar of assets. Ownership is separate from management. Management is a calling. It's something we train ourselves to do. It is something we get a degree in, such as in business administration or some other form of organizational science. Ownership is an art. It has no association with any science. It is the strategic process of bringing together disparate information into some understandable form founded on a long-term vision that is itself the reflection of a creative, generative dream, which those who manage can act on.

To prepare successfully for the fifth generation and beyond, a family must grow great owners. There are no programs for that. No college course will teach anyone how to be a great owner. To learn how to be a great owner, family members must work with people who think strategically and who will mentor them through the process of understanding what owners actually do. The wisest choice a family can make is to teach its members how to be owners and leave the management questions to those who are called to management. In this way, the paradox is resolved.

In their book *Preparing Heirs*, Roy Williams and Vic Preisser write that 70 percent of all family succession plans fail. Of that 70 percent, 60 percent "were caused by a breakdown of communications and trust within the family unit" and 25 percent "were caused by inadequately prepared heirs." An incredible amount of suffering is reflected in these statistics. One could argue that these numbers tell us there is no way to prevent entropy from working its will in the process we call "shirtsleeves to shirtsleeves." I disagree. No family wishes to spend its life on the downhill slope of entropy. I believe that at the heart of many of these failures lies failed ownership, not failed management. Families must learn to be great owners if we are going to change this statistical pattern.

3) Freedom and Greater Self-Awareness Versus Enslavement. One excellent measure of how likely a family is to succeed is the nature of its commitment to its members. Does it ask, "What can each of us in the family do to enhance your individual journey of happiness before we ask you to help the family?" Or does it declare, "Help us and then we might help you"? This is a most pernicious paradox because it seems logical to put the welfare of the family first. Indeed, there are invariably lots of things a family would like to have new members do for the good of the family. But no human being will voluntarily join any organization unless he first perceives that he will be enhanced by it before having to contribute to it.

Each member of a succeeding generation is born or adopted into a family; the choice is not voluntary. Those who marry in choose one member; rarely would they have chosen all of the members. Freud, Jung, Maslow, Levinson, and Erikson tell us that each human being must individuate, that is, differentiate himself from others. In families that fail, the prevailing ethic is not about enhancing the individual's journey toward happiness; it's about living out someone else's dream. Trapped in a system in which there is no way to individuate or differentiate, the human spirit declines. This particular paradox goes deep into the workings of the human spirit by questioning what we want from family and what we don't want.

4) *Growing the Family's Human and Intellectual Capital, With Its Financial Capital Gently Pushing, Versus Growing Only Financial Capital.* Families have changed. Since the 1990s, they've come to look to their advisers for far more than financial education. Indeed, the education and development of a family's human and intellectual capital makes all the difference in its success. No family can manage risk of any kind—financial, personal, or familial—if it can't manage the risks of its own life. If family members don't understand fundamentally who they are, how can they answer the questions about how much risk to take?

If a family can grow its human and intellectual capital, and in doing so develop and manage the critical assets on the family's balance sheet, the family will thrive. Not surprisingly, as the family's human assets thrive, its financial life thrives too. That's because as educated stakeholder-owners of their financial capital, family members will ask better questions of each other and of the professionals who serve them.

Human and intellectual enhancement is a key part of my work with families. One of the first things I do when a family starts its journey with me is ask all its members to take a learning-styles inventory. I want to find out how each family member—from three generations—learns. It is unbelievably powerful work and goes right to the heart of the development of the human and intellectual capital of a family.

Thanks to great minds like Paramahansa Yogananda, the pioneer of yoga in the West; author Howard Gardner, whose work has changed the way people think in education; Daniel Goleman, author of *Emotional Intelligence*; organizational change theorist Peter Vaill; and Mel Levine, author of *A Mind at a Time*, we now have tools that can tell people how they learn. When each member of a family knows how all the others learn best, communicating is far easier and more effective. Information is presented in the way a person can most quickly absorb it, not necessarily in the way the presenter learned it. The results are so effective that I also have all the trustees and all the senior family officers take the assessment. They share their results with the family.

I also work with families to cultivate beginner's mind in their approach to learning. Members need to understand that if they're on a journey to get to the fifth generation and beyond in good shape—a journey with a two-hundred-year horizon—they cannot be in a hurry. They must "hasten slowly."

5) *Teaching Skepticism Versus Teaching That No One Is Trustworthy.* In its efforts to teach the third generation to be skeptical of others, the second generation inadvertently teaches it that no one is trustworthy. The suffering of this paradox is tremendous. The people you love the most teach you that no one is trustworthy. In doing so, they are in fact untrustworthy in their own behavior. A person cannot become a whole human being without trusting someone. With such a worldview, how does one form relationships? How can one live contentedly in a world that deserves no confidence?

Why would any generation do such damage to those who follow? This is a paradox of extraordinary power and extraordinary sadness. The second generation is the fulcrum that either takes a family on to the fifth generation or takes it down in the third. This is the generation that inherited; it did not create. In the second generation, the dream of another has been fulfilled. Now it must develop a new dream, but of a very different sort. "I want to study family and philanthropy," John D. Rockefeller Jr. told his father. "I don't want to be in the family business." "Great," Rockefeller Sr. said. "Go do it."

The new dream enables the second generation to become like the first generation, one with its own deep passions for discovery and creativity. If a new dream doesn't emerge, the result is a plateauing and stasis of the family's energy. That plateauing in the second generation is expressed in the emptiness of spirit that comes from stewarding someone else's dream but never one's own. If this generation does not find a way to become creative, if its human and intellectual capital does not thrive, its members become fearful. A person caught up in fear or desire is in an illusion. From that illusion follows the terrible tragedy of teaching those in the next generation that no one is trustworthy. That's because the second generation fears itself. It knows it is untrustworthy, because it failed in its own life to find a dream and through that dream to grow. It failed to know itself and thrive, and thus it failed in the fulfillment of its own human experience.

Family elders and their advisers must pay careful attention to this paradox. If its symptoms begin to manifest in a member of the third generation, they must keep that person from falling into its trap. That individual's personne de confiance may well be the one person that third-generation member can learn to trust. But trust is not dependence. Dependence is the opposite of trust. The ideal personne de confiance is the person to whom the family member can say, "I can trust you to enhance my individual journey of happiness. I can trust you to help me find the connections of affinity that will bring me a relationship that will prove that I can trust." An adviser called to work with such an individual has a heavy burden. That professional may be the only one who can reach into the decaying entropic situation of a family member nearing the emptiness and despair of being unable to trust and reverse it. It is an extraordinarily important challenge.

6) *Leading From Behind Versus Leading From the Front.* In the history of Chinese philosophy, as one idea emerged, a balancing idea would follow. We have the philosophy of Confucius, which values and defines the leader who leads from the front. In the West, General George Patton would be a good example of this form of leadership. As Confucius offered this view of the leader in front, a man named Lao Tzu offered the concept of leading from behind. General George Marshall would be a good example of this kind of leadership. When one of Lao Tzu's students asked him, "How do I recognize the greatest leader?" he answered, "This leader's followers say: 'We did it ourselves.'"

Family governance in the second generation and beyond is a horizontal process. In *Family Wealth*, I describe family governance as a matter of each generation, sequentially, making a new, horizontal social compact with the other members of its generation for the governance of the family during its time of responsibility. A horizontal social compact is necessary because family members all rise together as a part of a distinct generation of the family and they are, therefore, all equally responsible for how their generation survives or fails. Second and later generations are horizontal cohorts. They all inherit the same position. The leaders needed for such a collaborative form of governance are those able to convene the family rather than direct it. They must guide with a hand the others can't see or feel but which is there nevertheless to help the group make the best joint decisions. Consider, for example, the leader among the owners of a family enterprise. From the second generation on, all family members in each generation inherit equally their relationship to the enterprise's founder; thus, the only leader likely to succeed is one who seeks to raise the boats of all the members of his generation. To do that, he must work from behind.

7) *Function Leading Form Versus Form Leading Function.*
How often today do time pressures compel a professional adviser to translate a client's problem, particularly one requiring courage to resolve, into a standardized solution—a form that offers a knowledge-based answer to the issues the family faces? Time-billing issues frequently force a rapid solution, based on the assumption that the family will not pay for the time the professional needs to study the family's system. Indeed, it takes time to understand how that system works, the people it comprises, the transitions it's going through, and the state of the human and intellectual capital of the individuals within it and within the family as a whole. But without the answers that such an investigation brings, the professional cannot know how the family *functions*. When that study does not take place, and a form is applied to solve the family's problems, that form is leading function. All too often, the result of such a process is a family's nearly complete inability to integrate the form imposed on it into its family governance system. Chaos is the likely result.

I continue to receive requests from other professionals to try to assuage unhappy family clients whose newly fledged family limited

partnerships, irrevocable trusts, or family philanthropies don't seem
to work. These entities invariably achieve their tax goals. The problems lie in the fact that the families can't make them work. That's
because the family's internal relationships, particularly their family
governance systems, are not nearly as mature as these structured
solutions require. The structures are wonderfully crafted. They
are textbook examples of what form good health should take for an
organization with healthy relationships. However, the family is not
only wounded by them, it may be fatally injured by the chaos they
create in its relationships. Forms are created for the "average" set of
relationships. I have never met such an "average" family.

A classic example is the father-in-law shrieking to his counsel,
"You told me I had all the power as managing partner."

"Yes," says his counsel, "you do."

"But you didn't mention that my ne'er-do-well son-in-law could
question my decisions."

"Well," says the counsel, "I never thought to tell you that since it
wasn't germane to saving taxes."

This is an example of form leading function. The critical issue for
a family in adopting any new structure is how it affects the functioning of its relationships. The structure must integrate smoothly into
those relationships and the governance system they constitute so
that it promotes them. If that integration is to promote the family's
well-being, the process must be orderly, evolutionary, and contribute
to the family's highest functioning. Thus, form leading function in a
family's governance far too often imperils rather than promotes the
development of a family system and often is deeply entropic to its
relationships, governance, and happiness.

To do well, every family must recognize that every new structure
it creates can be thought of as an organism that it's asking its family members and the family's system of governance to embrace and
integrate. It is therefore critical to family health that the organism be
a healthy complement to its well-being, rather than an agent of disease. A family must be sure that its professionals understand these
risks and encourage them to do the research required. The negative
results of not doing so are unacceptable. To object that the study of

these risks may be expensive is to misunderstand what is revenue producing for a family's balance sheet and what is a cost to it.

Every structure a family elects to create must create revenue by directly enhancing the family's system of growing its human and intellectual capital. A family should never create a structure to reduce taxes, which are, after all, a cost of business, unless it perceives that the lifetime of that structure will powerfully enhance its governance system and its purpose to drive the growth of its human and intellectual capital. All too often the tax savings to be achieved on day one of a structure's life is the only result anyone considers. It is essential to be aware that creating a perpetual trust, for example, will affect every family member who is a potential beneficiary of it every day of the rest of his life and every day of the life of every beneficiary in every generation to come. To fail to see this reality is to fail to understand such a structure's function and impact on the family. It ignores the risk that the structure will not be revenue creating, that it will not enhance the growth of the family's human and intellectual capital, or worse, that it will be entropic to its relationships and in fact be a cost. That form must follow function is a well-known rule. The question for a family's long-term success is whether its members, and particularly its leaders and the professionals who serve them, practice it.

—⁕—

PARADOX, AS IT appears in family systems and family governance, can open our eyes to issues of supreme importance to a family's well-being and its journey toward continued success over five generations and beyond. No doubt many other paradoxes inhibiting family success and promoting entropy remain to be discovered or the proverb wouldn't continue to prevail. The mutual task of the leaders of families and the professionals who serve them is to uncover these paradoxes.

Here are some questions families might ask themselves.

- When a certain behavior isn't working, what might happen if we considered doing the opposite?
- Can we as a family use our governance system to ask ourselves

questions using seventh-generation thinking and beginner's mind?

- Might those questions help us see that a certain behavior isn't enhancing our journey of happiness, isn't growing our human and intellectual capital, isn't solidifying our bonds of affinity?
- Is the behavior instead validating the possibility that no one is trustworthy?
- Is the behavior causing a leader in front to rapidly lose all followers, even as our family lacks a leader from behind?
- Is it, in fact, a form of behavior that is keeping our family from functioning well?

If a family has its beginner's mind tuned to such questions and uses seventh-generation thinking to answer them, there is a very high probability that it will recognize these paradoxes, discover new ones, and find the means to turn them to its advantage.

Chapter Four

The Physics of Affinity

When scientists state that something is possible, they are almost certainly right. When they state that something is impossible, they are very probably wrong.

—ARTHUR C. CLARKE, British writer

EINSTEIN'S EQUATION $E=mc^2$ tells us that the universe is made up of energy and that matter is therefore made up of energy. Essentially, we are creatures of light in an animate form we call matter. The reality that we are all integral parts of this universe—bundles of exactly the same energy as everything else in the universe—is a humbling one. It undermines any hubris one might harbor about being more important than anyone else, because at the most fundamental level, we are all exactly the same. I like to suggest to families that they start their journeys with this reality in mind.

The lessons of physics offer effective ways of conceptualizing the principles of affinity. Imagining that we are creatures made up of particles of light helps our individual spirits comprehend how we relate to all other energetic bodies. I see a family of affinity as a bundle of the individual family members' particles of light bonded by positive attraction into a larger body of light in animate form as matter. A family can put these lessons to practical use in its efforts to dynamically preserve itself and to manage the growth and decision making essential to such preservation.

Against Entropy: Postponing the Inevitable

The strength or weakness of a family's bonds of affinity will determine whether the collective family body of energy is journeying toward greatness or toward disappearance. In physics, the second law of thermodynamics teaches us that once energy has transformed itself into matter, that matter will seek to return to a state of pure energy through a process of decay of the bonds that hold that matter together. That process is called entropy. The law dictates that all matter in the universe is always and immutably destined to decay back into energy.

The process of entropy underlies all of life and deeply informs all of my work with families. Every chapter of this book deals with the reality of the law of entropy at some level, because the law dictates that long-term dynamic preservation of any form of matter is impossible. Every family seeking to dynamically preserve itself must start its journey with great humility because it will be attempting to avoid the effects of the law of entropy. To try to defy Mother Nature's laws of the universe is an act of Icarian folly. But to try with a beginner's mind and with seventh-generation thinking to discover how one's family can find the means to get along with Mother Nature by accepting her rules and managing them within their predictive realities seems to be a very sensible endeavor.

Fusion: The Power of Connection

Another lesson from physics that can help a family understand its journey is the principle from atomic physics called fusion. During the early twentieth century, physics initially defined the smallest unit of matter as an atom. Later, it found that within each atom is a nucleus that governs it and, even later, that the atom and its nucleus are themselves made up of even smaller particles of matter. The study of these virtual bits of matter-cum-energy and their interactions is called quantum physics. Continuing from their studies of the atom, physicists determined three possibilities for the interactions of atoms when they meet in space: fission, inertia, and fusion. Fusion is rich with valuable insights for families.

Fusion is the process by which two atoms join together through affinity to form a greater energetic whole. Fusion forges connections formed through the bonds of affinity between two energetic bodies positively attracted to each other, which create a new entity of greater energy and therefore having greater possibility for dynamic growth than either of the entities from which it evolved.

This idea that one plus one equals slightly more than two in terms of energy has captivated physicists for many years. But what are some of the elements of fusion that inform our family journeys?

• The reality that connection between two independent particles of light can produce an energy far greater than they had separately is beautiful in itself. The process illustrates for a family of affinity the limitless increases that can occur as its individual family members bind with each other in multiple ways to create a greater energetic whole.

• Fusion reminds a family of the Asian idea of "harmony as beauty." Clearly, the bonds of affinity leading to fusion are, in an aesthetic sense, the realization of harmony among the individual parts, which all of us can see is truly beautiful. It helps a family see the virtue of beauty in its aspiration to be a mosaic of light created from its members' individual particles of light.

• The principle helps us better understand theoretical biologist Stuart Kauffman's idea of the point at which life is sustainable: just above pure order (or inertia) and just into chaos (or fission) but not so far that we blow up in uncontrolled cellular growth. The perfect metaphor for this reality is the three forms of water as they apply to human life. When water is ice, it is in pure order and almost nothing can live in it. When it's steam, it's in pure chaos and evaporates, offering little or no nurturance to life. As water, however, it sustains life. The temperature (heat is energy) at which H_2O becomes liquid water is the life-giving point. I call it another "Goldilocks point" (where risk and reward combine perfectly for never-ending growth), not too hot and not too cold but "just right."

The principle of fusion can work in a family's favor in its attempt to energize its life forces—its internal relationships—to the Goldilocks point. That is the point at which its energy is alive as a result of the fusion of the positive connections of its affinity. From that point the family can grow its life forces, but not so fast as to cause fission or so slowly that it falls into inertia and ceases to have any relationships at all. Indeed, the life of a family can go on infinitely as it employs an understanding of fusion in its relationships.[1]

The Pace of Growth

Einstein's ideas shed light on the challenge a family encounters as it advances on its journey: maintaining a prudent pace of growth. Einstein proposed that the universe is growing from its initial "big bang" spark of energy at exactly the rate necessary for it to grow forever, without growing so fast that it explodes or slowing down so much it implodes. No physicist yet knows if Einstein's insight is true; however, many observations and measurements based on this concept suggest that it may well be. Einstein's proposition is the cosmic equivalent to Kauffman's conception regarding the point at which life begins and can be sustained.

Even if Einstein is correct, eventually entropy must win and our universe will collapse. In the meantime, Einstein's idea gives a family a beautiful way of imagining its energy being set at a point of generativity, at which it neither explodes nor implodes. Setting the governor of its energy at the Goldilocks point is critical to a family's long-term survival and prosperity. It must seek to grow, like the universe, at the gentle point at which energy continues to infuse growth. As we'll see when we discuss family governance in chapter 10, "A System for Joint Decision Making," a family's "governors" are its systems of governance and its willingness to be governed by them toward the sustenance of its bonds of affinity and their continual positive generation of family fusion.

Feedback Systems
Is it possible to manage growth? Physics can help a family with this question, too. From the science of complexities we encounter the notion that to have the capacity to evolve, all composites of two or

more entities must develop positive, controlled feedback systems.[2] These systems permit them to grow without deteriorating into chaos or closing themselves down and imploding into inertia. In other words, a complex system is an open system that admits new energetic elements by forging new bonds of affinity, all in controlled environments (founded on consistent, positive decision making about the system's well-being) that help it grow safely. A closed system has no way of admitting the new energy it needs to evolve to meet new issues.

The concept of complex systems as used to describe successful organic forms is extremely useful in helping to convey the process of controlled positive growth in a family relationship, that is, the fusion that's critical to family perpetuation. Every family develops a complex system of relationships. As each member joins the family, the number of relationships the family incorporates increases geometrically and the complexity of the family system increases as well. In the process of growing a family system, the family replicates the organic process described by complexity theory.

An understanding of how complex systems develop and function gives us a tool we can use to describe how a family is currently functioning and how it will likely function in the future. With it, we can better appreciate why family systems must be open and capable of successfully joining new members to their existing system. By offering new adherents the concept of affinity as the philosophy underlying its organic process of growth—and by practicing that philosophy—a family incorporates the principle of fusion into its complex systems. In so doing, it minimizes the likelihood of putting its systems into chaos and having them explode, as well as the odds of the system's closing down. A family that defines its connections only in terms of blood relation will eventually implode.

The Sphere of a Family's Energy

When I seek to explain the lessons of physics discussed here to families I work with, I go to a white board and draw a picture. The image is a sphere of pulsing energy depicting the size of a family's energetic self, with multiple atoms, shown as dots inside and representing each of the individuals making up the family (see **FIGURE 4.1**). In some cases, I even label the dots with the names of the family members. I explain that as each atom grows in human and intellectual capital—bringing a concomitant increase in the flourishing and happiness of the individual atom—the size of the energy body expands, causing a corresponding growth in the size of the sphere. Reciprocally, if a member of the family loses human and intellectual capital, the atom representing that individual shrinks and the size of the sphere diminishes. If the bonds of affinity among the atoms within the sphere are strengthening, then there will be an even greater expansion of the sphere's size through the fusion process of energetic growth. **FIGURE 4.1** uses different circles for the growing atoms, the declining atoms, and the bonds of affinity.

Given that family members have varied learning styles as discussed in chapter 19, "Educational Assessment Tools," certain family members will grasp these concepts more readily through the illustration in Figure 4.1 than they might from reading text. It's

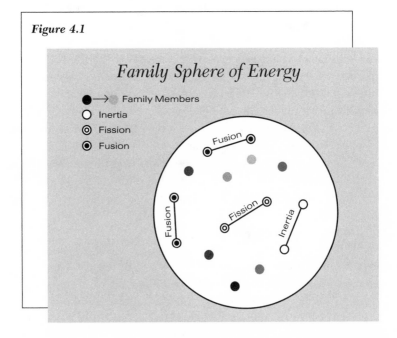

Figure 4.1

Family Sphere of Energy

●—→ ○ Family Members
○ Inertia
◉ Fission
◉ Fusion

important to illustrate complex ideas with a picture so that a family learning together can achieve its greatest depth of integration and use of the subject matter.

To depict the arrival of new family members, **FIGURE 4.2** adds their atoms in different shades of grey, representing the possibilities inherent in these new arrivals. For a family seeking to imagine reaching the fifth generation, it's extremely helpful that the future family members be represented in the picture. I do not assign a different color to deceased members or remove them, because keeping their memories alive through a family's stories retains their energy in the family's energetic sphere.

Finally, I add a circle representing a hollow sphere of energy, just barely outside the core sphere of energy (see **FIGURE 4.3**). In that outside sphere rests all of the family's privy councilors, its personnes de confiance. I'll define this group further in chapter 20, "The Personne de Confiance: Service Redefined." Although their energy is outside the core sphere, they nevertheless add energy to it, and

Figure 4.2

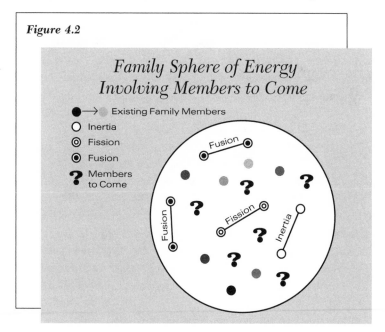

Family Sphere of Energy
Involving Members to Come

● → Existing Family Members
○ Inertia
◉ Fission
◉ Fusion
❓ Members to Come

Figure 4.3

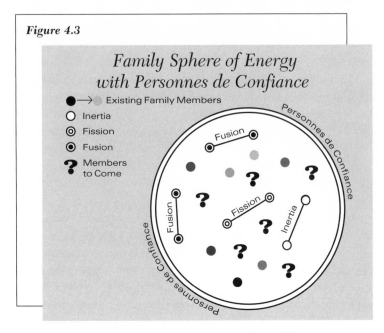

Family Sphere of Energy with Personnes de Confiance

their integrity and commitment to the family's well-being creates a strong outer defense ring to protect the permeable membrane of the sphere in which the family evolves. Equally and reciprocally, the inner sphere, as patron, sends energy to the outer circle, saluting the personne de confiance's journey and connection to the successful growth of the family, thereby deeply enhancing its personne de confiance's calling to a life of service.

With these illustrations, I try to demonstrate the time it takes a family to reach a fifth generation and what its demography could look like by then. Helping a family see how big its energetic body will need to be to accommodate all of the atoms it will comprise gives it a way of imagining itself as a physical presence floating in a universe of all sentient beings.

The illustrations also help a family see that it will need a strategy in the Darwinian competition for the space and life shared with all other families and sentient beings. It will need to choose between a strategy based on war making or one based on peacemaking. I remind them that some people of wisdom have defined our culture as basically driven by aggression and, therefore, believe that the normal state of our societies is to be at war. Other wise observers have said we are basically peace-loving and at war only as a last resort for survival. I explain that this is their choice to make, but that choosing peace—and resorting to war only when all other options have been tried and no other choice is possible—has always seemed to me to be the best Darwinian compromise. War, after all, risks the extinction of a family's human, intellectual, and financial capital. Waiting out all opponents and seeking peace, while always being prepared to fight and win, offers the greatest likelihood that a family will prevail.

Sun Tzu, the great Chinese writer on war, taught that the greatest general is the one who never has to fight. There is no need. That's because either he always has overwhelming superiority, and thus his opponent concedes and makes peace, or he acknowledges his enemy's superiority and leaves the field, living to fight another day. In its long transition, a family will sometimes find itself on the defensive and sometimes on the offensive. A family that considers which strategy is best for the particular cycle it is facing will do well. Longevity and success lie in knowing the competition and being able to use one's skills to overcome it. Better yet is to evolve with other families, seeking fusion with them in an opportunistic way, especially with those whose visions and virtues make them natural allies. A family should avoid the kind of competition that causes the fission that puts a family's survival at risk. With these priorities, a family can form a winning strategy for long-term positive evolution that's more likely to be effective as it seeks to reach beyond its fifth generation.

The Calculus: Start Where You Are

How can a family know what stage it has reached in its journey? To what extent is it truly a family of affinity? For help with these questions, we can turn to the calculus.[3] By using the calculus as a measuring stick, a family can define—at the beginning of its journey together and from time to time thereafter—where on the continuum the family's and its members' behaviors, callings, visions, systems, and practices fall and what that indicates for their success. I have found it especially useful for families who are beginning their journey to use this kind of measurement as a way of imagining the beginner's mind.

In its linear form, –1, 0, +1, the calculus expresses for a family the reality that if it is at –1, it has essentially disintegrated and ceased to exist. If it is at +1, it has become a tribe whose existence extends backward to before written history and forward infinitely. Keep in mind that the calculus is founded on the principle that there is an infinity of spaces between –1 and 0 and an infinity of spaces between 0 and +1. In other words, no matter how small you slice the spaces between 0 and +1 or –1 in either direction, they can theoretically be sliced even thinner.

History offers multiple examples of families disappearing, families for whom the entropy alluded to in the proverb fulfilled its destiny. History offers no example of absolute +1 family success, although the Jewish, Lebanese, Iroquois, Mayan, San, !Kung, Hakka, Masai, and Parsi tribes come close.

I apply the calculus by suggesting that the family members look at the questions posed in the introduction and at the theorems of my philosophy proposed there to see how and in which ways their journey might incorporate these ideas. I ask that they imagine doing so with an open heart and an open mind. I also suggest that they consider the seven paradoxes presented in chapter 3, "Obstacles to Affinity: The Seven Paradoxes," and ask themselves whether they believe they can, as apprentices at the point of 0, appreciate the truths of these paradoxes and learn to incorporate their wisdom into their vision and system as they journey together.

For a family already on the journey, its annual review of itself offers a chance to use the calculus to calibrate how it's doing and to make whatever adjustments are needed to its systems to move toward +1. I invite these families to use the calculus to help define the long-term transitions they're in and to reimagine how they want the transition issues to be successfully resolved. They can plot on the calculus how well they feel they're managing those transitions.

These measurements help me choose the families I can serve best. Since my retirement, I can no longer offer the long-term commitment needed to help a family that is failing. And since I am not likely to encounter a family who has succeeded completely, I now dedicate my professional life to working with families who score at or slightly above 0 on the calculus.

My interest in families at 0—the point I define as the point of the beginner's mind—is to help them move toward +1 by using the methods discussed in this book, in *Family Wealth—Keeping It in the Family*, and in the works listed in the bibliography. I also help them to discover and engage the privy councilors they will need to give them the courage to start the journey and to stay on it when it gets difficult. These are families that I can help the most, because they are already partway to +1 and, by my definition, do not require the remediation or therapy needed in families below 0.

Although I am sympathetic to families below 0 and remain hopeful for them, in my experience a family whose individual members are below 0 do not get past 0 even with therapy, although those whose members reach 0 do improve a great deal. Indeed, helping a family to get to 0 with therapy and remediation is a noble task and should always be attempted for the relief of suffering it offers and for the possibilities for the future it opens.[4]

No family perfectly comprehends every role and relationship its system creates or maintains. All families have squabbles, competitions, historic baggage, integration of new members' issues, and governance blockages. These issues are part of the complex territory of human relationships a person enters when he starts down the road to creating a family of affinity by connecting his family history and individual personality to the family history and personality of another person. The 0 point on the calculus poses critical questions to a family: Do you and your fellow family journeyers have a transcending dream to create a great family and a vision for its success? Is your heart open to finding the best ways of dealing with the relationship and governance issues the materialization of the dream will present? Note that all the calculus asks at 0 is whether the family has such a goal and is open-minded in its search for the ideas, tools, and skills that will bring this dream to life and eventually to fifth-generation happiness. The 0 point doesn't ask for perfection; rather, it asks for a willingness to begin with an open heart, with an open mind, and with a vision that will lead to the discoveries, creations, and explorations of the spirit needed to make the dream come true. The 0 point asks family members to humbly declare themselves apprentices to the work of creating a great family and to the task of seeking the master mentors who can take them on the journey to bring the dream to life.

Families who are willing to evaluate themselves in these ways and then commit to growing themselves with what they learn are generally at the 0 point. They are on the positive path that comes with a beginner's mind and have the openness and the curiosity such a mind encourages, which they will need if they are to achieve their dream of +1 and the happiness it reflects. Measurement should never be feared but rather welcomed if a family is honestly seeking the truth. The calculus offers a wonderful tool for discovering many truths, but only if family members have the courage to employ it toward achieving happiness for the family as a whole.

Chapter Notes

1. As I completed the final chapter of this book, I was given an article by John Ward called "The Involvement Paradox" in which he also speaks of the power of the idea of fusion in growing successful families. I hope our individual paths to discovering this use of the principle of fusion indicates that it will prove a useful metaphor for families on their journeys.

2. Throughout this book, I use the terms *complex* or *complexity* to describe family systems. I talk about them as webs of interconnected individuals and their multiple relationships, which ebb and flow with the demography that defines their particular family. I also discuss family enterprises and families as similarly complex organisms whose lives reflect the constant additions and divisions of all forms of capital in their enterprises.

What is the nature of this word *complex*, as reflected in complexity theory and the relatively new twentieth-century science that studies it? In this context, "complex" is used to describe the evolutionary process in which any single organic, base, or foundational unit—let's say the initial two members who form a family of affinity—through the addition of new entities that become parts of it (for example, a child joining the parents) causes its system of relationships to become more complex. Another example would be the process by which a single fertilized cell through continuous division becomes a human being composed of trillions of cells.

The development of complexity is the ordered, evolutionary process by which new wholes grow out of new parts, often leading to geometric increases in the number of relationships among the parts that make up the new whole. Sometimes it is not a chaotic process of random addition or division leading to new forms in what is a revolutionary process but rather an ordered process of growth. This point is very important, since there is another very powerful twentieth-century science that deals with the nature and process of chaos and seeks to describe the process of change in the universe resulting from seemingly random combinations.

The spectacular growth of the use of the theory of complexity as a tool to study the evolution of all systems—whether biological, sociological, political, economic, or cultural—is a defining reality of the twenty-first century. We have come to see that every system that survives competition with all others of its kind will gradually have to become more complex to do so. Family systems are forever becoming more complex as they add new members and new assets. The increased complexity posed to family survival by the need to integrate new relationships and new assets for the survival of its enterprises is what necessitates ever more complex systems of family governance to enable the ever more complex decisions the family will have to make.

3. In keeping with a family's multiple learning styles, and because very few may have ever studied calculus, I always begin any exercise using the calculus by making a picture of it so that all family members can appreciate its infinity in length and its infinitely smaller slices of space between two parts.

4. I continue to worry most about families that are slightly below 0, particularly those who have sold their active enterprises and have become "financial families." These families have problems I have found to be more complex than those who retain an active business, but there are very few trained professionals who have actively studied and worked with families of this type. I am working with therapists who specialize in assisting such families; many of these therapists have studied at the Georgetown Family Center or the Ackerman Institute.

PART TWO

Defining the Journey

Chapter Five

Essentials for Success

I am certain of nothing but the holiness of the heart's affections and the truth of imagination—what the imagination seizes as beauty must be truth.

—JOHN KEATS, English poet

DESPITE ITS BEST efforts, a family may fail. By the third generation, its assets and its relationships may be stunted or worse. Pinpointing the reasons for such failures is difficult. But among the families that model success, a certain characteristic stands out: The family has found a way to promote not only the welfare of the family but also to honor the value of its individual members.

Each family finds its own way to do that, developing its own philosophy of inclusion. Some ways—taking varied forms among many peoples throughout the world—have stood the test of time: beauty as harmony, "the Way" of Taoism, and the Buddhist concepts of awareness and compassion. These methods of making sense of the human experience can speak to families today, opening whole new vistas to explore.

Beauty as Harmony

Defining beauty as harmony and making its practice a fundamental tenet of family life is a powerful driver of family success. Some years ago I visited Japan as a member of a group seeking to compare the understanding of several virtues in the East and West. One of the virtues we chose to study was beauty. The Westerners saw beauty as a thrusting upward line of creativity, flowing out of the unique vision of a single person. Our Eastern friends, however, saw beauty more as a circle and as the movement toward the harmony of a vibrant community.

To help us understand the Eastern concept of beauty, the group leader explained that in Japan, for example, if a person commits a murder, he will often commit suicide afterward, not as a way of escaping retribution but as a way of rebalancing life so that society as a whole regains its harmony. For Westerners, this was a novel and disturbing idea. However, as I reflected on this concept of harmony, I soon began to see that it is, in fact, beautiful. I also learned to see how profound and useful the concept of "beauty as harmony" is in forming a successful community. Indeed, as applied to the family as a community, it's a key virtue for a family to have. A family that is harmonious is beautiful.

In the East, the Confucians believe that the success of the family represents their highest calling. Frequently, when I ask an Easterner how he wishes to be remembered in his epitaph, the answer is, "That I left my family in better condition than I found it." Rarely has this been the first answer from a Western client. My Chinese clients nevertheless suffer the effects of the proverb in equal proportions to my clients in other cultures. My point is only that the Confucian cultural idea that in harmony we find the definition of beauty is demonstrated in the belief that beauty is found in a harmonious family. This is a very powerful concept.

Although I first learned about beauty as harmony in the East, the same concept explains the success of a number of America's greatest families. Most of us would probably agree that beauty as harmony is a female virtue in the West. In many of the families I've studied, those lucky enough to have had a second generation made up entirely of women—or in which they formed a significant majority—are often still happily growing in the fifth, sixth, and seventh generations. Each of these families expressed surprise when I pointed out this phenomenon in their genealogy, but all agreed that harmony as beauty is something they deeply believed in and practiced in their family governance systems.

These families are not without healthy conflict and dialogue about real individual differences. In settling those differences, however, they relate their dialogue to the issues rather than to the person, so that dialogue remains harmonious. They practice the "ouch rule," which requires discussions to end immediately if any family member feels attacked personally and says "ouch." What's more, they make a point of starting sentences with "and" rather than "but," so that discussions remain neutral and not defensive. Equally effective, they listen affirmatively, ensuring that the speaker knows he's been heard. They seek the kind of answers that seventh-generation thinking produces. Harmony as beauty helps these families find the consensual solutions to the normal issues of individual and family development needed for their long-term dynamic preservation.

"The Way" and Its Definition of Time

In the *Tao Te Ching*, a work attributed to Lao Tzu, the founder of Taoism, we find a description of "the Way." The Way is a mystical concept far too complex to fully explain here, but two ideas that are fundamental to it have helped me help families.

The first is the concept of life as an energetic force flowing slowly through each individual life form: a river that joins all individuals into one life force, much the way all rivers flow ultimately into the seas and into the whole of the connected oceans. I offer this image to family members as a way to help them experience their interconnectedness, their affinity to each other and to the larger communities of which they are a part. Most important, I offer it as a "way" of understanding time, especially the meaning of "long-term." A family needs to appreciate that time is its friend and that its relationship with time must be nurtured and used wisely. The families I help are willing to do twenty-, fifty-, and hundred-year visioning to comprehend the long-term, complex processes of their transitions—in other words, they do seventh-generation thinking.

To do such visioning well, a family's leaders, especially its elders, must see the family's journey as a quiet, peaceful progression of the life stages of each of its members and the long-term evolution of each generation into the next, like a flowing river of family energy. They need to imagine time as the current that ceaselessly flows gently within the depth of our planet's oceans, a current unaffected by the choppy seas of everyday life. If time is seen as static or as requiring urgent decisions, it may become a force for chaos. Time appreciated as a dynamic flowing agent offering opportunity for orderly evolutionary change is critical to the vision of a family of affinity seeking long-term success. The Way of Lao Tzu provides a deep, energetic, committed "way" of seeing, imagining, and feeling the process of change required for a family's success. It helps keep a family aware that it is connected to all the other energetic bodies that form the universe's common energetic heritage and with which it shares the flow of life.

Leadership

The most successful leader a family can have is one who leads from behind. Many years ago, I came upon Lao Tzu's description of the kind of leader he believed best served his followers. He described that leader as "one who is never seen, never heard, and never felt, but is revered for one thousand years by his followers for his excellent leadership." More commonly, the definition is translated as "the leader whose followers say, 'We did it ourselves.'"

For a family, this is the most effective form of leadership.[1] Leadership from behind is what's required if the happiness of each individual family member is to be enhanced by the family as a whole. The leader from behind is a "herder of cats" who knows that the family group doesn't grow in one direct path but rather in the multiple paths followed by each of its members. In each family member's wanderings down "roads less traveled," which make all the difference,[2] and in the possibilities for discovery, creativity, and seeking of the spirit offered by those wanderings, such a leader sees the means by which the family can succeed in preserving itself.

Leaders in front have a vision of discovery, creation, and seeking and are so empowered by that vision that they believe all family members will see it and follow them in an attempt to achieve it.

Sadly, although such a trip may be extraordinary for the followers, more often it is taken at the expense of their individual journeys, which remain unexplored. If a family understands that all individual boats must rise if the family as a whole is to rise, it needs leaders who are managing a complex, dynamic system that's propelling each individual's journey of discovery, creativity, and seeking. Therefore, what's needed is the leader from behind who isn't seen, heard, or felt but whose care and seventh-generation thinking facilitates each family member's individual journey. In this way, the bonds of affinity are maintained and strengthened as the silent hand of the leader interweaves these individual journeys into the fiber of the family as a whole. In this form of leadership, the family steward serves the needs of the family as a whole by serving the needs of each individual within it.

All families attempting to preserve themselves for multiple generations need individuals who will achieve great things and whose individual stories will offer succeeding generations inspiration. In a family seeking to preserve itself, however, the stories most likely to be retained in its oral history are those of leaders who inspired all the family members to achieve happiness. Individual feats of valor are exciting, but providing long-term benefit to others is where true leadership lies and what's most likely to be "honored for one thousand years."

Leadership from behind is leadership through altruism. That's the kind of leadership every family seeks when its elders choose a new chief for a critical role in family governance. For example, when family elders are seeking a new trustee to act as a mentor for the next generation, they should select the person in that generation whom its members have been using all along to convey their wishes. This is invariably a person of emotional intelligence, rather than the family's business or quantitative leader.

Aikido Leadership

Leadership Aikido, by John O'Neil, one of the world's leading authorities on the forms and processes of leadership, offers families a view of leadership in the form of the leader who is a master of the

Japanese defensive martial art called aikido. In this form of martial art, the master seeks to permit an opponent seeking to defeat him to use his own energy to defeat himself. The genius of this art of defense is to employ all energy—one's own and one's opponent's—toward the protection and well-being of oneself.

Aikido seeks to deplete the energy of all those attempting to oppose the positive motion of its practitioner's energy. The aikido warrior seeks to avoid the lethal danger of his opponent's energy by rechanneling it as a positive addition to his own energetic force.

Metaphorically, a family creates a defensive system for combating negative energy from without or within. That energy is opposed first by diverting its force away and letting it pass by without it wounding members and second by taking that energy into the family itself and thereby making it a positive force for its own self-preservation and growth. A family's aikido leaders will do this naturally if the family is willing to recognize that its leader's ability to convert defense to offense is the preferred way for a family system to defend itself, especially with the positive energy it obtains as aikido warriors. This approach is the opposite of the normal tendency to immediately attack an opponent, which misses the deep wisdom that such an attack may waste valuable energy and certainly will not add the energy of one's opponent to one's own. One system risks dissipation of energy, whereas the other cultivates and accretes energy. Aikido leadership offers a model to family-enterprise leadership that, in its subtlety, goes deep to discover what works. Aikido offers Western families a way into models of leadership that grow out of the Eastern intuition about how energy flows and of their deep understanding of its benefits when one flows with energy and never wastes it by flowing against it.

Sun Tzu and Competitive Leadership

The Chinese military strategist Sun Tzu's *The Art of War*, written sometime between 500 and 300 BC, is the most studied book ever written on war and the nature of the leaders most successful at winning them. Within this study lies great wisdom on relations between opposing individuals, communities, and states at all levels of compe-

tition and the results of the behaviors that succeed and of those that
fail. Sun Tzu offers a family many important principles of leadership
on how to prepare for and engage in competition, whether on the
defense against entropic challenges or on the offense to gain greater
freedom.

Perhaps Sun Tzu's greatest gift to a family's study of leadership is
his observation that the greatest general is the one who never fights
a battle either because he[3] has planned so well strategically, long
before any particular battle, that he is so well prepared, equipped,
and manned, that his opponent declares defeat without fighting, or
because his opponent is in a superior position and he withdraws to
ensure his army can fight another day. For this leader, long-term
strategic planning is everything and tactics are a means of bringing
strategy to life. Such a leader takes opportunities that arise from
long-term thinking—seventh-generation thinking—and knows that
no opportunity that risks the survival of his family, regardless of the
reward, is ever worth taking. Any man whose works are read two
millennia and more after they were written must be of extraordinary
genius, and Sun Tzu is such a man.

Transformational Leadership

Families can learn much from the book *Leadership* by James
MacGregor Burns, a presidential biographer and authority on
leadership studies. In it, he distinguishes between transactional
and transformational leaders. Families need both in their family
enterprises, just as they do in their families. However, generation
after generation, families need transformational leaders *most* if their
enterprises and their families are to successfully achieve the long-
term transformation required for long-term success.

Transactional leaders meet and overcome today's issues while
transformational leaders meet and overcome the issues of the
future. The former helps a family enterprise meet a family's need to
eat for a day; the latter, often through seventh-generation thinking,
not only helps a family eat for its current lifetime but also plans for
the enterprise to provide the food for all the generations to come.

Buddhist Insights

Awareness

A core concept in Buddhism is that much if not all of our lives are lived in illusion, beclouded by fear or desire, and that we suffer greatly as a result. This has been among the most enlightening of all the ideas I've encountered in my journey. To develop the ability to distinguish between life that's unfiltered and life that's experienced through the emotions of fear and desire and the illusions they present is to gain the awareness that comes with seeing clearly. Seeing what is truly going on in one's life can reduce the suffering illusions engender. When we measure the extent to which our thoughts and emotions are driven by fear or desire, we make better choices. To live life awakened is to make ourselves aware at all times of the thoughts and feelings that underlie our decisions. If we wish to become more self-aware, more awake, we must, as Buddhism recommends, seek to make our decisions in a state as free as possible from the illusions that fear and desire create.

Compassion

The Buddhists also believe that to be truly alive, we must live with compassion for ourselves first and for the illusion we're in and the suffering it engenders. We can then extend that compassion to all others in similar states of illusion. This insight guides the choices in my life, and I believe it can aid immeasurably in a family's journey.

The concept is best understood through the mystery of the bodhisattva. The bodhisattva is a spirit who upon attaining complete consciousness—that is, freedom from all illusion—*chooses* to reincarnate rather than escape from continual rebirth. This state of complete consciousness is what all Buddhists hope to attain as they try to free themselves from illusion and perpetual incarnations. The bodhisattva has achieved complete consciousness, but in passing from his final incarnation, he senses the suffering of all sentient beings whose consciousness remains in illusion. He then vows to return to life perpetually until all sentient beings are free from suffering.[4] The depth of compassion shown by such a spirit is the most beautiful idea I've ever encountered. It exemplifies the pure altruism of total caring for another. To embrace this kind of compassion seems to me the highest calling any human being can achieve. To successfully live this vow is the final step to complete awareness.

Illusion: The Journey's Obstacle

To harbor an illusion is to mistake this life's apparent reality for the actual reality of oneness that we all share. The Buddha, like Lao Tzu, teaches that we are all energetically linked to all other bodies of energy and, in this way, to the oneness of the energy of the universe. When we see ourselves as unique or separate, we are in illusion. When we see ourselves as an integrated, interconnected piece of the whole—the one—we are without illusion and we become whole ourselves. In our connectedness to the whole and to the infinite self, we find our true selves.[5]

The Buddha's ideas challenge us to recognize that most of what we believe to be real is likely to be an illusion resulting from the ego's fears and desires, which cloud our consciousness. With this awareness, I begin each day of my work helping families achieve better outcomes. With a beginner's mind, I ask, "What is real and what is illusory about what we think we know about family?" These ideas challenge me to act with compassion as I seek to help others to reduce the suffering arising from such illusions.

This process has disclosed many realities and illusions among families. Here are some of the most important for them to understand:

The Value of Human and Intellectual Capital

When a family considers itself to be connected by its financial capital—and worse, fails to comprehend that it is, in fact, a set of linkages between human beings and their human and intellectual capitals—it is harboring the most profound of illusions. Such a family will sputter out, often after deep emotional pain and with rampant chaos, as it decays in entropy back to the rice paddy.

Cultural anthropology and archaeology teach us that financial capital is a tool to ameliorate the conditions of life. The trading our ancestors did for better goods, for better barbs for fishing, or for amber to make jewelry is a process now well understood by archaeologists who study prehistoric cultures. Clearly, our species has understood for most of its history the meaning and uses of financial capital.

But why are these cultures remembered? What is most notable about them? Their barter and trading? Or is it their art, their ocher funeral ceremonies, their attempts at writing—in other words, the evidence of their humanity and of their curiosity? In fact, we value their human and intellectual capital, and we celebrate their humanity as demonstrated by such capital. We seek to comprehend their religious ideas and their concept of themselves as human. Understanding their connections to us teaches us how we came to be as a species both biologically and culturally. We seek the roots of their humanity and ours. That's why this illusion—to misunderstand what is valuable in a family, to fail to see that its foundational assets are its human beings and what they know, what they can learn, and whether they have a system for sharing and experiencing that learned knowledge—is so critical to address.

The Pursuit of Wisdom

Among the most harmful illusions is the "modern" family's belief that it can learn nothing about its present condition by studying cultural anthropology's teachings on the evolution of families or by studying the nature of the family as revealed in history, religion, politics, art, and ancient wisdom. What's more, many such families believe that only psychology as therapy has answers for them. A family is in illusion when it ignores what the many bodies of wisdom have to say about the most successful multigenerational families. Such a family is prepared to leave all of this wisdom aside, assuming that none of it can be relevant to the modern family. What hubris! What illusion! In fact, the rich discoveries these disciplines offer about how families evolve to greatness lie open to today's families if they can overcome the notion that they alone have the secrets to family success.

The same hubris underlies the assumption that biology, chemistry, physics, organizational science, mathematics, and demography have no application to family management. Much suffering could be avoided if we could dissolve the illusion that the only answer to a family's dilemmas is therapy. What progress might result if a family was instead introduced to the possibilities gained from understanding the history and nature of the family—especially when a family seeks that knowledge with the curiosity of a beginner's mind and the joy of the apprentice?

The Need for Learning

I believe that the virtues Buddhists prize—compassion and justice, as tempered by mercy toward every sentient being—are critical to a successful life. A family must include these virtues in its vision of itself as it works toward its dynamic preservation. The constant practice of compassion toward oneself and toward others reduces suffering for all and leads to the awakened state we each seek and which offers a family the "awakened" members it needs for long-term success.

Buddhists believe that the spirit reincarnates continually in its journey toward enlightenment. Finally, when it is pure compassion, it joins fully with the universal consciousness. I was once told that Tibetans believe that as a spirit is reentering bodily form, it chooses its parents in order to learn something from them that's essential to its unique development. Once that lesson is learned, the three become friends.

I choose to believe this is so, because this idea carries within it several beautiful truths concerning successful evolving families. First, it relieves parents of any guilt for the behavior and faults of their child, since it is the child's spirit that chose them. I've often presented this idea in family meetings when a child attempts to dwell on the faults of his parents in explaining his poor behavior. This insight always elicits a laugh from all parties and often extinguishes enough negative energy to permit new thinking to emerge. Second, the concept puts the parents and child into a positive beginner's mind as the family searches together for what the child's spirit chose to learn from them. Third, it encourages teaching rather than preaching. Fourth, it recognizes that when the child has learned what it needed from the parents, the parents and child can complete their joint work together. Fifth, the idea reaffirms the saying from the Greeks, "When the student is ready, the teacher will appear," and as I like to add, "When the student is ready, the teacher will disappear." Finally, it encourages the parents and the child to become friends when their teacher/student relationship is completed. What a powerful collection of virtues and benefits.

To the Western mind, the concepts of reincarnation and of a spirit choosing its parents may seem strange, even occult. But I encourage all families to use their imaginations and to suspend their disbelief. We don't have to prove scientifically that something is true before we can use it creatively. Much can be gained by intuiting what such a relationship between parent and child might be like and by envisioning the practices such a relationship might engender.

Guilt, a form of fear, clouds the heart and spirit and endangers the relationship between parent and child, causing suffering. Adopting a beginner's mind with an intention to create a relationship that fosters learning together starts the parties at 0 and encourages behavior that enhances their relationship as it moves them toward higher orders of happiness. This Tibetan insight simply and gently offers a way for parent and child to imagine a relationship based on the compassion of the beginner's mind. I believe in this wisdom, and I have found it to be a deeper, more productive way of imagining my relationship to my children than any other I have encountered.

Chapter Notes

1. Whether such leadership is the equivalent of "servant leadership," as defined by Robert K. Greenleaf, could be profitably discussed, and I suggest it is. To those interested in learning more about this concept, I recommend Greenleaf's *Servant Leadership*.

2. Robert Frost, "The Road Less Traveled."

3. Although I use masculine pronouns here, I wish to note that the skill of successfully surviving family wars is in my experience far more often a gift received from its

female members, founded on their practice of beauty as harmony, than from its male members' biologically evolved aggression as a conditioned survival response.

4. Many individuals take this vow before they ever achieve perfect consciousness. In doing so, they try to awaken their sense of what a fully conscious life might feel like and to reduce their own suffering by seeking to reduce the suffering of others. I myself have taken the vow.

5. It is fascinating that the Buddha experienced the reality of what we consider "modern" physics and cosmology in the sixth century BC: we are all energy, as Einstein suggested, materializing in the form of our bodies, eventually dematerializing, and again becoming energy, with the universe constantly maintaining the same amount of energy. Someone once said that philosophy is a search for what is true and that there is nothing new under the sun of man's consciousness. In terms of the consciousness of our species, time essentially stands still. We have evolved as a species to the point where we consciously know ourselves and seek to reconnect to our energetic beginnings and endings.

Chapter Six

Happiness
Finding the Spiritual Path

In our era, the road to holiness necessarily passes through the world of action.

— DAG HAMMARSKJÖLD, Swedish diplomat

IN HIS MAGNIFICENT work *Man's Search for Meaning*, Viktor Frankl, a concentration-camp survivor who lost almost all of his family, including his wife, in the Nazi death camps, relates the story of his time in the camp and how he survived. One day he and his fellow inmates were awakened in the middle of the night and forced out into the freezing cold on a work detail. The men helped each other struggle against the frozen tundra, since to fall or sit down would likely lead to death. During this walk, Frankl and another inmate conversed in whispers. The fellow told Frankl that he hoped his wife, who, like Frankl's, was in a women's camp, was faring better than he. As Frankl began to think of his wife, he felt the deep love she had for him and recognized that love is what gives us meaning and that even in the most hopeless situation, love offers us hope.

Families of affinity find their meaning through love, just as each one of us does. In pure love for another, we experience pure love for ourselves. We find ourselves through the mirror of the love we express to another. Frankl offers us the beacon of hope that through love we can find meaning and through love become free. To be free is to be awake, to become light. Thus love is the means to freedom and happiness and to the full lightness of being we seek to become.

Few people have succeeded so well in epitomizing such lightness of being as the late Mother Teresa. Her presence affirmed the joy of a life based on love and her connection to the generativity of the universe's energy. Meeting her was a lesson for me in how to recognize that joy, and a story worth telling here. Some years ago, I was returning to the United States from Rome, and just before getting on the plane, I received the delightful news that I had been bumped up to first class. I took my seat, on the left-side seats in the front row. Directly across the aisle from me a seat remained unoccupied. As we got closer and closer to takeoff, the single seat remained empty. Just as the doors were about to close, there was a murmuring among the flight attendants and to my amazement, a very small lady in a light blue nun's habit was ushered to that single seat. I did a double take, realizing it was Mother Teresa. My goodness, I thought, we're going to fly across the Atlantic with Mother Teresa as our fellow passenger, and we're going to be with her for eight hours.

Once we had reached altitude and the seat belt sign was switched off, the flight attendants set out to see that Mother Teresa had a special experience. But throughout the flight, the hustle and bustle surrounding this lady was extraordinary. People came to her to be blessed, and an offering was taken up for the Sisters of Charity. Early on, I noticed that her eyes flashed and that she never stopped smiling. She seemed, in fact, to be pure energy itself disguised in that tiny body.

About an hour out of JFK Airport, we were all presented with the routine U.S. Customs form. I had to laugh. Mother Teresa had to clear customs. She turned to me and said, "You look like a bright boy. Will you help me fill out this form?" I told her that I would be delighted to help her and proceeded to do so. When I had completed this task—noting that Mother Teresa had "nothing to declare"—I returned the form to her. She thanked me and then said she wanted to ask my thoughts on another matter that was troubling her. I wondered what it could possibly be. She then shared her concern. "Mayor Koch [then mayor of New York]," she confided, "doesn't like me." I protested that I was certain that this couldn't possibly be true, because she was universally loved.

"No," she insisted, "he doesn't like me, and he tells me regularly. You see," she explained, "Mayor Koch has asked me not to come and see him so regularly, because he can't deny me anything that I ask for. So you see, Mayor Koch doesn't like me."

I laughed as big a belly laugh as can be imagined, and her eyes sparkled with joy and love as she laughed with me. Soon thereafter, we parted. Her laugh, her joy, and her humor live with me every day, especially on the days of my deepest gloom and depression.

Let us look now at some of the many paths people have taken to find love and happiness—paths that are still available to families today.

Ancient Wisdom

I am a historian by avocation. The basic premise I follow in my life and my work is philosopher George Santayana's admonition that "Those who fail to study history are condemned to repeat it." As I began my study of what a family might do to combat the proverb, it seemed right to me to begin with the voices in history who have spoken to the question of how a human being might live a life to achieve greatest happiness. Perhaps in these voices we might hear the echo of patterns of human behavior that could guide individual families. By following these precepts, a family might help all of its members to thrive.

Philosophy teaches that all ideas remain worthy of consideration until and unless they are found to be fallacious. The study of old ideas, even those that prove false, through their constant testing by each generation provides the basis for new ideas to emerge. Thus even negative information is valuable information. Knowing that something is false offers clues to what might be true. A whole period of civilization, the Renaissance, was built on recovering the ideas—thought to be lost—of the Greeks, Hebrews, Persians, and Romans, which the Islamic civilization had preserved. Once recovered, these ideas became catalysts for the development of ideas we hold true to this day—this despite the fact that many of the recovered works were badly translated and thus completely misunderstood. Note also that the concept of Plato's cave, Aristotle's essays on politics and aesthetics, and Cicero's essays on life remain as fresh and useful today as when they were first written.

The wonder of ideas, as philosophy teaches us, is that they are timeless and therefore forever useful, as long as we use a beginner's mind to search them out from their historic archives. Only when we fail to look for them do they become lost to us. We are then, as Santayana tells us, condemned to repeat what those ideas could have helped us avoid. Only then do we fully understand how important it is that we be lifelong seekers of these truths.

In these ancient traditions, achieving happiness is seen as a process of the gradual evolution of our individual spirits through a continual effort to increase self-awareness, with perfection of self as the goal. Fulfillment has many names, such as *happiness* from Aristotle; *enlightenment* from the Hindu sages and the Buddha; *saintliness* from the Christians, Jews, and Muslims; and *integrity* and the *clearing of the mind and spirit of the Way* from the Tao. These words are frequently linked to living life as a journey in which one sees through illusion and discovers truth. All of these traditions, whether philosophical or spiritual, refer to certain kinds of behaviors as virtues. Although each may prize different virtues, their lists are remarkably similar regardless of the cultural milieu in which the tradition was immersed. Each suggests that the virtues of love, truth, beauty, goodness, justice, gratitude, and compassion are vital to an individual living a life devoted to the development of the self, regardless of whether one describes that self as a soul, a spirit, or a sentient being.

Because this book is for a secular audience, my mission is to convey what individuals and families can do in this lifetime to advance the development self-awareness, so I won't spend time on issues of a next life. Note, by the way, that Eastern philosophers' views on the question of proving God's existence vary 180 degrees from those of Western scholars. The earliest Eastern philosophers and religious thinkers decided that because God's existence could not be proved, it was not a useful question for consideration and, therefore, no time should be spent on it. Rather, they decided that what was useful was to study the questions of how to live one's life in this lifetime to achieve the highest order of perfection of one's self toward one's happiness and the happiness of one's family. Necessarily, this way of thinking results in a greater amount of concentration on the family than the West has offered. All traditions, however, stress that living one's life virtuously is critical to achieving personal happiness in this lifetime. I believe that goal is just as necessary for families seeking to dynamically preserve themselves.

Aristotle and the Idea of Happiness

The fourth-century BC Greek philosopher Aristotle is surely one of the leading voices for individuals in the West on how to live a fulfilled life. He was for a time the greatest disciple of Plato, another important Greek philosopher. A polymath who thoroughly mastered multiple academic disciplines, Aristotle wrote with equal brilliance on aesthetics, physics, chemistry, politics, and ethics. In his book *Nicomachean Ethics*, Aristotle sets out his philosophy for how we might live a life of virtue. He suggests that we define and measure the state of our life by measuring our state of happiness. In the pursuit of happiness, through living a life of virtue, he explains, we will live a fulfilled life. In practicing the virtues of justice, courage, and prudence—all in moderation—lies the chance to be happy. He believed that to be fulfilled, we must be able to understand the aesthetics of life, to understand beauty, and to actively participate in family and civil society. And we must live and practice these virtues to the very end of our days because we can only know if we've achieved happiness in this lifetime on the day following our death.

The idea of happiness as something of supreme value rather than as a giddy state of being was, for me, completely new. To go on to find that almost all of the philosophers and spiritual writers I read talked about happiness as the goal of life confirmed for me that it is the term of art for evaluating the fulfillment of a life's journey. I came to understand that the question, "Have I achieved happiness?" is the fundamental question a human being must ask to measure the fulfillment of life. The idea of pursuing it by living virtuously is an essential part of the answer to that question. I have, therefore, adopted the pursuit of happiness as a basic tenet of my own philosophy. And I believe that it is the essential goal a family and the individuals within it must strive to achieve if they are to be successful in their journey. In Aristotle, I found the idea that underlies my philosophy—that through the enhancement of the happiness of each individual family member, a family as a whole has the greatest chance of dynamically preserving itself.

Aristotle also answered a question I had been asking myself since I was a little boy: Why had Thomas Jefferson and the founding fathers in the Declaration of Independence added the pursuit of happiness to the fundamental rights of life and liberty for which they were prepared to sacrifice their lives? Clearly, they decided that Aristotle was right that the pursuit of happiness was so integral a part of human life that society had a duty to protect it.

The founders of our national family must have had an excellent sense of what a family needed for long-term success, since our American family is now well over two centuries old. The Hughes family, for one, now spans seven generations of Americans (there were at least five generations of British-American "colonials" before we became Americans). Counting forward, with my ten children and seven grandchildren of affinity, we have nine generations of Americans altogether. Our national family—with its affinity based on our promise to protect one another's lives, liberties, and pursuit of happiness—has more than beaten the three-generation proverb and appears likely to prevail for many generations to come.

Greek Mythology as Metaphor

In studying the Greek pantheon, families can appreciate through myths key aspects of the human character and the related behavior that each god or goddess represents. In this way, they can more readily recognize those traits in their own family members. If a family permits the Greeks' wisdom to inform its behavior, it will have a far greater understanding of the human condition to work with.

The Greeks created a mythology of gods and goddesses on Mount Olympus as images of the human condition. Each god or goddess represents a combination of different human traits, which span the entire palette of human characteristics and behavior.

Studying the gods or goddesses and the acts attributed to them often informs us about why we act as we do and how our actions reflect our character. In the stories of even a single god or goddess, we find deep reflections of the human condition, which can assist a family in its journey. The two examples that follow offer ways of understanding how Greek mythology can inform a family's journey.

Hubris. The minor goddess Hubris represents overwhelming ego. Hubris permitted herself to imagine that she was terribly important. I like to think that Zeus, the father of the Greek gods, looked down from Olympus and spied this lady strutting around, all puffed up with self-importance, and that he immediately sent a thunderbolt that hit Hubris right between the eyes—a gesture to remind Hubris that he, Zeus, was the Big Daddy of the gods while Hubris was exhibiting traits that constituted bad manners at best and lèse-majesté at worst.

The Greek philosophers Socrates, Plato, and Aristotle thought that hubris was the gravest error of false consciousness a human being could commit. Essentially, they saw hubris as a deep state of illusion, a lack of reason so profound it would deny a person any possibility of realizing who he really is. They were quite correct. An overwhelming sense of one's self-importance blocks the emergence of the larger self that arises out of humility and true comprehension of the human condition. True humility—not unctuousness or pusillanimity but a beginner's mind of acceptance of the truth of one's humanity—is the antithesis of hubris.

The Greeks believed that with reason guiding our journeys and with true humility about the human condition, we can, as Aristotle suggested, live lives that can achieve happiness. Happiness, in the Greeks' view, is the sense of the full awareness of self that they believed came through the practice of the great virtues founded on a life directed by reason. The goddess Hubris represented to them a person whose journey—through a lack of self-awareness caused by overwhelming ego and the lack of reason it reflects—could lead only to the unhappiness of the metaphoric thunderbolt and a wasted life.

In my experience, families that ground their values in humility and treat hubris as the illusion it is give themselves and their individual members a running start for a life journey that has a greater-than-average chance of achieving the success the Greeks sought.

Mentor. The Greek god Mentor is seen for the first time in Western literature as a character in Homer's poem *The Odyssey*. He appears as a wizened old man of wisdom who raises the boy Telemachus in the absence of his father, Odysseus. Later in the poem, Athena, the goddess of wisdom, takes over the shell of Mentor and uses it as a vehicle to enable her to offer wisdom about life, power, and peacemaking. Thus within the single image of Mentor, the Greeks, through Homer, offer us in one figure the combined sage intelligence of an old man and the intuition of the wise woman. Mentor reflects the characteristics of true wisdom, intelligence, and intuition joined in the form of a teacher of truth. Mentor, as image, embodies the characteristics we seek in our guides when we want to truly learn to be fully ourselves.

I believe that being a mentor is the highest calling of any relationship with another individual, higher than being a teacher, coach, elder, or best friend—although any one of these relationships can on occasion transcend its special characteristics and skill set and become one of mentoring. Mentors are people we entrust with the right to ask us the questions we least want to answer and most need to address. This is the most trusted relationship we can enter with another human being and is, if performed well, likely to lead to our deepest learning about ourselves. To have a mentor is to be in an enlightened place where our egos are left at the door and our beginner's mind can thrive.

I always suggest in my work with families that each member have a mentor as part of a commitment to personal growth. I strongly suggest that families not only encourage the use of mentors but actually assist family members in finding them. I also believe a family itself should have a mentor who asks the questions it least wants to answer.

The Greek god Mentor gives us a portrait of the qualities a mentor must have to carry out that work: intelligence and intuition in equal measure with the strongest commitment to the well-being of the mentee. Great mentors have a commitment to learn about themselves through the practice of the mentoring art. In this way, every mentee becomes his mentor's teacher. When such relationships of reciprocal discovery and growth occur, the fusion of energy they represent often leads to far deeper insights for each participant than either could ever have attained independently. This is a truly blessed union of two energies in a relationship of affinity.

The Hindu Gifts of Wisdom

In India, the Vedic traditions that inform the Hindu faith are based on an oral tradition, written down in Sanskrit millennia ago. These writings include the Vedas and, most important, the Rig Veda, the Upanishads, and the Bhagavad Gita. Within this tradition a fundamental idea is that of the triune God.[1] This is a unity of God represented in three forms: Brahma, the inspirer who breathes life into the infinity; Shiva, the creator and destroyer of life; and Vishnu, the preserver of life. In this profound view of the dance of creation, the sages explain what we now know about how the universe works. The everlasting reality of energy is ever present, ever materializing as the energy of creation and chaos, and ever decaying and dematerializing in the entropy of order and death, but with the purity of the inspired energy always present in everything.[2]

Shiva as Creator and Destroyer, Vishnu as Preserver. Hindu insights inform a family in several ways. First, if there is ever-present inspired energy, pregnant with possibility, what a beautiful metaphor for the possibilities for family members to tap into for inspiration as they begin their work together.

Second, if we are made up of energy and if we emerge from that energy in a created form that will later be eroded as entropy works its will, then we can understand the role of Shiva as he dances the dance of life as creator and destroyer.

Third, but most important metaphorically for family success, is the role of Vishnu, the preserver. In the Hindu vision, as I understand it, life begins with inspiration from Brahma and form is created by Shiva. Shiva then moves to destroy it. It is Vishnu who grasps life at the moment before it is destroyed and, preserving it, tosses it back to Shiva in his role as creator. Great matriarchs and patriarchs in their roles as elders epitomize in the life of families the role of Vishnu, the preserver. These are the spirits who help us when our families and tribes are threatened by Shiva, the destroyer. They preserve our communities for the possibilities that Shiva can offer as he creates new possibilities for life out of the energy of the future.

The Hindu inspiration about the process of creation and its dance between the chaos of the newly created, the epitome of Eros, and the ordered reality of the decay of exhausted energy, the epitome of Thanatos, reveals in a mythical form what science reveals in a mechanistic form. The parallels between the wisdom of the Hindus and the enlightened insights of the twentieth-century scientists about how our universe works are not an unlikely convergence. This is a synchronicity of truth that will, I believe, deeply inform the twenty-first century.

The depth of insight of the Vedic sages about energy, its ubiquity, and its process of emergence into form and of decay teach a family all it needs to know to understand where it comes from and where it is destined to go. The insight informs a family deeply about the full wisdom of the proverb that declares that in three generations a family plays out in a form of energetic tragedy the process of emergence, plateau, and decay that underlies life.

Within the powers of Vishnu, however, lies a family's hope that this process need not lead to destruction. Vishnu's dynamic act of preserving life and maintaining the possibility for a very long future based on the possibilities of new, creative energy is the model a family must imagine for long-term success. This possibility is the essence of the term *dynamic preservation*. It is Vishnu's energy that a family finds and employs as it seeks to retard the energy of Shiva waiting patiently to fulfill his predestined role as destroyer.

Although all families practicing humility accept the universe's laws as true and thereby accept that the entropic role of Shiva as destroyer cannot be removed from the last act of a family's play, they know that Shiva can be held in a state of long suspended animation if a family learns to use Vishnu's energy in the many acts of its play.

More Hindu Wisdom

In their understanding of the human developmental processes, the Hindu sages preempted Jung, Piaget, Erikson, Maslow, and Levinson by thousands of years. Hindus learn early in life that as a part of their spirit's fullest development in this lifetime, they must fully experience all that there is to learn in each phase of life before passing to the next. They learn firsthand that life is a series of transitions, not transactions. As young Hindus learn about each stage of life and what is expected in it, they appreciate the depth of learning their reincarnated spirit seeks in this lifetime and in its multiple lifetimes toward Nirvana. In the first stage of life, they feel with a profound beginner's mind what the life of a child is. In the second stage, they experience life as a student, as a husband or wife, and as a parent; work as a calling; and service to community. In the third stage, they experience life as an elder as they seek to grow the spirit, and finally in the fourth stage of life, they know the dissipation of the body.

In my work with families, I use the Hindu view of the stages of life as well as modern developmental psychology to help families understand who they are. I suggest that they consider the current stage of life of each of their members and help them focus on the issues they're likely to be facing. I invite them to see the three major stages of life as those of learning, doing, and being/giving back. They can use these definitions to ask questions of each family member. From the answers, they can determine which stage the person has reached.

One exercise I use at annual family gatherings and at every first session I have with a family is to ask each family member to make a list of his individual passions, his big dream, and what one gift the family could give that would most enhance that member's life at this stage. These lists are then shared with the entire family. My goal at these sessions is to help each family member understand how to integrate passions and dreams into the present stage of life.

One very important lesson I've learned from these exercises is that age is a useful guidepost in discovering an individual's stage of life but it's rarely a perfect predictor. That's because, sadly, all too often in our modern societies we think that doing is the only way of defining our lives. We lack the Hindu wisdom that it is in the third stage of life, the stage of being and seeking to grow our spirits, that we have a chance to be truly happy.

If an individual does not fully live the first or the second stage of life, he will not be ready for the transition to the next stage and will truncate his development. A family must be aware of the risk to the family as a whole when family members fail to complete a stage of life and are unable to move on healthily to the next. The stunted growth of one member stunts the growth of all, with real entropic effects on the family's development. Clearly, if a family can prepare its members for these transitions, they will be better able to integrate each stage's learning into their lives and allow their natural evolution to occur, which, as Hindus have told us, is the key to happiness.

The Hindu sages challenge a family to understand and practice the art of development of the spirit through the earlier stages of life as fully and completely as possible so that family members are ready for the third stage.[3] In this challenge, they tell a family how to develop the elders it needs for the well-being of the families and how wisdom forms. They show the family how natural the transition from the doing generation to the being generation can be. How sad it is that many families perish because their family systems do not encourage their members to make these life transitions and thereby stultify their families' natural developmental process.

Life as energy is always in transition. The Hindu sages know this and offer their wisdom to us for the natural opportunities it offers for our development. A family that seeks to grow its human and intellectual capital, and includes in its curriculum for doing so a developmental process for learning about the natural transitions of life, is likely to sharply improve the probability of dynamically preserving itself.

Judaism and Altruism

Judaism has many insights to offer on the virtues of altruism and gratitude and on philanthropy. The inspirations that inform the Jewish faith are the Old Testament of the Bible, the Talmud, and the many writings of the sages and rabbis of the faith. Although I am indebted to Judaism for many of its deep insights about how to live, one in particular has captured me: the commandment by God to be philanthropic,[4] meaning to seek justice, to practice *philos anthropos*, that is, to "love [of] one's fellow man." Judaism describes in two ways how a person shall best fulfill this commandment: "That to save one human life is to save the whole human race" and "Tikkun olam," that is, to seek to heal the brokenness of the world. These are deep insights into altruism and our obligation to preserve the gift of love that our human condition proclaims.

In the twelfth and thirteenth centuries, a Jewish sage named Maimonides listed what he perceived were the eight levels of how a person might meet his obligation to seek justice. (I believe this equates in part to being philanthropic in the sense that if one is compassionate and acts to seek justice, one is by definition loving one's fellow man.) Maimonides defined the highest level of giving as helping a man achieve a livelihood or profession. This has come down to us in modern parlance in its Chinese form as, "If you give a man fish, he will eat for a day; if you teach him to fish, he will eat for a lifetime." Maimonides took the Jewish negative injunction "to save a life" and made it positive—"to help a man achieve a livelihood." Both statements enjoin us to save a life, but the second is a more positive way to go about doing so.

Maimonides's insight informs all philanthropy today. It is the foundation of the development of a society's social capital and of each family's social capital as well. The Judaic tradition's commandment to be philanthropic is the deepest injunction I know about the benefit of altruism to the human spirit. This insight enables each of us to understand what we need to do for others if we are to live fully ourselves. If our goal is to achieve greater personal freedom in the form of greater self-awareness, it is through living this commandment that we're most likely to do so. Seeking to "save others' lives" is how we will come to know ourselves most deeply. It is the height of "selfishness."

A family that seeks to dynamically preserve itself and practices the commandment to be righteous through philanthropy is one of those moving its probability of success most heavily into the plus column. Through the process of seeking to know itself as it acts toward others, it learns deep insights about itself. Such a family acts out of gratitude for the gifts it has been given and with compassion toward others as it celebrates the sharing of those gifts. It does not act out of obligation or duty, which, as Maimonides explains, is to give grudgingly. The family knows that sharing as an act of love brings greater rewards to the development of its family members' spirits than any other act. It is engaged in increasing their energy as human beings, the same energy needed for the family's dynamic preservation.

Christianity and Three Parables

Three parables of Jesus of Nazareth, as related in the New Testament of the Bible, have informed my work with families.

The Eye of the Needle. The first parable I find helpful is the one about riches and getting into heaven: "It is more difficult for a rich man to enter the gates of heaven than for a camel to pass through the eye of a needle."[5] Recently, I learned what this statement meant, not just in metaphorical terms but in historical terms. For this insight I am indebted to author and Roman Catholic priest Father Myles O'Brian. Father Myles advised me that the eye of the needle was in fact a gate through which one entered historical Jerusalem.[6] This gate was constructed in such a way that a camel entering the city was obliged to kneel down and crawl through it. The opening was so narrow that the camel had to be divested of any pack it was carrying and of its saddle. People of Jesus' time would have experienced these same discomforts, because so many of them would have walked through it.

In this parable, Jesus was asking those with financial capital to understand that through the humility needed to crawl through this gate and the unburdening of possessions necessary to do so, they could imagine the state of simplicity required to enter heaven. Again we learn that humility rather than hubris and simplicity rather than the pursuit of financial capital are the virtues Jesus suggests we practice for the unburdening of self needed to pass through the narrow gates that lead to the Promised Land. The unburdening of illusion likewise comes with the cultivation of a beginner's mind, an unburdening that leads to a greater lightness of being. To be rich enough in spirit to embrace the humility needed to kneel and follow the unburdened camel through the eye of the needle is to acquire beginner's mind and to be truly rich. Families who understand the depth of Jesus' parable and who practice its teaching may well find that the path through the needle is, while narrow, the access to a land of milk and honey.

The Prodigal Son. The second parable is that of the prodigal son. Many of us have not only heard this story, we've witnessed it being lived out in our own families. Some of us have been the children who stayed home and followed the rules, and some have lived the life of the prodigal son. As we read this story, we apply our own experience to it. What can families learn from this parable? Perhaps it's that even those members of our family whom we perceive as lost can, by being shown love through an open heart, be rendered productive to themselves and to their families. This isn't about trying to be Christlike or believing in the possibility for redemption of every human being; that's simply too hard for most of us. Rather it's about the recognition that if we as struggling human beings can keep our hearts open to the possibility of a person's redemption, our own ability to love grows, leading to our own ultimate redemption.

Blaming and shaming, as exemplified by the son who stayed home, are useful ways of teaching. However, as psychologists tell us, to be useful for our development, four appreciations are needed to make up for one slam. I wonder if the son who stayed home knew this? Compassion for another's suffering is the essence of being merciful, something Jesus taught is critical to one's well-being. To forgive another who asks forgiveness is to increase positive energy enormously for both.

In the proverb of the prodigal son lies wisdom for a family struggling to understand the virtues of compassion, gratitude, and justice
tempered by mercy. It illustrates justice in that the remaining son is
not asked to share his inheritance with the prodigal son. Gratitude
is felt for the gift of the son's return. The father shows mercy and
compassion in his willingness to forgive his son and welcome him
back into the family. The parable informs a family of the possibility
to heal wounds through the forgiveness that grows out of a parent's
pure love for a child. This is the wisdom needed by families who
seek to dynamically preserve themselves. In this way, they navigate
the transitions that flow out of abandonment and breaking of bonds
and the possibility offered for reweaving those bonds when the
prodigal son seeks to return. Here we see altruism practiced within
the family and the increase of energy that flows into a family by acts
of love toward even its most difficult members.

The Good Samaritan. The third parable I find helpful for families
is that of the good Samaritan. In this story of the stranger who "did
not pass by," we find perhaps the deepest learning possible about
altruism and love. The parable describes how a stranger, the good
Samaritan, chooses to delay his journey to care for an injured man
who lies by the side of the road. Before the Samaritan arrived, two
local men had observed the suffering of their fellow citizen but
chose to pass by. The Samaritan had no reason to stop and care for
the man; rather, he had every reason to pass by. Instead, as an act of
pure love toward another, he stopped and cared for the man. In this
story, Jesus asks us to understand that in our love for our fellow man
lies our deepest learning about ourselves. The act of love toward a
stranger is the highest form of love, of pure altruism.

It should not be surprising that this parable from the New
Testament is perhaps the most well-known story in the Western canon.
Although few of us may be able in this lifetime to perform the pure act
of love of the good Samaritan, every one of us can imagine and feel the
power of such an act toward another. A family that seeks to help others
learns lessons about altruism that shape its relationships. As a family
learns and practices altruism, it increases its positive energy through

the positive feedback loops of reciprocal energy between itself and the lives of the strangers with whom it interacts.

It is natural to help those who share our genetic DNA. It is human consciousness at its highest, expressed as altruism, as love, that helps us perform the less-compelling act of helping the stranger. It is the latter, however, that creates new energy as we link ourselves to another. The act toward a stranger is creative because it expresses the affinity we have to all within our species and to all sentient beings. Such an act lifts us above the mundane to the universal as we experience the power of the injunction that to save one life is to save the whole human race.

—ɯ—

SOME YEARS AGO I was privileged to attend a board meeting of the Institute of Noetic Sciences that took place in the community known as Yogaville, Virginia. At that meeting we were blessed to have a number of visits with Swami Satchidananda, the founder of Yogaville. During one of those sessions a guest asked the swami why at Yogaville all the world's religions were accorded equal status, even though the swami was a Hindu. The swami's eyes flashed, reflecting the most extraordinary inner energy of purity and joy I've ever encountered in a human being. Then he offered this story, laughing all the while he told it. It was a laugh of bliss so genuine that no one in the room could fail to laugh with him. In fact, it felt as if the swami's inner self was connected to the creative energy of the universe and that his laugh was its reflection.

This is the story Swami Satchidananda told: One day a Hindu priest was standing in one of the sacred rivers of the Hindus, looking back at the sacred mountains from which the river flowed. He was waving his fists in the air at a Muslim holy man, who was standing in a river sacred to the Muslims, and shouting that the religion of the Muslim was a false religion. The Muslim, standing in his sacred river and looking at his sacred mountains from which his river flowed, was waving his fists in the air and shouting at the Hindu, telling him that his Hindu faith was false. There the two holy men stood, screaming imprecations at each other.

Along came a little boy walking his dog. He looked at the two men for a long time. After a while, when they were both exhausted, the boy said to them, "Please turn around." When they did, they found themselves standing at the edge of the boundless ocean into which both rivers flowed.

This story, illustrating that the paths of all ideas flow into the vastness of the universe, forming an equal part of it, will remain with me always. Thanks to Swami Satchidananda, I understand the depth of the truth that we are all spiritual pilgrims whose rivers of spirit flow into the spirit of the whole. No one idea is right; all ideas flow together along the banks to consciousness.

Learning about each path to awakening and finding the ideas from the particular path you choose is the way to the awakening of consciousness each of us seeks.[7] Freedom comes from understanding that all streams lead to the same ocean. Every sentient being is seeking that freedom and Swami Satchidananda's story shows us the way.

Chapter Notes

1. The profound wisdom of Hinduism includes for many of its adherents a belief in Brahman as the ultimate force, with the three forms I am discussing as ways of understanding the full nature of Brahman.

2. Some scientists of the twentieth century have enlightened us with the concept of the zero-point field. Their belief is that throughout the infinity of this and the multiple other universes there lies a field of energy that is always prepared with possibility and that is forever ready to become something and to receive such something back. Although I am not a Hindu and cannot imagine the depth of the Hindu insight, I do believe profoundly that the Hindu insight and the possibilities of the zero-point field as it emerges from quantum physics seem startlingly close. Another remarkable synergy among the ideas of the past, present, and future is that they emanate from apparently profoundly different times, geographies, and cultures and yet come to the same view of truth.

3. I am in the third stage of life, the stage of being. This is the period of life the Hindus refer to as the life of the spiritual seeker and is the most important for one's highest development in this lifetime. This is the stage we must prepare for all of our lives if we are to live it fully.

4. One of my Jewish mentors, Richard Bakal, informs me that one cannot define oneself as an observant Jew without accepting that to be Jewish is to seek justice, or else one would be outside God's most powerful commandment.

5. One of the most serious issues in modern families is the state of victimhood called entitlement. For those who wish to understand why gifts that are only transfers, or subsidies, increase significantly the risk of family members' falling into this syndrome and why true gifts are those which enhance their family members' journeys of happiness and reduce the risk of entitlement, see my reflection called "The Path of Altruism—A Reflection on the Nature of a Gift" on my Web site at www.james ehughes.com.

6. Some students of the history of Jerusalem do not believe there was such a gate. I choose to believe there was because it makes such a good story as the camel kneels and crawls.

7. My thanks to Edward Bastian, founder of the Spiritual Paths Foundation, for his gifts to me of this reality.

Chapter Seven

Self-Actualization
Lessons from Psychology

This above all: to thine own self be true,
And it must follow, as the night the day,
Thou cans't not be false to any man.
—WILLIAM SHAKESPEARE, *Hamlet,* Act I, Scene iii

PSYCHOLOGICAL WISDOM CAN accelerate an individual family member's journey toward happiness. Giants of modern psychology have turned their minds and spirits to the question of the stages of development of a human being's life. The modern psychologists whose work has informed me most in this area are Carl Jung, Jean Piaget, Erik Erikson, Daniel Levinson, Jeffrey Jensen Arnett, Alexandra Robbins and Abby Wilner, James Hollis, Martin Seligman, Abraham Maslow, Helen L. Bee, James Hillman, Alan Jones, John O'Neil, and Frances Vaughan.

The Developmental Stages of Life

In his book *Toward a Psychology of Being,* Abraham Maslow postulates that human beings pass through various developmental stages in their evolution toward self-actualization and that a human being has different needs at different stages of life. As these needs move from the most basic to the more complex, they form a hierarchy.

A human being's personal growth to the highest stage of development, or self-actualization, is a process Maslow defines as moving from "becoming" to "being." He defines the characteristics of self-actualization. To achieve our highest selves and to live our lives with the characteristics Maslow enunciates is to be truly alive, awakened, and living with a beginner's mind. To imagine all the members of a family of affinity with their human and intellectual capital developed to this level is to imagine a beautiful painting of minds, bodies, and spirits in transcendence. Let us hope all family members will achieve such a state.

In his book *Childhood and Society*, Erik Erikson postulates that human beings have eight defined stages of life. Erikson calls these the "eight ages of man." A dichotomy of developmental choices, one positive and one negative, define each stage. He demonstrates that if we can develop and integrate the positive aspect of the stage of life we're in and carry that into the next stage, we will develop to our full capacity over a lifetime. Sadly, if we are overcome by negativity, often through a crisis occurring at that stage of our development and we carry that negativity forward, it will seriously impinge on our ability to develop in the subsequent stages of our lives. Erikson concludes with an explanation of the process of development. He gives us a psychological and cultural anthropological developmental model for the evaluation of self and how that self expresses itself in society at each stage, or age, of development.

Erikson brings psychology to us as an evolutionary tool, seeking to define what we should expect as our minds and spirits evolve throughout a lifetime. In the seventh stage, he develops the concept of "generativity." This stage seems closely correlated with Maslow's highest stage of self-actualization, in which altruism is one of the most salient characteristics.

I believe human beings do have a gene for altruism and, therefore, we are not simply selfish genetic beings. Maslow and Erikson, in their work on our psychological developments, clearly agree and indicate that their studies of our species' most fully individuated and self-actualized members express this quality as a defining characteristic. It is not surprising to me that all religious traditions come to much the same conclusion when defining the highest spiritual development to which a person can aspire. It is a happy thought for me that our greatest spiritual teachers of the past and our greatest modern thinkers agree about how *Homo sapiens* express the highest stages of being human. They agree that we seek to become altruists, to express through love—and through joy, which is its expression—our desire to help others; by doing so, we help ourselves attain happiness.

The Challenge of Midlife

Great minds in psychology have also studied the question of the midlife crisis and its developmental possibilities for true human happiness in the second half of life. I've discussed in a number of other writings my own midlife crisis and elaborated on its contribution to the second stage of my life's utility to better serve others and to my well-being of mind, body, and spirit. Dante describes the midlife crisis as "finding himself in midlife in a dark wood with no place to go." His great poem recites the journey of his spirit from the profound depth of total despair, exemplified by the dark wood, through the clearing out of his old self to achieve the emptiness needed to receive the new knowledge necessary for the next stage of his spirit's development—knowledge leading to the bliss of achieving a newly awakened self. Such are the toils and tasks of the midlife crisis, and such its promise.

I believe Maslow's description of the process of growth is a modern elucidation of this process and its outcome. He and Dante are describing a process that corresponds to the path and purpose of ritual to effectuate the passages through our life's transitions. A ritual is defined as a three-stage process: the psychological breaking away from one stage of life, which, when complete, offers an opening for us to receive and incorporate the new information we'll need to live fully in the next stage of life. We can then return to the stream of our lives with that information fully integrated for use in living the next stage.

Although none of us looks forward to the deep cleansing of a midlife crisis, it's clear from the work of these great men and many others that we must accept its challenges if we are to flourish and achieve the highest level of self-awareness.

Carl Jung: Finding the Whole Person

I now turn to the work of one of the greatest of all psychologists, Carl Jung, and to the insightful writings of Gail Sheehy. Jung's work ranks among the most profound efforts to describe the process of human development, and Sheehy's explication of that work offers the means to bring it to a lay reader in a remarkably accessible way.

A significant school of modern psychology is based on Jung's work. He was Sigmund Freud's greatest student until he broke with Freud. He went on to disprove parts of Freud's theories and to develop his own philosophy and practice of how the mind and the unconscious work. Jung advises us that in midlife men are asked to confront their shadow female side, their anima, and women to confront their shadow masculine side, their animus. He suggests that these are the most important moments of possibility for our development. He believed that if the crises these confrontations normally produce are welcomed and if the work of the integration of our shadow sides is done well, then in the second half of our lives we will achieve the highest development and the highest orders of happiness and human flourishing.

In this modern explication of the two sides of ourselves—the masculine and the feminine—and the need for their integration, we discover the path to becoming a whole human being. I am in complete agreement with Jung, based on my own experience of life, that this is the most critical work we do. If we skip this work by suppressing our awareness of the crises that bring it to us in our late forties, we miss the deepest learning about who we are and the happiness that comes to us from that awareness. "Know thyself," Socrates admonished, and that is our individual journey's task; it is in this work that we are most likely to fully discover ourselves.

Embracing the crises, going deep into the self and the psyche to discover their gifts, and then returning with the new understanding of ourselves is the classic story recounted in many famous mythic journeys of development of the spirit. Jung was deeply influenced by these myths and by their representative journeys into the unconscious self. He saw that these myths recounted precisely the paths to wholeness most needed for our deepest well-being. The journey inward to discover the self fully is the task of every human being. The optimal moment for that journey comes when we find ourselves "in midlife in a dark wood with nowhere to go."

Another aspect of Jung's work that follows from the midlife crisis is linked to the spiritual teachings of Buddhism and Judaism. This aspect concerns the task of a male or female spirit seeking to achieve its highest calling. Buddhism and Judaism teach that the perfection of the male spirit lies in its becoming pure compassion. The perfection of the female spirit is becoming pure wisdom. Western readers may find this somehow strange, since the general Western view is that men are defined as wise and women as compassionate. However, many of the world's traditions of wisdom disagree.

Jung offers the view that the male who has fully integrated his female side seeks in the second stage of life to learn and integrate compassion, first for himself and then for all others with whom he is in a relationship. The female who has fully integrated her male side moves in the second stage of life to seek her calling and to learn who she is through work and to be a warrior for peace. As she fully integrates all the parts of her self in that process, she attains wisdom.

Jung knew that the Greeks depicted Athena as the goddess of wisdom, that the Jews depicted female energy as Sophia (wisdom), and that the Buddhists in their tankas depicted female energy as wisdom and male energy as compassion, showing the congress of the two energies forming a whole. Perhaps by seeing how the wisdom traditions understood the highest development of our natures and by combining their views with what his own studies revealed, Jung came to see that the second stage of men's life was defined by relationships leading to compassion, while women's was defined by work as their calling, leading to wisdom.

I find the idea that my work in this stage of my life is to learn to be fully compassionate is exactly what my heart longs for. I also find that the women I respect the most (particularly my life partner, Jacqueline Merrill) are those with true wisdom.

In her books *Passages* and *New Passages*, Gail Sheehy takes us through each of our life stages and the questions they pose as most of us perceive and characterize them. Sheehy's distillation of the exhaustive interviews she held with many people helps the reader comprehend these stages and the behaviors that define them in a very gentle and accessible way. For readers seeking a nonacademic understanding of why they seem to feel and act differently at different stages of their lives, Sheehy's books are the way into developmental, anthropological, and spiritual truths that explain those feelings and why we act as we do, whether in our teens or our eighties.

Of special significance to the matter of the midlife crisis in Sheehy's work is the remarkably helpful illustration she offers in *Passages* of what I call the journey of the double diamond. In the lower diamond, the male journey is defined as one of work-as-calling and the female journey as a journey of relationship. At the top of the lower diamond, the male and female lines intersect and then continue to flow into what I define as the upper diamond, now with the male journey as that of relationship and the female's that of work-as-calling. In this beautiful picture, Sheehy illustrates Jung's great observation about the male's journey and the female's reciprocal journey in the first and second stages of life. The point of first intersection is where the midlife crisis occurs, as the male and female move toward the integration of the shadow side and the journey that follows. If both parties reach their eighties and come back together at the top of what I believe would form an upper diamond as a second intersection, they will have wonderful stories of compassion and wisdom to share from their life journeys toward wholeness.

An example of what Jung and Sheehy are describing is found in an excellent book by Robert Fisher called *The Knight in Rusty Armor*. It depicts the male who starts out in shining armor, admired by his lady. Later, in midlife, his armor turns rusty in the eyes of his lady as she moves from her relationship side to the integration of her male side of work and he moves toward nurturance in relationships and compassion. Finally, his armor is in good shape again as he and she reconnect with their individual work.

I was incredibly blessed by the love of the second stage of my life, who gave me this book with the love and affection that came from having done her journeywork. That does not mean I don't get "honey, do" lists, fail to accomplish them, and get admonished about my rusty armor. But we can laugh about it, and that is what makes all the difference.

A Woman's Conflict

In women's psychological journeys, as described by Jung and illustrated by Sheehy, one issue that produces great strain in our modern life is the trap in which young women find themselves in the first stages of their developmental lives. That trap is the inner conflict in this stage between a career of life and a relationship as life partner and mother.

When I work with a family for the first time, I ask each member to write a résumé to be shared with his or her family members. I don't tell the family we're going to do this exercise because I want their responses to be spontaneous rather than rehearsed. I explain to them that there are no right answers, only *their* answers, and that all I ask is that they be as deep and expressive in considering their answers as possible. Generally, the men write half a page and the women multiple pages. Here are the questions:

a) What was your big dream when you were fourteen or fifteen?

b) What are you truly passionate about?

c) What do your friends know about you that your family doesn't?

d) If your family could give you one gift, what would it be?

Although each of these questions always elicits information that most family members don't know about one another, particularly the dream question, the question that's germane to the trap I'm discussing is the question of a gift. In every family, there are young women between the ages of twenty and forty-five who are parents, often but not always with careers. I write down the gift that at least one of these young women will ask for and put the paper face down in front of me. Invariably, at least one of the young women affirms my prediction. She asks for one day, by herself, in silence. The suffering represented by such a request is real and deep. In some terrible way, the path of young women's lives are in such states of chaos, of

freneticism, that they are drowning psychologically in the clamor
and constant movement and demands that define them.

How did this happen? In some wonderful ways, the women's
revolution of the last half of the twentieth century that emancipated
Western women was long overdue. The revolution opened many
new career opportunities to women that had been closed and fostered a healthy climate for women to pursue education and careers.
The resulting change in the percentages of women pursuing educations at all levels presages a social revolution in the twenty-first
century. I anticipate this century will see women's accomplishments
carry them into the senior levels of all professions and areas of
human activity. All of this is to be applauded.

However, as with the "theory of unintended consequences," the
pursuit of education and career carried with it unexpected competition with Jung's observation that a woman's journey in the first
stage of her life is the journey of relationship. Here lies a trap for
our young women. On one hand the women's revolution calls them
to work-as-calling, while on the other hand their psyches call them
to relationships. Unfortunately, the voices raised most strenuously
about women achieving status through work appear not to have
studied Jung and his disciples; if they did, they chose to ignore
them. So now we have the suffering of the resulting trap, with
young women burned out psychically by its demands and finding
all too often, as they tell me—including my daughter, Ellen—that
they "have no time, no time for anything" and absolutely no time for
themselves. If we do nothing, we will imperil these young women's
sense of self, with all the spiritual and intellectual deterioration it
implies. They are crying for help.

I suggest the first step in helping is acknowledging that the trap
isn't a time-and-motion-study issue to fix but rather a deep psychological wounding growing out of our lack of awareness of Jung's
work. Let me hasten to say that I am not leading you to the logical
conclusion that women shouldn't pursue education to whatever level
they wish or that they should opt for partnering and parenting over
work-as-calling. Rather, I am asking all family members, in seeking
to enhance the journeys of their young women, to understand Jung's

observation and be sure their young women understand what he suggested is the journey of a woman's first stage of life. For a young woman to fail to be made aware of Jung's work is a tragedy because it leaves her without a fundamental tool with which to measure why she feels as she does. With this information she will be able to make more deeply informed decisions in the first stage of her life and more likely, therefore, to make ones that lead to a higher quality of life.

Jung's observations may also be helpful to women as they look at the issues of the second stage of life. Because work-as-calling is likely to be a part of the second stage of a woman's life, she can look forward to a career in that stage of life as likely to be more developmentally her cup of tea than in the first stage. Given that the life expectancy for most women who come from the top economic tiers of society is about age ninety, it gives a woman something to consider. Again, I am making no suggestions whatsoever about what any woman should choose as her life journey, or any man for that matter. I am simply hoping that Jung's insights about how our psyches develop and about women's journeys of development are concepts that families have available to use in mentoring their young women so that this trap in their lives will be unsprung with the happiness that will be generated.

—∞—

PSYCHOLOGY IS IN part the study of human behavior in relationships, and its insights are among the most valuable to a family's journey. I hope what I've offered here from my own experience of human relationships and those of the great minds I've shared will lead to families' achieving higher orders of self-awareness, freedom, happiness, and flourishing.

Chapter Notes

1. For those wise elders who are interested in how Erikson's seventh stage might manifest in their lives and in the greater society, there is a remarkable set of essays on this subject contained in a book called *The Generative Society*, edited by Ed de St. Auben, Dan P. McAdams, and Tae-Chang Kim. Would that we could all live in a world founded on the characteristics of Erikson's seventh stage of life.

Chapter Eight

The Evolution of Family

A person may be indebted for a nose or an eye, for a graceful carriage, or for a voluble discourse to a great-aunt or uncle, whose existence he has scarcely heard of.
— WILLIAM HAZLITT, British essayist

THE PREHISTORY OF our species—the time before written communication—is a fascinating period that dramatizes the similarities in behavior throughout our later history. Indeed, archaeology and cultural anthropology teach us that our gregariousness, playfulness, and toolmaking skills repeatedly have enabled us to find the means to bring our curiosity and creativity to life in useful ways. As the French historian Fernand Braudel informs us, we are the result of a long cultural evolution through 50,000 years—and the 100,000 years that predated our species' use of language—all leavened by the different geographical areas in which our species' cultures flourished.

If we are to understand who we are today, we must understand who we were as our consciousness evolved. We need only go to France or Spain and see the cave paintings of 18,000 to 33,000 years ago to wonder if we were truly any less conscious 50,000 years ago than we are today. The humility of this observation frees us from the hubristic belief that we are better than our ancestors. Once evolutionary biology and cultural anthropology correct that view for us, however, our species' history and the study of the events that have taken us to the present moment can tell us who we are today.

The History of Families

The history of families is the history of our species. Once we recognize this, we gain access to a large inventory of historical stories that can inform us about how and why many families have overcome the proverb's prediction. We can study success stories of the families and peoples like the Rockefellers, the Rothschilds, the Capetians, the Norman English Plantagenets, the Tudors, the Windsors, the Hapsburgs, the Lydians and Carthaginians, the Mayans, the Moghuls, and multiple Chinese and Indian family dynasties. Equally informative are the great historical traditions of the families of the spirit—the Hindus, the Buddhists, the Jews, the Christians, the Muslims, the Confucians, and the Taoists.

Enlightening as well is the much larger inventory of the histories of failed families, who could not escape the fate of the proverb. These stories show us how, as entropy set in, so many successful families eventually dissolved. The American philosopher George Santayana wrote, "Those who fail to study history are condemned to repeat it." I believe the deep wisdom of this statement ought to be at the core of every family's thinking when it begins working toward the development of its human, intellectual, and financial capital and toward its dynamic preservation.[1]

Santayana's wisdom combined with Braudel's understanding of the long duration of human development offer great wisdom for a family's work. To understand how an individual family fits into the historical reality of the human family is to be humbled by how infinitesimal it is within the overall family of man and equally to be excited by what can be learned from the family experiences that directly relate to its own existence and possibilities. This is a fertile body of knowledge that a family should seek to have in its armamentarium. It ensures that a family will follow the paths charted by history's successful families and, most important, helps a family learn from the stories of others' mistakes and heed Santayana's warning.

History studies human systems as cultures and civilizations. The process of how they come into being helps us understand families of affinity and their birthing and evolutionary processes.

Oswald Spengler

In his multivolume work *The Decline of the West*, the German psychologist Oswald Spengler attempted to explain why cultures and the civilizations they spawn come into being and why they decay and disappear. Spengler suggests that a new culture is born because a few people arrive at a new, powerful idea they believe is transcendent and come to believe in that idea as an article of faith. Frequently, they elevate the idea to one of supernatural strength and, in doing so, lose sight of the fact that it originated with them. Eventually, the idea becomes strong enough to attract a second, larger group of followers, or disciples. These disciples constitute the initial community of believers and define the geographic area in which the idea, because of its widespread practice, predominates over all competing ideas. Over time, this community evolves a culture, and eventually a civilization—a second community—is formed, identified with the social, economic, political, religious, and aesthetic systems practiced by the disciples and their families of affinity. Each of these systems is the developed form of the practices spawned by the original idea.

Spengler also describes a third community, which I call the barbarians, or the others, related to the original cultural creators and their disciples. The barbarians live within the energetic field created by the culture and defined by the geographic area in which it predominates. This third group does not necessarily believe or even know the central culture and its practices but rather finds living within the civilization defined by these ideas and practices to be better than the alternatives. This community normally lives at what become the outer geographic boundaries that define the adherents of a particular culture and civilization.

Thus, Spengler defines the birth and expansion of any culture and civilization as three concentric circles of believers and adherents radiating out from the originators of the idea that gives birth to the new culture and civilization. He then attempts to show how all major cultures and civilizations follow this path and evolve into this system. He also describes the decay and ultimate death of each culture and civilization and why it happens. The decay, says Spengler, results when the idea on which the culture was founded either is discovered by its adherents to be untrue or is supplanted by a more complex idea that makes the central, founding idea seem limiting. The culture's power to expand will cease only when it reaches the boundaries of a community that believes in a different idea and is sufficiently powerful to defend that idea successfully against the encroaching idea. Once this new idea, carried by its adherents, reaches the final boundary of the human community willing to support it, its adherents settle down and create a culture to practice it and, if sufficiently strong, spawn a civilization identified with that culture.

A seventh-generation family represents a profound dream of two people whose affinity for each other is so deep that it creates fusion and materializes the dream as an idea. The idea has such power that it represents a vision of overarching beauty to which the second generation commits itself, as well as each succeeding generation. Only when the idea of family founded on the original dream dies away does the family cease to exist.

Arnold Toynbee

In his thirteen-volume work titled *A Study of History*, Arnold Toynbee attempted, like Spengler, to explain why cultures and the civilizations they spawn come into being and why they decay and disappear. Unlike Spengler, who favored history's evolution of ideas, Toynbee believed environments as well as ideas were at the root of the evolution of cultures and civilizations. Toynbee, a British historian who specialized in the philosophy of history, was taken with the idea that individual cultures come into being as a result of the difficult environments in which they are embedded and to a certain extent reflect those environments as they evolve into civilizations. He believed that peoples of great strength come from such struggles.

It seems to me that with families, as with civilizations, the birthing process is almost always difficult and that meeting and conquering early problems can temper a family's steel and facilitate its long-term success. Indeed, I find Toynbee's difficult-environment idea compelling, especially when combined with the ideas of Braudel. Rather than stopping, as Toynbee did, at each civilization's individual beginning, Braudel takes a step further and asks us to go as far back into the history of our species as possible to understand how our current cultures and civilizations, as reflections of the environments in which they emerged, relate to our earlier history as a species.

These two men offer us a way of seeing the human family and explaining how it has developed as a consequence of the unique environments reflected in its cultures and civilizations. It appears that all cultures and the civilizations they spawn begin with a few families, who often can trace their ancestries back to three or four common family antecedents embedded in a common location, whether the seacoast, the mountains, the rivers, or the desert.

Studying the formation of cultures and civilizations teaches us the history of how our extended human family has lived and evolved in the different locations on our planet. Going back, as Spengler does, to the "founding idea" helps us appreciate that all families of affinity begin with an idea of differentness created by the two people who founded it. In turn, in the second, third, and fourth generations, the concentric circles of disciples form around the stories emanating from the original idea. With the addition of advisers and other associates, the third circle evolves. From these three circles come the clans and tribes. And from these tribes come the cultures and later the civilizations that characterize the most successful of the original family ideas.

Toynbee and Braudel remind us that the suitability of an environment for an idea will have much to do with whether it can embed itself and thrive there. The family that's lucky enough to be governed at its birth by a profound idea—the idea of a family of affinity seeking to enhance the happiness of each of its members—and to be founded in an environment where it can flourish has history on its side. Such a family takes Santayana's admonition to heart and makes history its friend and ally on its journey toward greatness.

Religious Communities as Families

A family hoping to preserve itself would do well to consider some of the ideas that have inspired the longest-lived families on earth, the religious communities. I consider these communities the oldest category of families on earth. In fact, these families of affinity have been the most successful in dynamically preserving themselves and are, therefore, worth studying in our search for ideas on how an individual family might succeed in doing the same.

I consider religious communities to be families because they think of themselves as such. Indeed, in the rhetoric they use to describe themselves, they state that

- they are based on fundamental relationships of trust and love;
- they are linked by the affinity of their beliefs and the stories they spawn;
- in some cases, they evolved from an initial relationship of two entities creating a family—Abraham and Sarah for Jews and Christians, and Abraham and Hagar for Muslims—to include eventually billions or more members who can trace their genealogies back to a common source that defines their differentness as a community; and
- they are generally founded on altruism toward each other as members of the community and often to the larger community as well.[2]

I've argued that a family may be defined as two or more people linked by affinity. Religious "families" are different in that they are linked by an idea that founded their family rather than by a direct connection between two people. However, I believe that the vertical link between a higher power and an individual messenger, avatar, or child of that power establishes the founding of a family of two just as solidly as the horizontal linkage between two human beings who found a nuclear family.

The Keys to Longevity

I offer these groups as worthy examples because their ideas and models illustrate their substantially successful efforts to preserve themselves for five generations or more. Certainly, the five religious communities that comprise the planet's largest numbers of adherents are very long-lived and have dynamically preserved themselves. These communities, in order of their appearance on the earth, are the Hindus, Jews, Buddhists, Christians, and Islamists. They have some common characteristics:

• Each of these groups is distinguished by a set of ideas that constitute its beliefs and serve as a source of faith for its members.

• Each, with the exception of Hinduism and its many Vedic sages, had a human founder who acted as a channel for the set of ideas and whose voice inspired faith in the ideas and led others as disciples to his message, taking it far beyond the community in which he lived.

• Each has a complex system of practices embodying the doctrines of the faith that grew out of the founder's vision, often as communicated to him by a higher power.

• Each has a community of adherents who follow the laws and practices of the faith and consider themselves a family of believers. In Buddhism, for example, the Buddha (Siddhartha Gautama) is the founder; the dharma is its body of laws, or scripture; and the sangha, the community of its believers. In Christianity, Jesus Christ is the founder; the Bible, particularly the New Testament, is its scripture, narrating its laws and practices; and the congregation forms the body of its faithful.

• Most important for our comparison, each of these religious families is extremely long-lived, with the youngest being more than thirteen hundred years old. Each has discovered the keys to longevity:

— Belief, rising to faith, in a set of ideas and a willingness to support those ideas through one's lifetime as a part of the community.

— A communal sense of purpose and a conviction that there is something greater than oneself to which one can be attached.

— A communal way of being that can impel one to a higher level of existence and knowledge than one could attain in any other way.

— A sense of being a part of a complex communal system that offers a higher order of existence *if* one is willing to sublimate oneself to that system to gain access to it.

Here, the community, or family, is offering a way of being in which one can have faith that the family has genuine interest in you as an individual and offers a place to thrive to the fullest extent. The community/family asks only that you be willing to join in its endeavor to preserve its beliefs and practices and extend them to all individuals likewise committed so that they too may thrive. This process of seeking affinity promotes flourishing of the highest order for an individual, who in turn offers to all others the willingness to help them achieve the same thing in exchange. Altruism forms the core of these communities—the act of reaching out to help another to eschew selfishness and achieve a higher order of existence for all. This process is at the *heart* of what I believe every family seeking to dynamically preserve itself must do if it is to succeed. This idea and the practices derived from it lie at the *heart* of my first book, *Family Wealth*.

These communities also exhibit the features that represent a successful tribe. Tribes are the longest-lived organizations of human families. Every long-lived tribe starts out as two people with affinity who establish a family, have children, and then produce grandchildren and great-grandchildren. These descendants form clans, and in the fifth and six generations, some or all of these clans elect to stay together and form a tribe. Underpinning a very successful tribe is a set of ideas that energizes its community and informs its practices. These ideas must adapt and evolve if the tribe is to survive attacks on the integrity of its identity by tribes on its border, seeking to displace it.

Religious communities follow this pattern. They have a founder and disciples, whose ideas become the foundation for the religion's various sects, or clans, and finally for the family of the faithful who, as members of those sects, connect to form the tribe of faithful adherents known as Hindus or Islamists, and so on. Thus religious communities exhibit in their multigenerational families the same process of evolution as all other kinds of families—from nuclear family to clan to tribe. The likeness is certainly close enough to be informative about the process of creating long-term families.

Religious communities, like families, also have additions, mutations, and schisms. If the community is unable to deal with these transitions in its evolution, it eventually is overtaken by other religious ideas and it disappears. This process is often accelerated if a new religion, in the form of a new transcendent idea, begins to invade the religion's geographical boundaries. In this way, religious communities are subject to the same boundary risks and limits as human families are when other human families with different ideas attempt to take over their homelands. Perhaps the best example of this process is the disappearance of the "pagan" or polytheistic religions of Italy, Greece, and the Near East. These groups were supplanted by Christianity, which in turn was eventually displaced by Islam in the Near East and Northern Africa. The same process took place in India as the Vedic religion supplanted the Dravidian, as well as in China where Confucianism, Taoism, and Buddhism supplanted the previously embedded animistic religions they encountered.

Families seeking long-term preservation will face these same kinds of challenges. They will need to incorporate new ideas into their beliefs and practices if they are to continue to attract the additions to their families they need to stay strong. This will be especially true as they transition into clans. They will gradually incorporate the new ideas, practices, and sets of beliefs from the families of the spouses marrying in and from successive generations of children who will grow up in changing environments. Family communities, like religious communities, if they are to succeed, must have foundational ideas that are strong enough to retain the majority of their members. Inevitably, schisms occur as some family members leave because they cannot accept the validity of the ideas and practices the family has at its core.

The histories of religious communities reveal another characteristic that is helpful to families in understanding themselves. These communities exhibit a characteristic common to all of evolution: they must evolve systems of higher and higher orders of complexity if they are to compete with other communities. A religious community begins with a creative idea that persuades people. It becomes a religious family, which, as it adds more adherents, becomes ever more complex. Each new adherent adds, in biological terms, a new cell, and the addition of that cell/adherent creates an ever-more-complex organism/family. In successful religious communities, meaning those that are long-lived, each new adherent/cell strengthens the entire community through his commitment to the community's success and his faith in its purpose and through living out the ideas and practices of its founders. The successful religious communities have dealt with all the issues that can challenge an organization/organism and have evolved through them all over thousands of years. Each represents a living idea that transcended its founder, attracted disciples and adherents to practice its tenets, and eventually evolved to establish and vitalize the largest and longest-lived families the earth has ever seen.

Chapter Notes

1. Many of my colleagues, particularly my mentor and friend Peter Karoff, would add here the value to a family of the development of its social capital as well. Certainly, a family acting with humility and gratitude for its blessings, and with compassion toward other sentient beings, starts on a strong footing—a critical footing, if altruism rather than selfishness is the core requirement for success. I honor these deeply informed voices that the development of social capital is necessary for a family's well-being, and I agree with them that the development of a family's social capital is a very important building block for successful long-term family preservation. However, I do not list social capital here because I believe that capital is a *result* of a family's development of its human and intellectual capital rather than a source for that development. Successful families will build up stores of social capital reflected within their stories, *but* I believe they will be the result of the family's development of its human and intellectual capital, the result of a family's deep introspection and the learning that grows from it. It is this process that will inform families on how to act toward themselves before they act toward others.

For more on philanthropy, see Rob Lehman's "The Heart of Philanthropy" on my Web site.

2. I fully appreciate that many religious communities number among their members some who are only nominally faithful. That is, if asked what their religion is, they will give an answer sufficient to respond to what they believe the questioner wants to hear, while, in fact, they have no belief in the precepts of that religion whatsoever. I agree that such nominal adherents are not members of that religious community within my definition of family. Many who classify themselves as members of the religion but in fact are not are nevertheless members of the particular civilization founded on that religion's beliefs. Because they ascribe to the mores of that civilization, they are nominally connected to its religion.

Chapter Nine

From Family to Tribe
The Emergence of Governance

Miss not the discourse of the elders, for they also learned of their fathers.

—ECCLESIASTICUS 8:9

To UNDERSTAND HOW a family succeeds in becoming a tribe, we must look to the teachings of anthropology. The work of physical and paleo anthropologists shows us how we evolved to become the primate we call a human being. They offer the knowledge we need to understand *why* we came to be who we are. Through the study of the tools we made, our use of fire, the things we ate and wore, the things we built, the spirits we worshipped, and the art we created, we deepen our knowledge of *how* we came to our present state. We begin to understand why we survived as a species when others—like *Homo neanderthalensis*, for example—didn't. Anthropology also teaches us the physical and cultural truths that shaped us as a species. When we face life's hazardous moments, reconnecting to the skills our ancestors learned for their survival can help us to ensure our own. Without the knowledge of self and the awareness of how we interact with all other species, we could not be defined as *Homo sapiens*—the thinking, conscious, talking, writing simian.

Cultural anthropology seeks to understand the nature of our species and the groupings it creates, using a three-step process. First, through the study of a tribe's stories, special practices, myths, rituals, totems, taboos, and fetishes, it seeks to understand the tribe's particular customs, mores, and systems. It explores how that tribe functions and understands itself, all toward comprehending and elucidating its unique culture. Second, based on studies of cultures generally, it seeks to know how a particular tribe is defined culturally, its differentness, in light of all other tribes. Finally, it seeks to incorporate that knowledge into a larger study of all the world's cultures and to enrich its understanding of the human community as a whole.

A Family's Evolution

Every family has its own cultural anthropology, telling the story of how it functions as a group, as defined within the larger society to which it belongs and as a part of the species of primate called *Homo sapiens*. A family's cultural anthropology often defines its class, its political views, its family structures and systems, its views on gender, race, religion, allies, friends, and enemies, and its virtues and values. A family's history may also influence its choice of where to live, its sense of what it means to be human, and how humans interact with others. Fundamentally, cultural anthropology reveals how a family and the complex system into which it has evolved are mirrored in the experiences it describes. It explains how and why the human groups we call families form and how they evolve into tribes, groups of tribes, states, nations, and perhaps eventually into a global society.

As a family prepares to work toward long-term success and survival, its imagination rekindles family stories depicting the differences that set it apart from other families, bringing these differences more clearly into its awareness. Every time family members hear the stories and practice the rituals, they reinitiate into the family's worldview.

Each family tribe should seek to use the tools of cultural anthropology to know and define itself and its differentness and to comprehend how that differentness interacts with and is defined by the culture at large. In this effort, much can be learned from the remarkable book by Allen W. Johnson and Timothy Earle called *The Evolution of Human Societies: From Foraging Group to Agrarian State*. This is the seminal book on how human societies form, starting with a few individual families and how they progress to larger and larger groupings, eventually to what we might call nation-states. The authors explain that this process begins for reasons of survival; expands to include economic, social, and political reasons; and finally evolves to more complex purposes.

From Family to Clan to Tribe

The first steps in an individual family's evolution into larger social groupings occur in the cellular division of a family, with children dividing into clans as the third generation is born. Members of the third generation will not grow up in the same household as the founding first-generation couple and are, therefore, nominally the first members of the family of affinity, sharing a common genealogy.

The word *clan* often takes on a negative connotation when it's used to define family members whose ideas are sufficiently different from those of all other family members. In the context of cultural anthropology, however, the word *clan* is neither positive nor negative. It simply describes every family of affinity's natural evolution to a new grouping, as it grows from a nuclear family to a set of collective families in the third generation.

In the fifth and sometimes in the sixth generation of a family of affinity, these clans, now frequently quite separate, must decide whether to integrate and evolve into a tribe. Should they become a tribe, they can anticipate very long futures of hundreds and even thousands of years. Examples of such tribes include the Basques, the Jews, the Lebanese, the Hakka of China, the Parsis of India, the Yanomami of Brazil, the Masai, and the Iroquois, Zuni, and Navaho of North America. Interestingly, many of these long-lived tribes have creation myths featuring two people of affinity as their progenitors. While Johnson and Earle are principally interested in how these early groups became much larger and complex social groups, it is the transition from family of affinity to clan to tribe on which we focus here. During this evolutionary social process, a family discovers whether it can reach its fifth generation and go on from there, and it must replicate that process if it is to make its fifth-generation goals come true.

Transitions and Family Governance

Only through a long series of linked transitions can a family attain its goal of survival. And only through the development of a system of family governance—which guides the joint decisions family members must make to successfully complete those transitions—can it create the means to do so. A very helpful tool for imagining how to devise such a system of family governance is described in *Generation to Generation*[1] by Kelin Gersick, John Davis, Marion McCollom Hampton, and Ivan Lansberg. This book brings to the fore two terms for describing family governance decision-making systems: sibling systems and cousins consortiums.[2] The authors suggest that as a family evolves from its first generation to its second, the siblings of the second will devise a sibling system for joint decision making when they are the governors of the family. All of my work affirms the correctness of these insights. As the second generation evolves into the third, the authors offer the concept of a cousins' consortium as the family governance model that emerges as this generation's approach to governing. Naturally, since all generations after the third will be genealogically linked as cousins, this form of consortium governance is ongoing. The nature of a consortium is to connect equals and to be generally nonhierarchical. Such a system naturally defines a group of people who by lineage have equal standing at a round table and who have a common and shared purpose. The consortium also calls for leaders from behind to find consensus so that the system can work.

Becoming a tribe requires a family to adopt a form of decision making that seeks consensus about what actions will likely perpetuate the tribe's success and thus its survival. Indeed, every family I've known or studied that reached its fifth generation and thrived from there recognized and practiced this principle of governance by consortium. These families saw that once they had reached the third generation, that generation and every one thereafter would be a consortium of related people of affinity. They saw that if the family was to make the joint decisions needed for its long-term success, it had to evolve a system of governance by consensus.

A consortium does not exclude having a hierarchy regarding who speaks when in the family group. Japanese families and institutions I've worked with, for example, have a governance process of asking the youngest to speak first and the oldest to speak last. I've witnessed the benefit to positive decision making of that process. It offers a platform for each generation's perspectives and experiences in the appropriate order of its current authority in family decision making. The approach is founded on the belief that wisdom gained over a lifetime is valuable and increases the likelihood that those having such wisdom will make decisions with positive outcomes for the long-term well-being of the family. Further, it offers the tribe's elders the knowledge and ideas of those whose lives will be most affected by the decisions and their consequences. The youngest members will also bear witness for later generations as to how the decisions were made and to the care and diligence the family and its elders exercised in making them. Getting all the decision makers who make up a family's governance system into the decision-making consortium and listening to them speak their truths for the elders to hear is the root practice of family governance that works.

The Role of the Elder

The elder plays a critical role in family system of governance. Today, many families fail to thrive because they distort the functional role of elders. They ignorantly define elders only as "olders" and, worse, ask them to get "hip" and act like the younger generation. These two approaches to the role of a family's elders are tragic errors that doom a family to failure.

Often today, when a family seeks to formalize its system of governance, it provides no accommodation for the natural evolution of the oldest members. Elders are moving from a time of life when *doing* dominates to a third stage in which *being and giving back* dominate. Such a family acts as if doing is the only thing that matters to its success and defines no role for the eldest generation—at least none appropriate to its state of mind and heart. This error leads inevitably to three highly negative outcomes. First, the eldest generation, frightened of letting go of the responsibility of "doing," may simply abort the creation of a decision-making consortium altogether. These wise elders feel, rightly, that the system proposed by the doers will quickly leave them and their much-needed wisdom out of the decision-making process and render them powerless. Second, deprived of elders, whose essential and natural role is to execute the four areas of authority (see page 107), the development of the family's governance system fails. Finally, as the eldest generation balks—sadly, often not becoming elders at all but remaining trapped in the doing stage—it blocks the family's healthy evolution. Consequently, the second generation cannot evolve naturally into doing the work required for its generation's growth and for the family's future well-being.

If the responsibilities of the family are to be carried out by those most developmentally equipped to do so, then the gentle, natural evolution of second-generation family members into elders and the evolution of third-generation youths into adults must consistently occur. Aborting this process is the most consistent reason I've found that families fail and entropy prevails.

A Lesson From the Hindus

Hindu families make this evolutionary step more easily than many others because their religion offers them a model for how to do so. One Hindu friend of mine, who had just become a grandfather for the first time, explained that in his faith when a first grandchild is born, if the new grandparents have fully lived the second stage of their lives, they are free to spend the rest of life in spiritual quest as a sannyasin.[3]

I was deeply awakened by the wisdom of this Hindu tradition and by its developmental possibilities for all families. This view of evolution through stages of life illuminates human consciousness as it truly is and offers insight into the different ways we experience our lives as these stages unfold. The idea that each stage of life is special and that each must be lived fully if we are to successfully move to the greater freedom and self-awareness offered by the next is fundamentally sound. In my own experience, it has led to great happiness. Equally, the process accepts the difference between *doing* and *being* as natural and one to be hoped for rather than feared. Ultimately, it offers a way of seeing the third stage of life, the stage of the elder, as beautiful and full of the possibilities for wisdom, as so many stories inform us. Here is a way for a family to imagine the creative possibilities for the discovery and growth of self that the third stage of life offers and, in turn, to imagine with joy what people in this stage of life can offer its members as these elders tell the tales of their journeys through all of their life stages and share what they've learned.

The Four Authorities

Cultural anthropology teaches us that every successful tribe seeks to find and grow its elders, so as to have tribal members to whom it can entrust the tribe's sacred authority. There are four fundamental areas of authority:

a) The authority to mediate disputes within the tribe, so that all members feel heard. No judgment of a dispute should result in some feeling like winners and others like losers, which destroys the fabric of the tribe.

b) The authority to advise the entire tribe when it is not following the decision-making rules the tribe adopted. Elders never seek to make those rules themselves, however.

c) The authority to tell the tribe's stories.

d) The authority to maintain and implement practices for carrying on the tribe's rituals and the ceremonies that memorialize them. These rituals mark the tribe's most important transitions: children becoming adults, new members of affinity entering the tribe, tribal members achieving the status of elder, the death of tribal members, and electing new chiefs for peace and war.

Each of these authorities held by the elders is foundational to a family's governance system and to its successful journey. Let's consider each one more closely.

Mediating. Government by consortium suggests seeking consensus. Through such a governance system, the tribe, meeting in assembly in its legislative body, discerns and develops together the policies and procedures most likely to lead to its flourishing. It then empowers its executive body to implement these policies and procedures. All systems of human decision making, no matter how well thought out and practiced, will, from time to time, cause some of their constituents to feel unhappy with the decisions made by the larger body. Likewise, all human groupings will have individual idiosyncrasies that will lead to difficulties among their members. Whether the disagreement is between an individual member and the family as a whole or among several members of the family, disputes about decisions will occur and a process of family governance must have a way of resolving them so that the tribe will not be destroyed.

In successful tribes, elders are granted the authority by the tribe as a whole to mediate disputes involving the tribe's overall health and to protect it against the risk that such disputes will split up the tribe. With the ceremonial appointment by the entire tribe of a new elder, the tribe grants the authority to that elder to preserve its survival by empowering him to act as its mediator. In their many years with the tribe, elders have known all of the tribal members intimately as well as their strengths and weaknesses. This knowledge adds greatly to an elder's capacity to fulfill the role. Often these elders are consummate leaders from behind. In exercising their mediative roles, they practice the art of infinite patience by "hastening slowly" to help the tribe's members find the *best* answer to the question at hand rather than simply a *correct* answer. They recognize that frequently what may "de jure" (legally) be a correct answer to a particular problem—that is, a rules-based view—may "de facto" (in fact) lead to a result that will splinter the tribe rather than unify it.

In their role as mediators, elders seek to find equity for all rather than judgment for one. They see the nuances in situations and patiently help others appreciate them too. They are known by the tribe, through the lifetime record of their behavior, to seek the well-being of all and to put that welfare ahead of their own self-interests. They are the altruists within the tribe, the fusion seekers and creators, who see and practice tribal beauty as harmony. Because the tribe's survival is the elders' greatest concern, their mediation is one of the most profound ways the tribe avoids the internal fissions that would otherwise destroy it.

Protecting Decision-Making Rules. Families who go the distance will have many moments in their multigenerational lives when they will naturally break into majority and minority factions on certain very important decisions. From cultural anthropology and from my own experience, I know that successful tribes often have strongly held and very diverse views. This is a healthy sign of a tribe's well-being, because the dialogue on almost any important matter will bring forward at least two competing views of how it should be decided. Without both views being fully articulated by those who hold them passionately, the tribe will not gain the broadest understanding possible of the ramifications the question has for its well-being and thus for its security and survival. Equally, it is critical to the tribe's health that eveyone—even those who opposed the final outcome—be willing to fully accept such decisions once they're made and to actively participate in their implementation.

Since I assume that the tribe has begun its work by applying seventh-generation thinking, that any mediation needed between individuals has occurred, and that the likelihood of a good decision is present, a serious problem for family governance remains that of gaining the minority's participation. This problem occurs when the majority has thwarted the minority's right to be heard by failing to follow the rules for decision making that the tribe as a whole has adopted. This kind of behavior lies at the root of many stories of failed tribes, often culminating in the departure of whole clans because of their rightly held grievance with such a failed process. A tribe seeks to overcome this risk by giving its anointed elders the right to step into its decision-making process to enforce its rules and to do so by advising the tribe when it is not following them.

Elders don't make the tribe's rules; that is the responsibility of the whole tribe. A fundamental principle of consortiums is that for the members of such a system to be willing to be bound by its rules and decisions, each must have been a willing participant in the creation and adoption of those rules and have affirmed a willingness to be bound by them.

Telling the Tribe's Stories. Cultural anthropology teaches us that as a species we are principally linked by our oral tradition. Writing, which is about 5,500 years old, is a relatively modern system of communication. The earliest forms of writing may be as old as 20,000 years. Speech, however, appears to have evolved between 50,000 and 75,000 years ago, although it may, in fact, be as old as our species—somewhere between 150,000 and 200,000 years old. Thus, we have shared our stories orally far longer than in writing.

All tribes we can study have bards, or oral historians, who hold the story of the tribe's creation and journey in their memories and who, in turn, are the reporters of earlier bards' memories of those stories. They keep our individual memories alive as they name the names of those who have gone before. No tribe can exist as a unit if it does not know where it came from and how it arrived at its current place. In most tribes, an elder or a group of elders bears this bardic title and responsibility. Often, the person is one who demonstrated unusual capacities of memory from an early age and was therefore assigned to an existing bard to be trained in this skill so critical to the tribe's survival. The story-telling elder enables the tribe to understand its history and therefore to help it know how to safely get to its next developmental level.

Maintaining Rituals and Ceremonies. This last of the four authorities given to elders calls attention to the role of ritual in maintaining a family's well-being. Much of cultural anthropology is the study of how our ancestors initiated tribal members into the experiences their wisdom-keepers knew they would need to move safely through the significant passages of their lives, all toward the dynamic preservation of their tribal families as a whole.

All tribes, as extended families, have recognized that they need elders as shamans, medicine men and women, or priests and priestesses, as wisdom-keepers—today, we might call them secular priests[4]—to preserve and carry out the tribe's rituals. These tribal elders are needed to mentor individual tribal members and help them make the developmental changes needed for their individual growth at each stage of life. This process is essential to the tribe's well-being because it ensures that its members will achieve the competence to face and live each stage fully and happily and do the work of the tribe that will help it to flourish. Families should embrace a similar process. Indeed, having a group of family members charged with assuring high levels of competency among family members who have to do the family's work is a critical function in family governance.

For enlightenment on the nature of ritual, we have Arnold van Gennep's book, *The Rites of Passage*. Van Gennep teaches that the purpose of ritual is (1) to initiate an individual's breaking away from a current stage of life, (2) to provide new learning and experience of that learning for the new stage of life the individual is entering, and (3) to help that individual reintegrate with this new learning into society (in this case, family) and into that new stage of life. Thus, a particular ritual represents an experience, or set of lived experiences, to accomplish an individual's successful transition from one life stage to the next, often celebrated by a special ceremony to mark its successful completion. The elder's role is to implement the ritual in such a way that the space for such experiences is generally safe and the path clearly open to the next stage of life. I say "safe" with full awareness that all life transitions have elements of fear, chaos, and the pain of shedding one's skin to take on a larger skin. I also recognize that in some male rituals in Africa, in female circumcision, and in the military, not all survive. Regardless, most must survive or the tribe will perish, thus the elder's role is to hold the space as safe as possible for the initiate so nearly all will, in fact, make the transition successfully.

Some of the life transitions for which families devise rituals are births, birthdays, transitions from youth to adult, graduations, marriages, wedding anniversaries, deaths, the anointing of new elders, and the selection of chiefs for war and peace. Nations also establish rituals and ceremonies for their important passages: events such as making peace, holding elections and coronations, making war, and executions.

Cultural anthropology makes us aware that rituals, and the special ceremonies that define them—along with family totems, such as family crests, Bibles, portraits, videos, genealogies, family taboos, such as forbidding the discussion of money as gauche; and family fetishes, such as the special costumes, jewels, and heirlooms we employ in family ceremonies—are all universal cultural characteristics of our species.

The Spiritual Intermediary

As spiritual intermediaries, elders ensure through ritual that the life transitions of the tribes' members are successful, especially the rituals for children moving into adulthood. In the days when tribes survived by hunting and gathering, a tribal member who never became an adult developmentally—specifically, finding the work for which he was best suited—meant the tribe would be forever burdened with an unproductive member, one who could in times of crisis endanger the whole tribe's security and thus its survival. Although in modern times, a lifelong Peter Pan or Wendy won't necessarily doom a family, that member will be a continuously underinflated tire on the family's journey.

This role of elder as mentor/spiritual intermediary is needed in families today as much as ever for the individuation and development of family members. That role, however, has nearly disappeared. Families would do well to foster its revival. Cultural anthropology teaches that the quadrumvirate of bard, medicine person, shaman, and mediator form the highest level of tribal and family roles to which a family member can aspire. Unless these functions are performed by the family elders, the family will not flourish. Families need these four types of intermediaries from the start, because these enlightened spirits are needed for the family's successful journey, especially to carry its members smoothly through their life transitions. Families who seek early on to identify the members called to fill these critical roles and who nurture them toward performing the role of elders in the third stages of life will do very well.

Echoing the role of elder in many families is the traditional role that aunts and uncles play in the process of a girl or boy becoming an adult. In families with maiden aunts or bachelor uncles, these members often take the first keen interest in the success of a niece and nephew. They have the time for museum and zoo visits and, even more important, the time to inquire about dreams and passions. In my own childhood, it was my paternal aunt Dorothy (Sutter) who first sought to know who I was. Never for the rest of her life did she fail to be my most ardent fan, forgiving surrogate parent, and best friend. Every child would benefit tremendously from having such an aunt to read to them so that their imaginations don't atrophy, to tell them the stories of their ancestors and their history, to be poets with images to share with them, and to model the love of humanity and of the mind that will provide endless examples of what it is to be human.

Today, ritual and its ceremonies often seem to be irrelevant cultural artifacts, and many families thoroughly disdain them—that is, until they get on a plane on Christmas Eve and the family's form of sugar plums begin to dance in their heads. In this context, I think of my father's admonition that "there should be some progress from generation to generation." I heartily agree and ritually advise my children and now grandchildren of the same.

Chapter Notes

1. I also discuss this book in chapter 14, "Family as an Organization." These authors' insights into how family systems of governance evolve by generation speak as much to cultural anthropology's study of how all human families evolve as they do to families with businesses.

2. In his article "The Evolutionary Stages of Family Governance," John Ward suggests the terms "collective partnership and collaborative community " for these systems of governance. I believe both sets of terms define these systems very well.

3. In Hinduism, the role of the sannyasin, or forest dweller, is to take to the forest, metaphorically or actually, for the growth of his spirit. Because of the courage and diligence of this path, it is the highest level of spiritual seeker. Sometimes it is even described as a fourth stage of life.

4. In chapter 20, "The Personne de Confiance: Service Redefined," I describe the characteristics of such persons and their calling to service to families.

PART THREE

Principles of
Family Governance

Chapter Ten

A System for
Joint Decision Making

Let the people think they govern, and they will be governed.
—WILLIAM PENN, founder of Pennsylvania

WHAT WE ALL too often have in the governance system of a family is an incredibly complex set of human relationships, with little or no education of family members on how to fill the roles and responsibilities of these relationships. This leads to very poor boundaries, with all the confusion that follows. Family systems with these infirmities ultimately exhibit tremendous fatigue, as family members try to make the decisions required by each relationship. Entropy, exhibited by the exhausted decision-making process in these governance systems, is working its will at the core of these families. To find some answers to these problems, let's begin by looking at the seminal work of Murray Bowen and his family systems theory.[1]

Family Systems Theory

Bowen was a clinical psychologist who specialized in working with families. He practiced from 1940 into the 1970s. Before that time, few psychologists had practices focusing nearly exclusively on the family.

A pioneer, Bowen saw that families were systems. He realized that by applying to family relationships the newly emerging scientific theories of systems and of complexity, he could determine how their complex webs of relationships functioned. He saw that in cases where families needed therapy, he could apply ideas from those disciplines to help them achieve well-being. He established a laboratory to work out his ideas, and in a series of discoveries, relying on intricate questioning of each family member and the close observation of their behavior toward each other, he developed definitions and descriptions of many unhealthy family behaviors and offered therapeutic suggestions for their improvement.

Although his contributions to the psychology and health of families and their systems of decision making are seminal, one area of his work is particularly helpful to families seeking to achieve good health, and that is the concept of "triangulation" he introduced to family systems theory. Bowen suggests that although the triangle, as Buckminster Fuller concluded, is the strongest form in the universe, in family relationships it is the weakest. He brilliantly saw that if he could find the third party to what otherwise appeared to be a two-person relationship and determine how that third party interacted to disable the relationship of the other two, he could often work to dismantle the unhealthy triangle. He did this by helping the two parties to see that their relationship was being disabled by the third. This new awareness of triangulation changed forever family therapists' understanding of how a form of dysfunctional behavior can arise in a family. This theory also elucidated the idea of a "family" system, because the interaction of three parties is one definition of a beginning system.

Today, the ideas of triangulation and systems have been adopted in the clinical practices of all family therapists, leading to the reduction of suffering in many families. These ideas have spread into all kinds of human-relationship work because triangles are as prevalent in other human systems as they are in family systems.

The family that sees itself as a complex system of human relationships, and then avails itself of the knowledge in this field and adapts its wisdom, can significantly facilitate the process of joint decision making. It will help members understand what the family system consists of, how the relationships within it actually work, and consequently how its decision-making process works.

Family Decision Making

A useful technique—taken from the study of psychology—which I offer families is the system I learned of labeling different relationships when we're about to engage in decision making. As a family enters its system of intrafamily decision making, or enters such a process with another family or social system, this tool asks the family member to define its allies, its friends, and its "others."

There are no enemies to be labeled in this process. That's because in the many, many years of a family's journey, those who seem to be enemies today may well be our allies tomorrow. A family of affinity making a positive intrafamily decision with the seventh generation in mind must act so that all individuals and family members' boats can rise. That's why there can be no enemies in a family of affinity. They can dialogue and disagree. It is useful to good decision making to assure that all arguments are on the table. But if it is to be successful, a family of affinity cannot have family enemies.

This system allows the individual to see the different points of view likely to be presented when a decision is being made. It helps define everyone who will take part in the process by categorizing those who are not likely to be in favor of a position as "others," those who are neutral as "friends," and those who agree as "allies." Empowered with this knowledge of the likely views of all the participants in the process, a family member should be able to find those most likely to help the family achieve the outcome it seeks. The process also frequently uncovers friends members didn't know they had, who become allies, and this requires them to fully appreciate the views of others who might become friends. Giving serious consideration to each decision maker's point of view enhances our ability to determine where consensus is likely to appear, while helping us ask ourselves whether our arguments and those of our allies are really the best for the whole family or whether better arguments are held by friends or even by others.

In *Family Wealth*, I discuss rules for family meetings—listening affirmatively, speaking one's truth without fear of blame or judgment, and being flexible about outcomes, which are critical foundational skills for a family to make decisions successfully. Preparing for meetings using the allies/friends/others process not only sharpens the sense of where a good decision lies but also helps family members prepare to participate in the decision-making dialogue at the meeting in a way that will enhance their ability to use these three skills to achieve the best possible decisions for the family's well-being and its future.

Analyzing the System. A second technique I use to help families facing an important decision combines psychology, complexity theory, and my view that families have transitions and not transactions. Using the approach described in chapter 4, "The Physics of Affinity," I illustrate the family system. I consider what transitions the family is undergoing and how the decision to be made will integrate into those transitions in the most gentle, evolutionary way. I list the members of the family who will be most affected by the decision and ask which of the three or four goals each person might have for the decision's outcome is likely to have the highest priority for that person.[2] I try to understand where the family member is likely to stand on the decision by trying to understand what he is most likely to wish to personally gain from the decision's outcome. By starting from the macro—the whole scope of the family system—and moving to its transitions, then including its relationships, and finally the aspirations of those within the system, I gain a deep insight into how the system can best work to achieve the optimal outcome for the family's well-being.

Of course, my having this knowledge is useless unless I can communicate it to the family's elders and help them learn and apply its technique to the family they lead. I find this isn't difficult, because the best outcome for the family suggested by my process is usually mirrored by the intuitive answer the elders have reached on their own. That's why they're the elders.

Principles of Governance

In *The Politics*, Aristotle observes that to comprehend how any system of human governance works, one must begin with an analysis of each family unit within the system and how it makes decisions. He recognized that if families, which are the building blocks of more complex systems of governance, cannot govern themselves well, the larger systems will fail. My own work in assisting families with governance systems affirms this.

For a family of affinity to have a successful decision-making system in its third and later generations, its governance system must be founded on the positive functioning of the constituent families' decision-making systems. Without its own strong decision-making

Eight Principles of Governance

1) The art of governance is making sure that over a long period of time, joint decisions with positive outcomes slightly outnumber those with negative outcomes.

2) The best system of governance for a family of affinity is an Aristotelian republic, or what would be known today as a representative democracy.

3) A governance system should be based on universal suffrage for all adult members of a family of affinity.

4) When its turn to govern the family arises, each generation must reaffirm the horizontal Lockean social compact that underlies the first generation's governance system.

5) A governance system must have three branches—the legislative, the executive, and the elders/judicial—and the interaction of these branches must be regulated by checks and balances.

6) A governance system is most effectively based on a confederation of clans with a weak tribal center rather than a strong tribal center.

7) A governance system should operate with the understanding that a family's own relationship system is always in flux, in transition. It should be based on Burkian not Jacobin principles.

8) A governance system should be founded on the idea of Benjamin Franklin's statement, "As we are certain to hang separately, we are far better to hang together."

process, a constituent family can't be an active, helpful participant in the larger family governance system. Effective joint decision making at all levels of governance must be in place if a family is to have long-term success.

My philosophy on systems of family governance for families of affinity is founded on eight major principles derived from political science.

Let's consider what each of these principles means for a family of affinity's system of governance.

Joint Decision Making

> **Principle 1.** *The art of governance of a family of affinity is no more and no less than the art of joint decision making.*

Every family begins with two people. It is necessarily, therefore, from its inception making joint decisions through the interactions of these two persons. For example, two people's decision to form a family is simply the first joint decision they make, followed by many others. In the case of a mother and her child, the decisions may appear to be perfectly vertical, with the mother making all the decisions. In fact, the child, expressing his needs by crying, is participating, and they're making the decisions jointly. Each of these decisions represents the acting out of a system of governance created and chosen by the parties. Thus, family governance is no more or less than an extension of these first joint decisions and reflects the process used to make them.

Recognizing that each family within a system of family governance is practicing the art of joint decision making often helps a family see what governance actually is. Demythologizing the term "governance" and separating it from the idea of big government pares it down to its roots: the nuclear family. This clarification often helps families understand that the practice of governance is simply joint decision making, not some complex structure of intersecting lines and boxes.

When a family can appreciate that its governance system represents a way of making decisions together, it can begin to imagine how to make better decisions. Successful family governance is the art of making sure that over a long period of time joint decisions with positive outcomes slightly outnumber those with negative outcomes. The positive compounding of anything reaps enormous eventual returns. Families of affinity who make their joint decisions looking at the long-term compounded benefit of each decision are likely to do better than other families in terms of survival and growth. These families recognize that each decision they make is founded on all those that have gone before and use the histories of those earlier decisions to inform their current ones.

The Aristotelian Republic

> *Principle 2. The best form of governance for a family of affinity is an Aristotelian republic, or representative democracy.*

Aristotle identifies in *The Politics* five systems of governance that he believed exemplified all the forms of governance that then existed. I find it fascinating that, although he was writing circa 350 BC, no political scientist since has added or subtracted from his list. The five systems were an aristocracy, an oligarchy, a republic (representative democracy), democracy (anarchy), and tyranny (dictatorship/totalitarianism). Aristotle believed a republic to be the best system of governance for human beings. I agree. And I believe that it is also the best form for families of affinity.

How a Republic Works
In viewing the balance of strengths and weaknesses of human beings, Aristotle believed that to ensure the most people within any society the highest likelihood that they will be well governed meant giving as many people in the system as possible the right to choose

representatives and to be well represented by them. A republic, or representative democracy, is a system of governance in which a group of citizens, in open elections with secret ballots, selects individuals to represent them. Persons chosen to act as representatives are chosen for specific terms and are accountable to the citizen/voters for their actions. All such representatives are free after selection to act within the governing body as they best determine for the good of the whole. In other words, they are free to act as their consciences dictate for the betterment of the whole system.

Normally, a representative democracy has a strong judicial branch that provides the means to remove representatives who commit acts against the good of the society as a whole. The system is based on the rule of law and presumes that a high percentage of the adult population participates in the selection of representatives during elections. The system also presumes that those selected will have shown special aptitude for political leadership, often based on their education and previous success in positions of authority. The system is usually founded on a voluntary written agreement or compact, often referred to as a constitution, among the people who agree to be governed under them, defined as constituents. Frequently provided within such a constitution are the rules for the process of governance and for the checks and balances needed for such systems to work.

Aristotle saw that systems of governance based on exclusivity, such as aristocracies and oligarchies, were not sufficiently inclusive of the total population to succeed in gaining the needed support of the members for effective long-term governance. He made it clear that he didn't view republics as perfect; he clearly saw and described their faults. But he saw that a republic's including most constituents as voters and electing the likely best constituents as representatives offer the best hope for a society's effective governance.[3] He remained highly skeptical of human beings' ability to live virtuously and altruistically and, therefore, to govern themselves and others with any degree of success.

The Successful Governance System

In my work with families, I've observed that those who govern themselves best have systems with five outstanding characteristics:

1) The system is highly inclusive, asking as many as possible of those who will be governed to actively participate in it. It also seeks to minimize the waiting time for a new family member to begin participating fully in its processes.

2) It has highly articulated practices for the development of representatives, and as early as possible, it recruits members of the family who show leadership characteristics for roles in family governance as potential career choices.

3) It has active training and development programs to provide the coaching and mentoring necessary for a family member to be ready to act as a family representative when asked to do so. It provides clear succession guidelines[4] so that serving members know exactly how long their tenure will be.

4) It has highly developed educational programs to ensure that all family members are able to fully participate in family governance and to comprehend the decisions made by the family's legislative, judicial, and executive bodies.

5) It has procedures in place, using elders, to ensure that the minority view on any issue is protected. It gives the elders the authority to advise the family when it is not following the rules it has made for its governance.

Families whose representative democratic systems actively support these five practices do much better than families with any other system. As Aristotle observed, none of the five systems he described is perfect. Certainly, a republic presents the risk that its representatives may become tyrants or fools or, worse, that the majority of family member constituents may adopt any or all of these characteristics and lead the entire family into the chaos of anarchy. Regardless, Aristotle is right that most of us want to participate in the decisions of the group rather than have others make decisions for us. Equally, most of us know that others "called" to governance work will serve as better representatives of the needs of the whole group than we would.

Each of us realizes that in a world where risk to ourselves and to our dreams is inherent, we should in prudence find a group to join that seems to offer us security within its system so that we can fulfill those dreams. Each of us recognizes that by ceding some of our individual freedom of choice to a group we've chosen to join and to its representatives whom we helped to choose, we are joining in a government that is most likely to be interested in our individual safety and in assisting us in the achievement of our individual aspirations. This understanding is likely to prompt us to choose, as Aristotle did, a republic, or system of representative democracy, as the most effective governance system.

At the core of my philosophy is the principle that to live life fully—that is, to attain the highest fulfillment of our individual callings and to achieve our highest levels of self-awareness—we must be willing to make our own choices, with all the risks they entail. Choosing the system of governance within which that fulfillment is most likely to be achieved is one of life's important decisions. To achieve greatness in the long term, a family must understand how important it is to attract new members. A family that chooses a republic as its system of governance is likely to be making the best choice to achieve that goal.

The perfect family governance system is one that provides the means not only for individual members to achieve their personal goals but also for the group as a whole to meet its needs. Of course, no governance system will ever achieve such perfection. But I believe that Aristotle's recognition that a group's strengths and weaknesses could be best managed within a republic is as valid today as it was in 350 BC. We can all hope that we might live one day in Plato's Utopia, a kingdom ruled by philosophers, but for today we need to get on with governing the space we're in and to do so as best as we can through representation by others who, while not philosopher-kings, will at least do what needs to be done.

Chapter Notes

1. For those who wish to go deeper into Bowen's theory, the books to read are his *Family Theory in Clinical Practice* and his disciple Edwin Friedman's *A Failure of Nerve*. An ideal institution for study in this area is the Georgetown Family Center, in Georgetown, DC.

2. Goals, for example, might be egoistic, self-esteem, a personal financial goal, status in the family, or status outside the family.

3. I have always loved Churchill's statement, which I'll paraphrase: "Although representative democracy is a terrible form of government, it is better than all the rest."

4. I have come to believe that the better term is "transition," but I use the more understood term here. In general, I advise families to rename their succession committee a transition committee. This enables the family to see a change of representatives as interconnected with and integral to its successful long-term transitions and not as transactions without consequence to these transitions.

Chapter Eleven

Participation and Commitment

That government is the strongest of which every man feels himself a part.

—THOMAS JEFFERSON
third president of the United States

IN POLITICAL SCIENCE, the term for full participation in the decision-making process within a governance system is *suffrage*. Suffrage can be as narrow as in an aristocracy, where only a very few participate, or as wide as in anarchy, where everyone has equal say. In general, as Aristotle suggested, wider participation among those affected by the governing system is likely to lead to a higher proportion of citizens who willingly accept its decisions.

Certainly, for Americans, the idea of universal adult suffrage is a fundamental prerequisite to the willingness to participate in and be governed by the various levels of governance affecting their lives. Although this view of wide participation among the governed is now generally accepted throughout the world, and is a mark of a free society, it was not always so. Throughout most of written history, aristocracies, oligarchies, and dictatorships all offered very few of the governed the right of participation. Only since the nineteenth century has universal adult suffrage emerged as part of the preferred system of governance and only in the twentieth has it been achieved in most societies.

One would expect the same preference for universal suffrage among family members in designing a governance system. So it amazes me how often in our deepest relationships—even in a marriage—we voluntarily enter a family governance system and find that we are excluded from direct participation in it. Clearly we will never be able to make the greatest possible contribution to that system; nor will we ever be completely comfortable being governed by it. In fact, we're likely to abhor it and seek to neutralize its effects on us. We are also unlikely to encourage our children and grandchildren to participate in it since we perceive it as unfair.

Let's look at how a family can avoid such an outcome.

The Value of Inclusion

> **Principle 3.** *A family of affinity's governance system should be based on the principle of universal suffrage of all adult family members. Inclusion offers the means through which all voices are heard, thereby reducing the risk of loss of family members through lack of participation or, worse, through their permanent departure from the family.*

Families guided by the principle of including as many family members as possible in their governance systems will do better in successfully achieving their fifth generation and beyond than those with governance systems based on excluding all but a few family members. Why, then, do so many families have such an aversion to the principle of universal suffrage? I believe it results from the failure to perceive that the principle of affinity—rather than blood relation—must be the defining characteristic of a family. Holding tight to the principle that only shared "blood" entitles a member to participate in family governance requires that many persons be excluded from it and thus from family decision making. Ironically, this out-group consists of people who consider themselves family members and whom the family considers in all other respects to be family members. In a world in which we seek individual freedom and in which that freedom is largely defined by our direct participation in the decisions that affect us, such exclusion guarantees that many family members will feel that they're at best "nonfamily members" and at worst slaves to the governance system. No one chooses either role voluntarily. Nevertheless, in many families, members by "blood" happily impose such restrictions on those they ostensibly most love—their new family members—often forgetting that these new members were asked to join.

Given the difficulty of attempting to become a family that lasts five generations, it is highly doubtful that a system of family governance that excludes many of the members governed by it will lead to success. A family needs the human and intellectual assets of every member to enhance the group's well-being and to achieve its mission of greatness. Requiring any subset of family members to be governed by a system that bars their direct participation is unlikely to encourage the commitment and contribution of their human and intellectual assets. Rather, it will certainly discourage it.

Individual family governance systems, like systems that govern multiple families, must replicate the wishes of those governed by them if they are to be successful. Systems of family governance that encourage active participation by the largest number of family members are the ones most likely to foster their members' willingness to be governed. Such systems speak best to an individual's freedom of choice and thus to the pursuit of personal freedom. Families whose governance systems encourage and practice the principle of universal adult suffrage are best able to meet their family members' individual desires. Members enter such systems willingly. The more willing the family members are, the greater the likelihood that they will forgo their personal desires for the good of the family when difficult times require it.

A family seeking to achieve its fifth generation is not likely to do so unless all facets of its family system are working optimally. A family governance system that encourages the widest possible participation through universal suffrage is most likely to achieve that optimal result.

Universal Suffrage

The achievement of greater individual freedom for all individuals has led gradually to systems of governance that encourage that freedom through direct participation in the decisions affecting their freedom. All systems of governance assume that the lives of the governed, within the societies of which they are a part, will be ordered by them. Clearly, nations have decided that in return for giving up some individual freedom of choice to a common governance, citizens achieve the higher level of security for the individual and families this governance offers. In making this decision, citizens also recognize that they must directly participate in the process of how that freedom is devolved if society is to be truly preserved. Perhaps this is self-evident in the world today, but it has certainly not always been so; nor, more important, has such a choice been available to all who wished to have it. Sadly, there are many in the world who still lack and are seeking this choice.

Freedom to participate in the governance decisions that affect us is today something most of us cherish and almost all of us will even go to war to preserve. The system of governance that includes the widest possible participation is the definition of the governance system that provides us the freedom we so strongly want. Universal suffrage within such a system is how maximum freedom of participation by those governed is achieved.

Governance as a Compact

> **Principle 4.** *As each generation of a family of affinity reaches its turn to govern, it must renew the horizontal Lockean social compact that underlies the founding generation's governance system.*

In *Two Treatises on Government*, John Locke offers the view that governance systems reflect a "social compact" made by those governed by them. Locke suggests that those to be governed by a system are most likely to be governed willingly if they have a part in its formation. Systems of governance, he explains, require us to give up some personal freedom for the greater personal security offered by joining with others. This mutual security is the underlying reason we're willing to be governed by others in the first place. By presenting governance as a compact among free persons for their improved joint success, Locke's view of governance provides an understanding of why we might be willing to give up some personal freedom and why, by entering voluntarily into a compact with other like-minded people, we are most likely to be successfully governed by the rules of that voluntary compact. Locke's vision of governance as a social compact by free persons toward the greater good of all is the strongest statement to the modern mind of what governance is about. Naturally, Locke was greatly influenced by Aristotle, since it is a simple evolution from the idea of a voluntary social compact to a system of representative government that brings that compact to life. Locke is simply explaining what underlies a republic, the fundamental consent of the governed to be governed by *their* compact and then by the choice of representatives to make it work.

Families seeking to govern themselves well for many generations will recognize that adopting the concept of governance as a social compact is likely to create a governance system that will thrive. As cultural anthropology teaches, families in their third, fourth, and fifth generations are individual clans that have voluntarily elected to govern themselves together and thus become tribes. The voluntary decisions of the individual clans to join together for their mutual security and prosperity are social compacts in John Locke's sense. These compacts are the foundation for long-term systems of tribal governance. The individual family units combine to create long-lived families who practice seventh-generation thinking.

These compacts are profoundly horizontal rather than vertical. They represent the leveling of hierarchy among all of the original clans that voluntarily enter into them. They are normally the acts of the members of the same generation of each clan within a group of clans that grew out of an original nuclear family of affinity. Often such compacts can be made as early as the second generation of a family reaching adulthood. They can also form as late as the fifth generation.

Horizontal social compacts provide the foundation for long-term family governance. They exemplify the voluntary nature of family systems of governance. Through the commitment to that compact, each family member accepts the limitations on personal freedom of action that the family of affinity's governance system will require to govern the family successfully far into its future.

Preparing for Leadership

For a family's governance system to be most effective, each generation of the family of affinity should reaffirm the family's original foundational social compact as its turn to govern the family arises. If a family encourages each generation to understand its governance system and the role of each individual within it, the family's intellectual capabilities will grow and the chances for the system's success will improve. Just as civics courses in American high schools teach about the American system of governance, the members of a family must be taught their roles and responsibilities within the system that governs them. Without a full understanding of family governance, members will be unable to fully exercise their authority within that system and will be unable to be fully represented within it. Successful families will encourage all family members as they reach the age of full participation in the governance system to voluntarily commit to following its governance principles and to being fully active in the system.

Families of affinity should also offer rituals whereby maturing adults are welcomed into the system. With such education and rituals, the family will encourage family members to appreciate the special benefits they will enjoy by actively participating in the system. Rituals that recognize the attainment of the rights and privileges of participation should be developed and practiced so the depth of the family's commitment to its governance system and to the social compact that underlies it will be fully integrated into the consciousness of its maturing family members.

Likewise, each generation, as the time arrives for it to assume leadership of the family, should renew the original social compact that lies at the foundation of the family governance system. Often it will be unclear exactly when the wheel of family generations has revolved to bring the new generation of leaders into place. The family's elders can help a family recognize when that time has come, and the history of the family's earlier generational transitions can serve as guide. When it is time for the new generation to assume leadership, an important and powerful way to celebrate that moment will be for the entire family to join together in a ritual ceremony, reaffirming the family's social compact and affirming its willingness to be governed by that compact.[1]

Re-imagining the family's past, as reflected in its foundational social compact, and then imagining the family's future based on that compact give the governing generation the greatest possible understanding of its heritage and of the system it will lead. Seeing that heritage as a horizontal compact of equal family members seeking to find a better way to grow as individuals through the security offered by the group is critical to success in governing the family. Comprehending that membership in the family governance system is voluntary follows from a recognition of the free nature of the social compact that gave birth to it. Having each generation renew that compact is profoundly reenergizing for the family as a whole. The new generation pledges its energy to the common good of the family and pledges to be governed by the original energy of the family's affinity, represented by the original family compact.

Chapter Notes

1. Participation in this ritual should include all family members age ten and older. Giving a family's youth the opportunity to participate in its most important transitional rituals as early as possible is essential to fostering a feeling of belonging and to building bonds of affinity. I have seen the age for full voting participation set between eighteen and twenty-five.

Chapter Twelve

Function and Structure

In framing a government, the great difficulty lies in this: You must enable the government to control the governed and oblige it to control itself.

—ALEXANDER HAMILTON, American statesman

DURING THE EIGHTEENTH century, two figures emerged who played an extraordinary role in the development of the art and practice of governance: the French writer Charles-Louis de Secondat, baron de Montesquieu, and James Madison, the fourth president of the United States. These two men developed systems of governance founded on their beliefs that governance performs three essential functions and that those three functions must be separate yet fully interconnected. Although Montesquieu's work preceded Madison's and was foundational to it, Madison's views of the practice of governance, as reflected in the Constitution of the United States of America, are more accessible to readers generally, so I will use his iteration of their views.

> *Principle 5. A family governance system must have three branches: the legislative, the executive, and the elders/judicial, similar to those suggested by Montesquieu and Madison. The interaction of these branches must be regulated by checks and balances similar to those outlined in the Constitution of the United States. The vision and practice of a family governance system should be contained in a written constitution.*

The Family Assembly

In guiding the framers of the Constitution, Madison understood that governance requires three separate sets of actors to fulfill its roles. First, governance requires making laws that define the rules and practices of the system. This branch of government is generally called the legislative branch. In family governance, this branch is often called the family assembly, or family forum.

This branch of the system normally comprises all members who have reached the age for full participation in governance. It normally creates committees, drawn from its members, to study and sometimes administer various areas of family activity and to inform the larger family assembly about those matters. Frequently, committees include executive, elders, nominations, education, trustee/beneficiary relations, family philanthropy, family heritage, and family meetings.

As the policy-making branch, the family assembly also has the right to initiate and approve amendments to the family's constitution. This branch is the core of the family's governance process, and it approves the family's budget for governance costs and gives family members access to these funds. The assembly also has the responsibility for selecting elders from the various family clans, to whom the family will grant judicial authority.

The Family Council

Governance requires a branch to carry out the decisions made by the legislative branch, and this is called the executive branch. In family governance, this branch is frequently called the family council, or the executive committee. Normally, a family does not have a permanent executive body; instead, the legislative branch selects representatives to carry out its decisions as needed. These representatives are usually selected by the members of the family for a term of years and are accountable to the legislative branch, and thus to the family as a whole, for their actions.

The executive branch generally serves as the voice of the family, interacting with outside professionals, including employees of the family office. The executive branch will often be tasked by the various family committees to search out experts to assist them in their work, to help them form their agendas, and to share information about the best practices learned from their interactions with other families and outside professional organizations. Typically, the executive branch is responsible for managing family finances, including investments, unless there is a strategic investment committee authorized by the legislative branch, a practice I strongly encourage. Related responsibilities include the collection of family assessments and paying the costs of family governance.

The Elders

Governance requires a branch to settle disputes and to determine when the family is not following the rules of its governance system. This branch is parallel to the judicial branch in other governance systems, but with certain key differences. In family governance, this branch is frequently called the elders branch, rather than the judicial branch. The difference in terminology is not semantic; it is fundamental. Families are unique in that they have no transactions or short-term events; they have only long-term transitions. They must recognize in their governance that "settling" a dispute rather than "mediating" it puts the fabric of the family at risk.

Judicial branches of societal governance systems are reflected in the courts and judicial systems they administer. Societies need to settle disputes for their good order. They require finality. They consider the loss of members that might occur if losing parties choose to opt out of the system far less of a risk than not having finality in resolving disputes. These societal judicial systems are founded on the hope that their innate fairness and objectivity will hold losing parties within the system. They are based on the rule of law.[1]

Although in societal governance the judicial branch resolves disputes, it also assumes that one party to every dispute will lose. That's why this branch makes great efforts to settle disputes rather than adjudicate them. Societies, like families, know that their good order, and indeed survival, depends on their citizens' willingness to stay within the system and that this will happen only if its citizens believe in the system's innate fairness.

Families of affinity expand this view to recognize that losing any member because he perceives the family's governance system to be unfair is a threat to the whole family. Remember, a family needs every member's human and intellectual capital to attain greatness. No family can afford to lose these assets. A family of affinity recognizes that its governance system must provide for dispute resolution by mediation among members because it's the method most likely to retain family harmony. However, the family also recognizes that it must have systems to ensure the uniform enforcement of the rules and impartial access to the legislative process to ensure fairness for both the majority and the minority. These families understand that the resolution of every dispute bears on the successful transitions the family must make to ensure it will arrive at its fifth generation and flourish thereafter. Thus, families realize that their judicial branch must do three things:

a) mediate rather than resolve disputes,

b) advise the family when it is not following its own enacted rules, thereby protecting individual members and minority family groups from the tyranny of the majority, while assuring impartial enforcement of its decisions, and

c) provide the family with a storyteller who can recount its history and explain why it does things in this way—that is, why it is "different."

Families who revere their elders by granting them the authority to do these three things are emulating the success of the longest-lived tribes as extended families of affinity. All families have elders. Often they are the older members who have gained wisdom about themselves and others from life's experiences. More rarely, but more often than we might imagine, they are young people who are wise before their time. Regardless, the family knows who they are and comfortably grants them the authority to settle its disputes, to opine on its rules, and to tell its stories.

The family knows that its elders will do all in their power to help its members feel that they are part of traditions and experiences that put into context the transitions in which they find themselves. They see the nuances in a situation and, with patience, help all others see them too. They seek equity for the long-term gain of all. They avoid ever having any dispute or rule interpretation become a transaction that might cause a family member to perceive that he has lost and decide to abandon the tribe. In helping family members to see disputes as transitions rather than transactions, elders act more as peacekeepers than as jurists.[2]

Checks and Balances

Among the three branches, checks and balances must be in place to regulate their interaction. The legislative branch regulates the executive branch by maintaining it as one of its own committees, setting the terms of its members, deciding on its budget, nominating its members, and holding them accountable for their actions.

Since in a family governance system, the executive branch is an arm of the legislative branch, the risks of the tyranny of the executive are not nearly as prevalent as in more complex systems of governance, in which the executive branch is fully independent of the legislative branch.

The legislative branch regulates the elders branch by choosing the elders as one of its own committees, setting the terms of its members, and holding them accountable for their actions. The elders, however, are normally nominated, not by the nominating committee of the legislative branch, but by the individual clans that make up the family. In the working of the elders branch, the need for some degree of independence from the group as a whole is as strong in family governance as it is in societal governance. The elders' terms are typically longer than those of members of the executive branch or members of the other committees of the legislative branch. Also, the decisions of the elders branch are final on the issue at hand and may not be appealed to the family as a whole. Its selection process affords this branch an independence that provides a special protection to each clan by ensuring that each clan's views on disputes will be honored. It also guarantees the ability of the elders to act in the highest and best interests of the family as a whole, while protecting all individual family members from the possibility of the tyranny of a runaway majority.

As Madison wrote, there are three fundamental tasks for government to accomplish—legislative, executive, and judicial—and if these tasks are to be performed for the greatest good of the governed, the branches that perform them must be regulated so that all are coequal and none can dominate the actions of the others.

A Constitution

History has shown that writing down the agreements contained in the social compacts on governance offers all the parties to those compacts the greatest protection of the rights and responsibilities they confer. Of course, writing down rules doesn't ensure that those governed by them will comply. Indeed, writing them down is only meaningful if the parties have agreed to act according to those rules. Among tribes that predated writing, oral histories of the rules of governance appear to have served their societies quite well. However, they were small communities in which the voice of the bard, the tribal historian, could be heard by all tribal members when they convened. In our times, with family members scattered geographically, such a system will not suffice. And we are accustomed to having written documents, provided that we've been consulted as they were written or have agreed to be governed by those already in place.

These written documents containing the rules and practices of particular systems of governance are called constitutions. They are the written affirmations of the horizontal social compacts by those who agree to be governed by them. A constitution may be a single document, as in the United States, or it may be a series of documents, as in Great Britain. Either way, it expresses the wishes and desires reflected in the compact of the governed. Many families have found that recording their compact for joint governance in written form gives their agreements greater depth and reality. The writing process also helps them clarify and refine their intentions and thereby deepen the utility of those agreements.

A Confederation of Clans

Principle 6. *A governance system based on a confederation of clans with a weak tribal center, rather than a federation of clans with a strong tribal center, provides the greatest likelihood of successful long-term family governance.*

For Americans it is almost axiomatic that a strong federal system with weak component states is the preferred form of government. This view results from the North's victory in the Civil War, which resulted in the North's capital of Washington, DC, becoming the capital of the entire system. Great Britain, until very recently, had the same preference for federal versus confederate systems, as the English succeeded in conquering and merging the Welsh, the Scots, and the Northern Irish into a very strong federal system based in the historic English capital of London.

Although history, in these two examples, appears to have favored strong federal republics, there are other, longer-running republics, which indicate that a confederation of strong states and weak federal centers are also successful. Switzerland is both the longest-lived republic on earth and the model for a successful confederation.

What do these systems of government offer us as analogies for successful family government? Cultural anthropology can help us here. At the most basic level of human societal behavior, families evolve into clans in their third and fourth generations and into tribes in their fifth and sixth. As families evolve from a single household with parents and children to multiple households formed by the children and grandchildren, each household forms its own identity. Part of that identity relates back to the founding couple of affinity and part is influenced by marriage to other families of affinity. Each of these new households is simultaneously a new family on its own and the second or third generations of the original family of affinity. As these households in turn spawn new families of affinity out of the third and fourth generations, clans are born. In turn, as these clans, by the fifth and sixth generation, differentiate from the original family of affinity, they develop separate, strong individual identities. At this point in the evolution of the original family of affinity, if some or all of the clans have stayed cemented to other clans from the original family, these clans may elect to join together and—in cultural anthropological terms—form a tribe. Such tribes can go on for multiple generations.

What forms of governance do most tribes adopt? Again, cultural anthropology would suggest that as clans come together to create tribes, they seek to retain their clan identities in tribal governance, while ceding to the tribe those powers necessary to enhance their security. In other words, they relinquish to the center only those powers necessary for the limited general purpose of mutual security, while retaining for all other purposes their clan governance systems.

In my work with families, I have noted that this same process goes on today. Clan structures offer their members the close ties necessary for resolution of most individual issues of family relationship. Equally, clans recognize that they often execute tasks such as education of family members, pooling of assets for financial investment, formation of private trust companies, and relations with outside professionals more efficiently when they join with other clans to understand and underwrite these activities. Clans recognize that by ceding some authority to the tribal center they can accomplish many things that would be impossible on their own. These opportunities prompt clans to form tribes with other clans from the original family of affinity.

Given that the clans seek only limited assistance from the tribe, they prefer to retain strong individual positions, with the tribal center serving more as a place of discussion than of decision making. Such systems of governance are known as confederations rather than federations. In my experience, such systems serve the individual clans well and do not require them to give up individual clan identities to some larger tribal identity in order to gain the advantages of mutual cooperation.

A hallmark of such systems is the selection of elders who will form the governance system's judicial branch. Here, the power of tribal dispute resolution is not lodged with the legislative branch but rather with the elders. And the power to determine when the majority is not following its own rules but instead is acting in a way that would trample clan authority is likewise lodged with the elders. Often in these systems, each clan places its elder on the elders committee and includes in its own clan's governance plan the process of nomination and selection of that elder.

Families that balance the separate identities of their clans in the elders branch and integrate the needs of the whole tribe by including all families in the legislative branch seem to do best in governing themselves. For these reasons, I believe family governance systems based on the confederation model of strong clans solving most issues of governance within their own systems and ceding to the tribal center the authority to deal only with the particular issues—namely, those dealing with the positive development of family members and with greater personal security—serve families better than systems based on the federation model.

Chapter Notes

1. I believe that America's greatest contribution to the history and science of governance is the success of our Supreme Court in establishing and enforcing the principle that the judicial branch of government's highest purpose is to assure all citizens it will enforce their individual rights, as described in the Constitution, against acts by the legislative or executive branches that impinge on or abrogate those rights.

2. Thanks to the American jurist John Marshall, Americans enjoy the special benefits of the supremacy of the rule of law not as an ideal to be sought but as a fact of life. Not surprisingly, members of the U.S. Supreme Court are invariably the most admired American personalities in every opinion poll. It's also no surprise that very few citizens in America fear their government and feel forced to expatriate as a result. Therefore, the American system has historically lost very few members, compared with the millions who have moved to America to gain the individual protection it offers.

Chapter Thirteen

Change and Accommodation

Democracy is a process, not a static condition. It is becoming, rather than being. Its essence is eternal struggle.
—WILLIAM H. HASTIE, American jurist and pioneer of the civil rights movement

WHEN A FAMILY can imagine the transitions inherent in its evolution from a founding affinity pair to the multiple members of the fifth generation, it can begin to form the vision necessary to grow a great family. In every family I meet, someone asks me how it's possible to envision this sort of transition so far into the future. Because each of us learns and experiences things differently, there is no single answer to this question. I've found, however, that such visioning comes easier if I ask the questioner to imagine the family far back in its past. Taking the long view, the "longue durée," in both directions helps.

An Evolutionary System

Principle 7. A family governance system should operate with the understanding that a family's entire system is always in flux, in transition. The system, therefore, must be sufficiently flexible to constantly evolve toward higher levels of complexity as the family it serves becomes more complex. Successful family governance systems are based on Edmund

Burke's principles of evolutionary governance rather than on revolutionary principles. A Burkian system of liberal conservatism seeks perpetually to enable greater individual freedom for each of its members to pursue their individual journey of happiness in an orderly, systematic, evolutionary way.

In this seventh proposition, I suggest that the most successful family systems of governance are those that allow positive evolutionary change and seek to avoid the risk of being destroyed through revolutionary change. I have found that a family journeying toward success recognizes that it has no transactions but only transitions. Sadly, I have also observed families experiencing events as transactions (for example, selling their business enterprises for "godfather offers," without realizing they're selling their dreams and their stories along with them). These actions are short term, with a defined beginning and ending. The trauma of the ending, when the family is unable to integrate the outcome of the event into its system, frequently leads to the family's demise.[1] Families who take the long view plan for transitions so that no event will ever so imperil the family's fabric that it will be permanently weakened. Transactions suggest final endings; transitions suggest ever-open new possibilities.

Family governance systems cannot overcome revolutionary change because revolutions are transactions. Revolution, by definition, means change at the root of the system and the overthrow of that system to substitute a different system for it. Clearly, change at the root of a family and its overthrow mean its demise, since nothing can be "substituted" for it. A family exists, and, if it is overthrown, it ceases to exist. No family governance system can possibly be useful to a family if its nature is to favor revolution, because revolution is predestined to destroy the family. Fomenting revolution is the antithesis of seventh-generation thinking. I believe a successful family governance system must be Burkian and not Jacobin; its philosophy should, therefore, be that of liberal conservatism.

In political science, the great Irish statesman Edmund Burke stands for a belief in ordered evolutionary change rather than revolutionary change. His views stand for the principle that government should seek to ensure the greatest degree of personal freedom and security for its constituents by providing an orderly society where change is evolutionary, founded on the basic history, culture, ideas, and ideals that form that society. He recognized that a system in which each individual acts for his own interests in his own way leads to chaos for all. In this sense, Burke is a liberal conservative. As a conservative he stands for orderly social change, founded on the history of the society being governed, and as a liberal he supports a system that allows an individual the greatest degree of freedom to seek his own future, consistent with harming no one else in that pursuit. The Burkian view recognizes that such an ordered evolution may not provide freedom fast enough for some people; still, the pace will be best for the vast majority of the people who live within that system. Burke also believed strongly that those chosen to represent their constituents should be encouraged to do so in the manner that best served the entire community, not just their own narrow interests. Burke was a true believer in the concept of a republic as a representative democracy.[2]

The alternative view of governance is the so-called Jacobin view. It takes its name from the Jacobin Club, active during the French Revolution of 1789, and is used to describe governance systems that believe that constant change at the root of their systems is necessary for successful achievement of the highest degree of personal freedom. This approach endorses revolution, seeing it as good and necessary for the system to work. This philosophy has been expressed by both Thomas Jefferson and Mao Tse-tung. Although change is necessary to accommodate family transitions, the disorderly approach of blowing up the center has never, in my experience, been successful in the dynamic preservation of a family. Whether it has been good for societies as a whole is debatable.

The Continuum of Past and Future

When I talk to family members about envisioning transitions and change, I tell a family story to make the point. On the day my first granddaughter, Margaret, was born, I telephoned my father to tell him the good news. Margaret was his first great-grandchild so our family wheel was revolving to welcome a new generation. I told him that I had been thinking of what I would tell Margaret about her family and that I had decided to tell her about my great-grandmother Epatha Sharp Berry, who died when I was six years old. I knew her quite well. She was proud to tell me that she had been born in Missouri of Southern sympathizers who had emigrated there from Virginia through Kentucky and that she had lived there during the Civil War. She remembered very well having to leave her home three times as the different armies passed through her town. My father replied that he had been thinking the same thing. He had known his great-grandmother, Mary McGhee Sharp, very well, and she had been born in 1820—before Napoleon died. We laughed as we imagined starting Margaret on her journey with family stories of our ancestors whose histories dated back 175 years.

I suggest families do this exercise to see how far back in time they can go, usually four to five generations. We then fast-forward from the present the same distance into the future to imagine our family four or five generations ahead. Winston Churchill said, and I paraphrase, "The wisest people I know are those who can imagine back the farthest because they are those most able to imagine farthest ahead."

Another tool I use in helping families imagine the future of the family is to ask them to imagine what joint decisions they could make with their family of affinity in the next month that would make them feel more positive about the contributions they could make together to this long-term process. When I help a family combine the long view with current short-term decision making, I am offering a process that provides lessons discoverable by almost all who try it. This combination also helps family members see that the art and practice of their governance is not some complex, jargon-ridden academic subject but rather the simple act of seeking to make a few more daily joint decisions with the foresight of seventh-generation thinking.

As a family moves forward from this simple process, I help them probe the "how" question by gently coaching family members to appreciate that their participation in acts of joint decision making represents their direct contribution to the family governance system. It helps them see how they're involved in it. They're able to feel the deep currents of continuity that flow through the system as they imagine the contributions made by earlier generations. As they remember hearing family stories about these people, they can imagine the new people who will become part of the system in years to come. This kind of thinking helps family members appreciate how an already-intricate system evolves to become more complex as each new member joins it. Complexity then ceases to be a subject for academic study and becomes a perfectly natural, normal idea that fits what family members already know about how the family works. At this point, they can easily imagine the concepts of joint decision making, evolutionary change, systems theory, and complexity theory without having to know anything academic about any of them. This isn't magic; it comes from experience.

Families seeking to dynamically preserve themselves know intuitively that a system of liberal conservatism, exemplified by taking the long view of successfully managing its multiple transitions, will be the governance philosophy that serves its purposes best. These successful families are Burkian at their core. They seek to promote the individual searches for happiness of each of their members through a system of evolutionary, ordered family governance. They offer their members the safety and confidence that they will have a lifetime in which to attain the highest level of self-awareness and the personal freedom and happiness that come with it. And they will do so without anxiety that their family's governance system will be undermined by constant changes to the system's roots. Adopting a Burkian belief in liberal conservatism to ensure an orderly evolution of the governance system creates a platform that offers the greatest number of family members the greatest possibility that each will achieve the greatest happiness attainable.

All for One

Principle 8. *A family governance system should be founded on the reality of Benjamin Franklin's statement at the signing of the American Declaration of Independence: "As we are certain to hang separately, we are far better to hang together."*

Imagine a group of white males gathered to consider a long document that rests on a table in a beautiful Georgian red brick building in the city of Philadelphia, Pennsylvania, on July 4, 1776. The document is to become the American Declaration of Independence. It is quite hot inside the room, and they've been in Philadelphia, most of them having traveled there on horseback, for two months with only two or three changes of clothes and they normally did not bathe. If they should lose the war they're fighting to remove the British king, George III, from his position as their sovereign and declare themselves an independent nation, signing the document in front of them means signing their death warrants. The stale, acrid odor of fear and anxiety permeates the room. Yes, this is an entirely different reality from the heroic Joseph Trumbull painting of decades later, showing men in beautiful brocades and satins happily signing the historic document.

Benjamin Franklin, who by 1776 was already an old man by the standards of the time, became irritated that no one was coming forward to sign the declaration. He had a room full of "Alphonses and Gastons," types who hang back and say, "If you'll sign, then I will" or "Please go forward and I'll follow." No one wanted to sign his death warrant but each knew that unless he did, Americans would never achieve the freedom they deserved. Franklin is then reported to have said, "Gentlemen, as we are certain to hang separately, we are far better to hang together," whereupon they all stepped forward and signed, thereby pledging their lives, their liberties, their property, and their sacred honor to the preservation of life, liberty, and the pursuit of happiness for all Americans.

The Trade-Off

Franklin's observation lies at the heart of family governance. All human beings know that they must find a group to join if they are to survive, yet each fears the loss of individual freedom that joining any group entails. Each intuits that giving up some individual freedom for the sake of the success of the group is the price that must be paid to gain the group's support in achieving personal happiness.

Successful family governance lies in positive attraction. If a family can imagine itself surviving many generations hence, it will see the wisdom of incorporating Franklin's "hanging together" principle in that pursuit. We all know that if we find no group to "hang with," we are very likely to hang separately. We need the support of others if we are to succeed ourselves, while we fear that in choosing a group to "hang with" we may choose wrongly and lose all freedom and happiness in the bargain. Early in our life journey, we each will find ourselves having to choose which group to join for our journey and we appreciate how profound the choice is.

A family of affinity, by its nature, exists to help its members achieve the realization of their individual dreams. Equally, it asks them to promise to make the same effort to help all other members attain theirs. Members of the group are positively attracted through the promises they've made. The group asks its members to participate in the joint decision making of their systems of family governance, and so, yes, they ask them to give up some personal freedom toward successful achievement of the group's goals. However, if these goals include promoting the individual journey toward happiness of each member, this loss seems a small sacrifice for the benefits that being in a family of affinity brings.

Franklin's statement reminds us of the perils of hanging together when we imagine that roomful of anxious men, but it reminds us more deeply that hanging together is essential if we are to avoid the ever-present risk of hanging separately.

Chapter Notes

1. My "Reflection on the Sale of a Family Business as an Event of Trauma," accessible on my Web site, www.jamesehughes.com, offers insight into this all-too-frequent event.

2. My senior thesis, presented to the History Department at Princeton University, was titled "A Study of the Conservative Reaction to the French Revolution of 1848 Through Its Leadership, the Union de la rue de Poitiers." Perhaps it gave even in 1964 a hint of my future life in politics in which I've stood, in both elected and appointed positions, for the principles of liberal conservatism, the principles of Theodore Roosevelt of fiscal conservatism, progressive social liberalism, and what is today globalism. I believe that each of these three must be tempered by the view that the government should stay as much out of the lives of its citizens as possible while providing the greatest possible security to permit the orderly evolutionary change that society requires if it is to use the creativity of its citizens to meet the challenges that new times require and to encourage the highest flourishing of each citizen.

I believe a system of government must avoid promoting the growth of a narrow "rights-based" society of rules with no flexibility, which promotes only one individual's or group's goals and requires a larger and larger government to administer. I believe such a system leads eventually to the anarchy of everyone believing that their own "rights" are paramount, with the fission that follows.

A system of government that seeks to act with the greatest flexibility to discover the solutions that benefit all and thereby increases everyone's liberty is a far better system and one far more likely to survive and prosper. For such a system to work, its representatives must be able to act for all rather than in the narrow self-interest of only a few. I agree with Burke, Madison, Hamilton, Jay, and Theodore Roosevelt.

PART FOUR

Family
Leadership

Chapter 14

Family as an Organization

Man is but a network of relationships, and these alone matter to him.

—ANTOINE DE SAINT-EXUPÉRY
French writer and aviator

THE SINGLE LARGEST factor contributing to a family of affinity's failure is the inability to organize and manage the multiple relationships that its enterprise system demands. Organizational science offers the methodology to dissect any set of relationships, define them, and explain the rules and practices that govern them. Unfortunately, families of affinity have not traditionally applied that science to their family governance systems.

During the past twenty years, however, that reality has changed:

• As business and organizational scientists have assisted families with their business enterprises, families have gained a better understanding of the ideas and practices of organizational management.

• Similar ideas from family systems theorists found their way into family organizations through psychology as family members sought advice on how to make their relationships, including financial relationships, more successful and happier.

These two streams of ideas, both offering skills for developing and maintaining better relationships, are now significantly improving families' abilities to govern and manage themselves. Families of affinity are blessed to be in a world where the ideas of these two sciences are available to them.

Organizations and Their Management

The study of organizations and how they operate began in the early twentieth century with the time and motion studies of Frederick Taylor for various industrial enterprises, as well as other studies, such as those for Ford Motor Company, when Henry Ford was developing the assembly-line system of production. In an age of just-in-time computerized inventory systems and its links to the production line, we see the results of those early studies.

There are, however, earlier historical precedents for the study of how organizations work. Many individuals such as Sun Tzu, Julius Caesar, Carl von Clausewitz, Napoleon, and Mao Tse-tung studied how organizations worked so they could improve how they made war. Others—the Greeks, the Macedonians, the Romans, the Chinese, the Mongols, the Japanese, the French, and the British—studied how to manage and operate empires. Some groups studied how to manage and run global religious enterprises; the Islamic Caliphate and the Roman Catholic Church were perhaps the best examples. In these three theaters of activity, the need to manage complex far-flung enterprises—whether, armies, kingdoms, or episcopates—required a deep understanding of how to build, manage, and run large-scale organizations.

Family Business

What relevance do organizational and management sciences have to the study of a family of affinity? In the 1960s, when I first began to work with families, I knew of no one who was using business terms or the sciences of organization and management to understand and explain the dynamics of family organizations. The family and the system were thought not to be businesslike, much less businesses, and therefore were apparently thought to have no relevance to the family. Much later, I learned that Peter Davis and Howard Stephenson were doing such work at the Wharton School and at Harvard, respectively.

Today, such a view is seen as impossibly antiquated. In fact, one cannot attend a conference dealing with the family without encountering four terms that come straight from these sciences and are now used to define the nature of a family:

1) The business of the family is its well-being and development.

2) The assets of the family are the human beings who make it up.

3) The goal of the family is the growth of its wealth—its human, intellectual, financial, and social capitals.

4) A family is an enterprise, and to be successful it must be enterprising.

These ideas about the family and its practices are taken directly from these sciences. Again, to my knowledge, no such terms defining a family and its practices were in general use before 1980. Since then, they have become ubiquitous.

Nevertheless, a question that arises for a family of affinity seeking skills and practices to facilitate its development and survive for many generations is whether organizational and management sciences can truly help a family achieve long-term success. Or are their principles merely easy to apply and intended only as a way to impose on the family system a particular consultant's hubristic view, by equating his professional work with families to that of great business advisers, like Peter Drucker, John Ward, and James Collins? In my experience, these sciences are of significant benefit in helping a family comprehend how its system—its family organization—can work more efficiently toward the family's dynamic preservation. The reasons are straightforward:

• Families are self-governing and self-regulating organizations of increasing complexity and therefore candidates for the application of systems theory.

• In many ways, families behave like enterprises.

• Families are complex systems, working toward an outcome that's intended to make a profit: the greater happiness of each succeeding generation.

• Families seek measurable results.

• Having systems of governance that grow in complexity through the constant accretion of members, families must necessarily organize themselves in highly structured ways to accomplish very long-term goals in line with the visions and outcomes they plan for.

Applied Sciences

How can a family of affinity employ these sciences and their operating concepts toward increasing its success? Organizational and management sciences can help a family recognize how complex the process of its governance and preservation is organizationally because of the multiplicity of its relationships. And they can help the family structure and manage those relationships well. A family of affinity represents a system of multiple relationships, each of which must be managed excellently over a long period of time if the family is to dynamically preserve itself.

Let's look at the scope of family organizations within the context of organizational and management sciences and at how these sciences can offer systems and skills to enhance a family's multiple relationships. Within families I've studied that are in their third, fourth, and later generations, members often have as many as twenty-one different relationships with one another. In almost all cases, those relationships fall into two divisions: I call them "me" relationships and "we" relationships. In defining the multiplicity of family relationships and in explaining them I am deeply indebted to the work of my colleague Joanie Bronfman, a psychologist and author.

In a "me" relationship, the family member has a role as an individual in direct relationship to another. These include one's relationship as a son or daughter, grandson or granddaughter, great-grandson or great-granddaughter, cousins (often first, second, and third), parent, spouse, grandparent, aunt or uncle (often great and great-grand), son- or daughter-in-law, godson or goddaughter, godparent, and step relationships of all kinds.

In a "we" relationship, the individual interacts as a member of a designated family group that includes other family members. Such roles might include beneficiary; trustee; owner of shares of a family corporation; member of the board of a family corporation; employee of a family corporation; owner of a partnership interest in a family partnership; general or limited partner of a family partnership; employee of a family partnership; general or limited member of a family limited liability company; employee of a family limited liability company; or employee, member of the board, or member of the grants committee of a family philanthropy formed as a not-for-profit corporation.

The variety of these relationships can span quite a range, indicating just how complex the organizational management of a family's multiple relationships really is. It's no secret how difficult it is to manage one relationship well. Trying to be an excellent spouse, or parent, or elder, or owner often requires superhuman efforts over a lifetime to do any one of them well. Rarely is a road map given at the inception of such a relationship to help us do a reasonable job. Only through trial and error do we discover the means to make the relationship successful.

Does this mean I'm saying that to successfully organize and manage a family's dynamic preservation, we have to understand and manage perhaps as many as twenty-one or more relationships perfectly? Have I set an impossible hurdle? Is family enterprise governance, in fact, impossible? Certainly not. However, a family whose members do not understand the complexity of the relationship systems in which they're embedded, who cannot pull apart and describe each of their relationships with family members, who cannot understand what must be learned about the nature and rules of each relationship will fail.

Relationship by Edict
How might family members begin to understand how to make all these relationships work? To successfully engage in any relationship, they must

• know themselves and define their goals and aspirations in terms of what they will gain in their understanding of themselves by entering into the relationship;

• understand the goals and aspirations of the other party to the relationship;

• be educated about the nature of the relationship they intend to form—that is, the values, rules, and practices that underlie and define it; and

• be prepared to organize and maintain such a relationship around those values, rules, and practices—often for an entire lifetime.

Sadly, in most families, the multiple relationships formed are not entered into with any awareness about these rules of engagement. More often in a family, individuals don't even foresee these issues because they're born into many of these relationships and recognize the complexity of them only when it begins to hinder the individual's efforts toward individualization and happiness.

Many "we" relationships in a family are formed by third-party advisers. The individuals in these relationships are frequently co-opted into them by family leaders rather than voluntarily forming them. Just as often, they're a matter of genealogy, because many of these relationships, such as long-term family trusts, may predate the member's birth, giving him no chance at all to decide whether he wishes to be in the relationship created for him. However these "we" relationships come into being, members are simply drawn into them by virtue of their having a "me" relationship to the person whose financial assets fund the relationship. Rarely are individuals asked whether they'd like to join, and even more rarely are they given the educational tools to understand what's entailed in being part of such an organism and the complex, legal, ethical, human, intellectual, and family relationships that are part of it. It is not surprising, therefore, that most families fail because they can't organize and manage the multiple relationships that their enterprise systems demand.

Case in Point

Let's have a look at the complexity of just one of these roles: the role of owner as opposed to manager. Many families fail to understand that long-term success in dynamically preserving financial capital lies in making certain that every member of each generation learns to be a dynamic steward-conservator-stakeholder[1] *owner* of the family's financial capital, rather than someone who is chosen merely to *manage* that capital.

My father and I, having spent a combined ninety years helping families tackle these issues, often noted that many—indeed, probably most—of the failed family business enterprises we observed failed *not* because of poor management but because of failed ownership. At the root of this reality lies the Cheshire cat's question to Alice. Yes, a family enterprise is bound to arrive somewhere in its life's journey, but if its owners are not providing the strategic vision for where it should go, it will arrive wherever its management leads it. And that place, in my father's and my experience, will rarely be a safe harbor for the family that owns it. Of course, a family enterprise perpetually at sea is no fault of management—barring corruption, which is the rarest of reasons for a company to founder.

Management's role in a family enterprise is to serve as the crew and perform the tactical maneuvers needed to keep the ship afloat and in good condition. Its task is not to determine the ship's strategic goals. Strategy is the responsibility of the family owners. If the owners are not performing their strategic roles and responsibilities and providing direction, the enterprise will experience the entropy that all rudderless ships face. These enterprises do eventually wind up somewhere, but never where their owners hoped they'd be.

Tough Lessons

Why does this paradox of focusing on management at the expense of active ownership in a family enterprise—and the subsequent entropic effect on a family's financial capital—constantly replay itself in so many family enterprises?[2] There are multiple reasons:

• Failure to educate owner-inheritors on their roles and responsibilities as dynamic steward-conservator-stakeholder owners

• Failure to perceive that ownership is the stewarding responsibility of every adult family member regardless of how that member joined the family of affinity; management, on the other hand, is a calling

• Failure to perceive the different nature of the role of a passive shareholder versus an active stakeholder, as well as the failure to foresee the gradual running down of the enterprise's energy by its management if all owners are passive

- Failure to appreciate that managing risk is a complex discipline that every owner must undertake and that the difference between taking too much risk (thereby throwing the enterprise into chaos) and taking too little risk (thereby putting it in a state of profound inertia) is one that can be learned and managed
- Failure to perceive that trustees, by virtue of their duty to be prudent, are entropic owners because they cannot take the same risks as the stakeholder owners of competing enterprises
- Failure to perceive that the beneficiaries of trusts that own family enterprises are the true stakeholder owners of those enterprises; these beneficiaries often have no understanding of how to be great beneficiaries much less how to be great stakeholder owners
- Failure to provide owners with an understanding of systems theory and of the ever-increasing complexity of systems as they evolve
- Failure to expose owners to organizational science as it relates to leadership transitions within family organizations and to the various forms of leadership from in front and from behind that might be best for the enterprise at different points in its evolution
- Failure to educate owners about the business tools of evaluation and assessment they'll need if the enterprise and its management are to thrive
- Failure to enable dynamic steward-conservator-stakeholder owners to develop their dreams for the enterprise as it evolves beyond the dream of the founder/creator generation, leaving management with a historical rather than a current dream to fulfill
- Failure to offer dynamic steward-conservator-stakeholders the wisdom that the family, in its goal to reach its fifth generation and beyond, has a few critical long-term transitions to manage in every generation and that no short-term transaction is likely to make a difference in its success except negatively
- Failure of family elders to help the owners perceive the need for strategic seventh-generation thinking with a beginner's mind instead of the tactical management thinking appropriate to short-term problems. If owners are not educated to maintain the boundaries between these two approaches, short-term concerns and management's need for short-term rewards will prevail. Only trouble can

follow from such a misprision

• Failure to expose dynamic steward-conservator-stakeholder owners to the knowledge and implementation tools needed for the role of stewardship in overseeing the family's enterprises, such as

a) Family balance sheets as well as financial statements

b) Family income statements as well as enterprise income statements

c) Family banks

d) Modern portfolio theory

e) Investor allocation as well as strategic asset allocation

f) Vision and mission statements for the family and the need for them to be congruent with the mission statements of each of the family's enterprises

g) Rules for family and family enterprise meetings

h) Policies on secrecy and/or confidentiality and the fundamental difference in outcome of the two

i) Valuation, evaluation, and assessment systems

j) Family systems theory and business systems theory

k) Roles and responsibilities within family enterprises

l) Human resources knowledge of how to recruit, retain, compensate, and change both family management and external management

m) Modern governance tools for improving family oversight of trusts.

The list is extensive, but it represents my view of the components that—if neglected or mishandled—lead to failure in the life cycles of family enterprises. These are areas essential to an owner's education.

Remarkably, however, all too often the problem of a family member's education as owner never arises because the leaders of the family's enterprise don't realize that dynamic steward-conservator-stakeholder ownership is critical to an enterprise's long-term success. Instead of teaching ownership skills, many of these families fight endlessly over who gets to manage the enterprise, thinking that this is where success lies.

In this struggle, the family often makes two tragic and deeply entropic errors. First, it eventually selects a manager from within the family, who is not called to management as a life journey but who is simply good at intrigue. Often, this selection results in the founder's replaying Shakespeare's King Lear, with similar tragic consequences to the family. A manager who is good at intrigue, for whom management is not a calling, and who is competing with all other managers in the business, will eventually lose that competition because he'll be up against managers whose life calling is to win such rivalries. Ultimately, choosing this kind of management leads to the weakening of the competitive position of the business enterprise itself and often to its failure.

Another mistake on this path takes place when the family wants to avoid the conflict of choosing among competing family members and selects instead external management as a compromise. Such management, sensing, correctly, that it does not have the confidence of the family owners—after all, it was not the family's first choice for leadership—elects not to advise the owners of the difficult risks they need to take to face their competitors dynamically. Such managers never feel certain that the divided family owners will back them up, especially if they suggest taking the risks that the business environment of the family enterprise requires. As Abraham Lincoln said, "A house divided against itself cannot stand."

Only competent and thoughtful ownership, not management, determines the fate of family enterprises. Uneducated owners lead inevitably to the entropic downfall of their family enterprises. Within this reality we can begin to understand why only 15 percent of family enterprises reach the third generation of the family that founded them and only 30 percent of the succession plans developed for family enterprises actually work.[3] With statistics like these, the problems of entropic ownership become a challenging reality rather than merely an interesting theory.[4]

Chapter Notes

1. *Dynamic* means to avoid stasis and to grow; a steward as inheritor is someone with an obligation to the family and to the world at large to responsibly increase and use his inheritance for the good of all; a conservator is one who turns over an inheritance to the next generation in equal or better condition than it was received; a stakeholder is an active, caring participant, as opposed to a passive, disinterested investor.

2. The term *family enterprise* here includes both active businesses and family enterprises consisting solely of financial assets.

3. This first statistic is widely cited; for this second proposition, see page 161 of *Preparing Heirs* by Roy Williams and Vic Preisser.

4. There is no doubt that many of these businesses are sold successfully and contribute to this statistic. However, fewer are sold at the prices they would have commanded had they had great owners.

Chapter Fifteen

Ensuring Dynamic Ownership

Education is the mother of leadership.
—WENDELL LEWIS WILLKIE
American industrialist and political leader

CLEARLY, THERE ARE many ways a family can go astray in family governance. Organizational science and management science offer many helpful antidotes to the range of difficulties families face. These disciplines also offer the skills and practices needed to address the educational deficiencies that bring on these sad developments. Here, I'll present these remedies in generally the same order as I listed the failures in chapter 14, "Family as an Organization" (pages 163–166). Some responses cover a number of the failures.

Lessons From Organizational Management

Educated Owners

Owners must receive the education they need to understand the many strategic roles cast for them in the rules and systems governing the operation of a family enterprise. In their enterprise relationships, whether through corporations, limited liability corporations, limited liability partnerships, or general partnerships, they generally represent a majority of the financial capital invested in that entity, thus they are the principal owners of that entity. At present, the creation of one of these entities rarely comes with any education on how to become an excellent dynamic steward-conservator-stakeholder. In fact, normally no education of any kind occurs. The same does not apply to those chosen to *manage* the entity. Generally, management is well educated. This imbalance sets up governance conversations in which the parties have no common ground of knowledge. The confusion that results is inevitable, and the subsequent loss of financial capital is predictable.

Owners must be educated particularly on what the roles and responsibilities of a stakeholder owner are and specifically on their responsibility to take an active role in the governance of the entity, as opposed to the more passive role of a shareholder-investor owner who waits for his dividend check as an infinitesimal percentage owner of Exxon/Mobil.[1]

Managers' tasks are tactical; dynamic steward-conservator-stakeholders' tasks are strategic. Owners who ask managers to take over their duties lose connection with the governance of their financial wealth, which leads to the entropy that befalls the absentee owner of any asset. All too often, such owners ask their managers to serve in strategic roles that may have nothing to do with their managers' calling to manage or with their education. Management is a science for which one can get a degree in business administration; ownership is an art, as all true entrepreneurs discover. There is no reason to support the view that a calling to management is a calling to entrepreneurship. Even if a particular manager is gifted with the skill of an entrepreneur, how will the owners know how to govern the enterprise if someone else is fulfilling their role as owners?[2] Clearly, the poor-boundary issues of such a business relationship will cause significant friction within governance; that friction is a form of entropy. Best to educate owners from the beginning on their roles and responsibilities toward becoming dynamic steward-conservators-stakeholders of the family enterprise. To the extent they are educated to fulfill their proper and expected role in the entity's governance, the enterprise will function more effectively and the possibilities for its success will be enhanced.

The governance of family enterprise fails when it abrogates the fundamental rule that form follows function. For example, personnes d'affaires help the families they serve organize the proper legal *forms* they need for the management of their financial enterprises, but they ignore the *functioning* of such structures when they fail to educate its owners on how to make them work. These professionals presume that because they know how such enterprises work and the family's managers who hire them know how they work, all of the family members who own them will also know how they work. This simply isn't true. A moment's thought on the adviser's part about the reality of who actually knows what about how the entity functions, as opposed to its appropriateness in its legal form, would avoid the significant risk of financial capital entropy that flows from the owner's lack of education. That awareness could turn that risk into growth simply by providing the family owners with the education they need to govern these structures successfully. So, education of owners to become dynamic steward-conservator-stakeholders of every family entity is the first step in avoiding the catalog of failures listed in chapter 14.

Full Participation

Every member of a family of affinity, whether born, married, or invited into it, automatically becomes a participant in the stewarding-conserving-stakeholding role of owner of the family's enterprises upon joining the family.

Every family must recognize that every family member, regardless of physical ownership of a family enterprise, is a member of its governance system and thus deeply intertwined with the governance of every entity affected by that system. Failure to understand everyone's stake in the system leads to educating only those who own direct interests in the enterprises, if any education occurs at all. Such a system withholds that education from those who may own the enterprise in the future. In doing so, it diminishes the overall competence of all the family members to fully participate in the owners' decisions, which will be directly, or indirectly, the focus of the family's governance of its financial capital.

Teaching all family members to become dynamic steward-conservator-stakeholders of the family's financial capital increases the family's store of knowledge as it increases the intellectual capital of its members. Families that recognize this perceive how to make highly valuable additions to their asset base. Such families also appreciate that increasing individual family members' understanding of how the family's financial capital is owned and managed will enhance their ability to participate in its governance and increase the likelihood of better financial decisions.

Active Stakeholders

Having active stakeholder owners as opposed to passive shareholder owners makes a positive difference in the long-term performance of a family enterprise. Management's capacity—and its interest—in managing the family enterprises will be heightened by reporting to active stakeholder owners. Management's calling is to bring to life the owners' entrepreneurial dream, not to achieve its own dream. When a family enterprise has owners who believe they are stakeholders in bringing to life the dream that the enterprise was given as its birthright and who actively participate in its governance, that enterprise is likely to be dynamic. Management in turn will be stimulated by the owners' efforts to bring the dream to life and be energized by that process.

Sadly, family enterprises dominated by passive shareholder owners are often enterprises in which the dreams of the founder of the enterprise have gone flat or disappeared. No new dream has emerged, and the growing stasis of the enterprise reflects the lack of dynamism of its owners. The managers of such an enterprise will themselves go stale as they realize that there is no dream to bring to life; the dream vanished with its earlier stakeholder owners. In this case, good management will leave and poor management will thrive as the whole structure slumps into the land of Lethe. Families who practice stakeholder ownership, and thereby practice dynamic steward-conservator ownership and leadership, will positively attract to their enterprises management that will be energized by them and whose energy will reciprocally enhance the family energy. This is the positive spiral of entrepreneurial energy that family owners need to overcome the entropic failure to which the enterprise will otherwise succumb.

Risk and Reward

From evolutionary biology we know that the code for life lies in the double helix of DNA. Risk and its double-helix partner, reward, spiral on forever together as the code for the dynamic steward-con-servator-stakeholder process of ownership. Families seeking to avoid the failure of their enterprises need to understand the never-ending and ever-changing conundrum of how much risk to take to achieve the reward of growing a family enterprise each year. They must govern the enterprise to be slightly more profitable every year, so the power of compounding can work its potent magic for their family's long-term success.

Today, many economists' professional lives are occupied with trying to prove statistically that their system of managing risk and reward will equal "Goldilocks" perfection—the ability to know consistently when risk and reward are in the exact balance necessary for continual nonvolatile growth of financial assets. So far, no system has done so. Their efforts, however, add to the increasing probability that we're getting closer to discovering the "Goldilocks'" golden formula and the holy grail of investing it represents to all investors.

In the meantime, I've observed some rules that guide the most successful dynamic steward-conservator-stakeholder owners in managing this challenge:

• They recognize that taking *no* risk puts a fortune into inertia, with the family's capital losing its spending power and thereby eroding the capital base. This problem is even more critical for trustees. At the other extreme, believing that one can beat the markets' odds is gambling, not investing, and such an approach disregards the rule that the house always comes out ahead of the gambler. Wise investors seek to act dynamically, within the rules of prudence that modern portfolio theory teaches, while noting that no theory (including that one) is ever infallible. Instead, they use that theory like a pressure cooker's valve, to be sure that their investment pots are steaming with energy but not blowing up.

- They understand that as stewards they must do seventh-generation thinking if they are to honor the future. They take the risks that will permit their financial capital to meet the needs created by the likely growth of their family.
- As stewards, they help the family understand risk by using family stories to inform them about the risks taken by earlier generations to achieve the current rewards they enjoy.
- As stewards, they take advice about trends that could affect the future of investment markets from the wisest people they can find, whose experience represents the highest level of success in investing. They often employ these advisers as part of a strategic investment committee for long-term guidance.
- As conservators, they recognize that they are required to meet the conservators' credo "to pass on to the next owner whatever comes into my hands in equal or better condition than I received it."[3]

Combining the steward's sense of the family's history and future with the willingness to take sound advice on investing and the conservator's credo of maintaining and improving family assets, all in a controlled way, offers family owners deep insight into the process of managing the double helix of risk and reward. In an intuitive way, they bring "Goldilocks" to life.

Dynamic Succession

Many succession plans[4] for the continued control of family enterprises for two or three generations beyond the life of the founder are based on placing the owners' interest in the enterprises into a trust. My father and I, over the course of our careers, frequently suggested such plans to our clients. However, my father taught me that there is a shadow side to the clear benefits of trusts as succession devices: trustees, by law, are not permitted to take the same investment risks as stakeholder-owners. As fiduciaries, trustees are acting for the beneficiaries and not for themselves, and the law requires them to act as prudent investors so as to conserve the assets of the trust for the lives of their beneficiaries and those who succeed them.

As the rules of prudent investing have evolved, trustees have been counseled that while the law permits them to make any investment they deem prudent, investments such as in venture capital, private equity, oil and gas, and real estate—particularly the early financing rounds of these types of investments—carry higher levels of risk and are not likely to be considered prudent. Trustees are taught that broad diversification of the assets under their control is the best way to meet the duty of prudence. This policy translates into a risk/reward program that often and properly (since they are dealing with someone else's money) provides for less risk and thus less reward. Individuals and particularly entrepreneurs often are willing to take more risk, especially when they concentrate all of their fortunes in their active enterprises, all toward greater reward. Ironically, the entrepreneur's policy of concentration, if implemented by a trustee, would legally be "per se" imprudent and raise a serious risk of the trustee's surcharge by a judge for any trust losses should the policy fail.[5]

Prudence in investment is often equated in law with diversification. This leads all trustees to seek to diversify their investment portfolios as much as possible. In the case of family trusts holding single or multiple closely held enterprises, the trustees will try to diversify away from such positions by selling them, a policy directly contrary to the entrepreneur's. Since trustees will always be sellers to protect themselves, in setting the trust's investment policy, a significant tension arises over which should prevail: the trustee's concern about liability for lack of diversification or the enterprise's possibilities for greater reward if the investments remain concentrated.

Whenever such tensions arise, entropy enters the system because they interfere with clear decision making. Entrepreneurs, when competing with trustees for reward, have no such tension and will, therefore, be likely to prevail in competition with trustees in the marketplace.

So here is the paradox: Many family-business founders choose trusts as the vehicle for the ownership of their enterprises because they believe maintaining long-term control of these enterprises in the hands of family owners will help their families grow their financial capital. Yet there is a legal requirement that a trust be invested prudently and thus diversified, thereby making a trust perhaps the wrong ownership vehicle altogether for taking the higher risks needed to achieve the enterprise's success. The tension between the human and fiscal benefits of trusts and the investment limitations imposed on them by law, particularly in the case of a trust's concentration of ownership in active business enterprises, is a reality that many families don't see or experience until the trusts have existed for many years. Eventually, the business enterprises begin to reflect the entropy of the trustee's worries about liability as the enterprises cease to take the risks necessary for them to continue to grow.

So far I have found no perfect remedy for this paradox, and I believe this to be rightly so.[6] Trustees are round-hole investors who find the continued ownership and success of the business a square-peg problem. They try, unsuccessfully, to fit the business enterprise's need to take risks into their responsibilities of managing the trust's assets with prudence.

My legal colleagues often opine that drafting a trust properly will significantly reduce this tension. They suggest that the trust deed should give the trustees special permission to retain closely held active business assets and to make further investments in them. What's more, it should direct that the trustees need not diversify away from such investments or diversify at all. I agree that such language helps, and I often made it part of the trusts I wrote. However, even with this language, I have never met a trustee, including myself, who, when advised by counsel of the duty of prudence, did not thereafter, implicitly or explicitly, seek to find a way to diversify the trust's portfolio. Although I appreciate that entrepreneurs—who establish trusts to achieve long-term family ownership of their businesses—don't like to hear this, it remains true. The desires that trust founders express are deeply important, but legal risks to one's own assets (read the trustee's fear of surcharge) will always trump them.

Although there may be no perfect solution to this paradox, taking it into consideration when planning for the transition of a business enterprise's ownership and control will shift the probabilities of finding the right transition plan and the correct risk-and-reward profile for the enterprise's success. Using a trust solves some problems but raises others. Finding the balance is the task of great family leaders as they seek to be dynamic steward-conservators working toward strengthening the family's financial capital.

Stakeholder-Owners

A partial solution to the trustee's dilemma in managing risk and reward within a trust that owns an active family enterprise often comes from having enlightened beneficiaries who see themselves as the stakeholder-owners of the enterprise. Under trust law, if the beneficiaries of the trust are all adults of sound mind, the beneficiaries can release the trustees from the normal limitations on risk governing the trust. This legal principle recognizes that because the trustees are ultimately accountable to the beneficiaries for their actions, the beneficiaries can determine in advance how they would prefer the trustees to act and release them from liability for that action if the trustees follow their requests.

This approach would appear to solve much of the problem in the trust's tension. Sadly, in most cases, it does not. That's because family members find themselves in the role of beneficiary by dint of birth or marriage, not by choice, and with no education to prepare them for the roles and responsibilities required of the position. In my experience, of all of the relationships requiring education, that of beneficiary creates the greatest risk to a family's long-term success when the family member is not properly prepared. Why? Because among wealthy families, the largest proportion of financial capital is generally placed in trust to "solve" tax and control issues. Given that trusts are the most frequently chosen means to resolve the questions posed in transition planning, the most critical question for the success of these plans must be whether the beneficiaries and trustees can manage the relationship well. Clearly, if they can't, the entropy of a failed relationship will eventually doom the plan the trust was designed to foster for the dynamic preservation of all of the family's various forms of capital.

In three reflections on my Web site, I pose the questions I believe are most likely to lead a family with trusts to a more success-ful outcome.[7] All are questions of governance regarding the relationship between the beneficiaries and their trustees, and specifically the necessity that the current beneficiaries dominate the process of trust governance unless and until the trustee decides that he must act to protect all of the interests presented by the beneficiaries. I add here the admonition to trustees that perfect beneficiary/trustee governance should never require the trustee to exercise discretion in a way that appears to the beneficiaries to be a veto. These essays stress the reality that today, as in the past, there is no single path of education that beneficiaries can follow to become great beneficiaries. Regardless of how the beneficiaries learn, it's clear that educating them about the function of the trust—that it exists to enhance their lives—and about how to play their roles within its system of governance, rather than educating them about the trust's form, will enhance the process of beneficiary/trustee governance.

Beneficiary education is not a panacea for the ills of family enterprises held in trust, but it is a critical requirement for enterprise success. How can an enterprise owned by a trust thrive if its de facto owners, the beneficiaries of the trusts—as opposed to the trustees, who, de jure, own and control it—are absent from their roles in trust governance or, worse, have been rendered dependent instead of independent by their trustees? Without excellent beneficiaries who can fully participate in and approve the risks their trustees are taking, a trust will become entropic—that is, its energy will run down as its trustees avoid making any decision that puts them at risk. As this process of avoidance becomes embedded, the family's enterprises will cease growing and the family's financial capital will enter a period of long-term dissolution.

Succession Planning

The issue of succession for family businesses has challenged a range of professionals: leading academics, management consultants, organizational dynamics specialists, attorneys, accountants, and a myriad of career coaches, counselors, and pundits. Unfortunately, the vast majority of succession plans and systems they develop don't work, as we saw earlier in the Williams and Preisser statistics. *The consensus on why they don't work is this: the rational solutions they offer can't overcome the irrational human behavior they must modify.*

At the heart of the problem are the following issues:

a) Failed ownership as a result of decisions made by family members who lack education about the roles and responsibilities of owners and the different roles and responsibilities of management

b) The need for owners to learn how to govern the multiple relationships they inherit, especially between beneficiary and trustee

c) The idea that management is a personal calling whereas ownership is a process of becoming a dynamic steward-conservator-stakeholder

The family system, particularly its governance system—regardless of the state of order or chaos it may be in—is, of course, deeply involved with how successfully the family is able to carry out its role as dynamic steward-conservator because it is the family's vehicle for providing education. In the end, the lack of education will be a principal reason family relationships fail and these systems go into chaos.

The wisdom offered by a number of great minds in the domain of organizational and management sciences can offer a very powerful advantage in the attempt to reverse these odds. Essential to that advantage, however, is that these ideas be fostered, developed, and used within the family ownership system in an educational process that begins at least ten years before the next likely succession transition. Once embraced by the current adult generation, these ideas become a permanent core curriculum taught to every rising generation of dynamic steward-conservator-stakeholder owners.

If succession occurs without being integrated with all the other long-term family transitions, it will not succeed—although it may possibly solve whatever short-term issues the family enterprise faces. Succession in such cases will be seen as a transaction to solve an immediate problem the enterprise is experiencing, rather than an integrated act within the family's long-term strategic goal of dynamically preserving its financial capital. Seeing succession as part of a twenty- to fifty-year long-term plan for the success of the enterprise is likely to produce a candidate interested in long-term bridge building that can provide a way of consistently crossing the river of risks that threaten the enterprise. Seeing succession as a transaction is likely to produce a very different kind of candidate—one who quickly finds a low point in the river to ford it but offers no long-term solution to the risks it poses when, as always happens, the river rises. Transitional thinking is seventh-generation thinking; transactional thinking is its antithesis.

The best way I know to illustrate this point is to describe my father's process of welcoming a new chief executive officer to a company when he was on its board of directors. He would approach the CEO and congratulate him and then immediately ask, "Who is your successor?" Dad knew that the answer to this question should be the principal occupation of the new CEO, beyond all other issues he would face. He felt that this question was equally important to all sorts of enterprises, but it was a particularly vital issue for family enterprises. He saw that the succession (transition) planning process and the need for it were appreciated and studied carefully in public enterprises as a result of the life choices and the experiences of their shareholders, boards, and management. They recognized the importance of transition to the long-term well-being of the enterprise and therefore kept the question of succession high on the agenda of every meeting.

In family enterprises, however, he observed that very few owners were educated on these subjects, nor did the family culture endorse this learning. Families of this type feared the subject of succession, appreciating the risks it presented but having neither the education nor the culture to deal with it. Their strategic agendas rarely included this question until it was forced on them by events outside of their control, often when they were least able to deal with it. The failed succession in these cases validated my father's concerns and his wisdom.

Model Leadership

A family of affinity needs to understand the world's models for leadership. This is an essential part of the education of choosing the model of leadership best adapted to the family's system of governance and to the governance of its business enterprises. As a part of its education on governance, it needs to learn how such systems can transition from the form of leadership that was best for the founder's generation to a form that's best for the next generation—one that can work as part of a sibling partnership and later as part of a cousins consortium for the third and later generations. The study of leadership helps develop business enterprise leadership that is both reflective of and integrated into the leadership of the family governance system while still appropriate to the needs of the enterprise. This integration leads to significantly higher functioning of both systems, because the learned skills of leadership within the family then flow naturally into the governance system of the family enterprises.

Areas of Study

Certain areas of the study of leadership—both of a family governance system and of its enterprises—are vital to include in a family's education on this subject:

• The combat of ideas on what type of leader is best between Confucius and Lao Tzu is discussed in chapter 5, "Essentials for Success." The leader from behind is more successful than the leader in front for a family, and for the family enterprise once the family moves into its sibling partnership and cousins consortium generations. I believe it was Confucius himself who said that Lao Tzu's model won the debate between them over which type of leader is best. To have the followers of a great family leader from behind continually feel as if they "did it themselves" is the highest commendation any family leader can receive. A good chairman of the board of a family enterprise who leads from behind, gently urging all parts of the enterprise system forward yet never seen or heard, will be revered by that enterprise's owners for more than one thousand years.

• Families can learn much from the distinction between transactional and transformational leaders, both of whom are needed in family enterprises and in family governance systems. Generation after generation, however, a family needs transformational leaders *most* if its enterprise and family governance system are to achieve the long-term transformation it will need for long-term success. Transactional leaders meet and overcome today's issues, whereas transformational leaders meet and overcome future issues. The first type helps a family enterprise meet its needs to last through the day; the latter type, often through seventh-generation thinking, helps a family enterprise last the lifetimes of all the generations to come.

There is a place for leaders in front and for transactional skills in winning battles. However, it is the transformational leader who wins the war and, even more important, the peace. Peace, after all, carries the family and its enterprises through the long transitions that come with the struggles of reaching the fifth generation.[8]

Business Tools

Families must educate their enterprise's steward-conservator-stakeholder owners to use the business tools of evaluation and assessment that can help these owners determine whether the management and the enterprises they're leading are thriving (see "Tools for Implementation," on page 185). Without such a determination, owners will be in the dark on the most important knowledge they need about an enterprise's management and the state of its human and intellectual capital.

Servant leaders use a variety of tools to measure progress and evaluate themselves. Edward Koch, when he was the mayor of New York City, had a rather straightforward one. He asked everyone he met, "How am I doing?" As mayor, he believed this was the only relevant question in measuring his performance toward achieving a higher quality of life for his constituents. Koch had the humility of a servant leader both to ask the question and to *hear* the answer, regardless of whether that answer was what he hoped it would be. During his tenure, Koch was viewed by most New Yorkers as an attentive and positive leader, and he was reelected twice with large majorities. He is also remembered as having been a great mayor.

In evaluating and assessing their performance, all leaders of family enterprises, whether owners or managers, can benefit greatly by practicing the form of leadership epitomized by Koch's great question. In my experience, if a family enterprise's leadership knows—by virtue of the enterprise's vision statement—where it wants the enterprise to go and how to get there, leads from behind, has a process to assess and evaluate whether its management is sound and growing, and has a process for growing dynamic steward-conservator-stakeholder owners, it will succeed.

Integrating Dreams

As a family and its enterprises evolve beyond the dream of the founder and creator, the family should seek to enable its steward-conservator-stakeholder owners in each generation to develop their own dreams for the goals of its enterprises. A family enterprise is the fruit of the dream of family founders whose work led to the creation and growth of the family's financial capital. All human beings have personal dreams. Those dreams need to be ours, not someone else's. So why should any generation seek to enable the dream of an earlier generation at the expense of its own? This reality poses a serious conflict in the development of a family over whose dream should take priority. All too often this conflict leads to entropic symptoms in the life cycle of the family's enterprises. Entropy here manifests in the enterprise failing to evolve when the dream that gave birth to it fails to give way and integrate the emerging dreams of subsequent generations. Often, the failure occurs because the family's older generations manage to abort this natural process when they don't permit new dreams to replace the old.

But making room for new dreams need not be entropic to the family's enterprises if the family's dynamic steward-conservator-stakeholder owners can be educated to appreciate the need for it. The potential for conflict in this process is easily intuited. The critical question for the family leadership is whether it identifies the conflicts early and, after defusing them, gently uses persuasion to integrate the new dreams into the family's vision. If it doesn't, it may see these conflicts as challenges to a historical legacy that it must maintain, even at the expense of the family's own dreams. The family must be open to the generativity reflected in the upcoming generation's dreams. Unless it incorporates the aspirations of new generations, it cannot attract them. Positive attraction is fundamental to a family's long-term well-being.

Integration notwithstanding, every new dream need not be selected to survive in competition with the older one, because when it emerges, nothing guarantees that it will more creatively accommodate the issues of the family and its enterprise. Clearly, a founding dream that led to the creation of a significant financial fortune is a very powerful dream. All new family dreams must stand in its powerful shadow; they will have to be highly robust and strongly generative to long-term family success to supplant it. My purpose here is simply to raise a family's awareness of this natural conflict that arises from the evolution of generations. It need not fear this evolution; instead, it can aim to manage the competition of the creative dreams of different generations toward an integration of the best of them into the family system. In this arena, seventh-generation thinking by elders can do much to guide the family, helping it recognize the positive creative aspects of generational change and helping it manage change as a transition. Elders can let the transition energize the family system rather than impeding it by ignoring it or blocking it. The latter presents a great risk to the family's well-being. What's needed are open systems within the family enterprises that welcome new ideas while honoring older ones.

This view embodies Austrian economist Joseph Schumpeter's intuition about capitalism. Schumpeter suggests that creative destruction is at the heart of capitalism and that this concept is reflected in the set of beliefs that guide capitalist owners and the business systems and processes they bring to life to practice those beliefs. In this process, as new ideas are born and integrated into their enterprises, they meet the future challenges to the enterprise's well-being. This process recognizes the creative chaos new ideas often present to orderly systems. These capitalists, therefore, ensure that the systems governing their enterprises are constructed with such flexibility that they can accommodate new ideas without being destroyed by them. In other words, their business systems are being built so flexibly that the new ideas can creatively destroy the old without destroying the entity in the process. Schumpeter suggests that capitalism is the only economic system that can physically destroy the old and create the new without destroying itself. I see Vishnu the preserver hiding here, with his gift of enabling Shiva's destruction and creation without death intervening. The process of creative destruction requires an open system in which old dreams compete for light with new dreams, all toward the sustainability and strengthening of the organism in which they're competing.

A family that seeks to encourage the discovery, creation, and quest that new dreams bring into its system does well to practice creative destruction. The process of successful natural selection Darwin taught is at the heart of life. A family must honor the dreams of its founders, as reflected in the enterprises their dreams brought forth, but never at the expense of the future dreams of later generations. These must be nurtured if the whole family enterprise organism is to be able to evolve to be the survivor of the fittest among all similar enterprises with which it competes for survival.

Tools for Implementation

Earlier in this chapter, I suggested areas in which dynamic steward-conservator-stakeholder owners may educate themselves and the tools for implementing what they learn. Here, I'll point to resources where discussions of some of these tools can be found. In all cases, a family member with a beginner's mind can understand these tools as an apprentice, without the need of expert assistance. To be mastered, however, they do require a coach to help develop the skills in that area.

- Family balance sheets, see chapter 4 of *Family Wealth*
- Family income statements, see chapter 4 of *Family Wealth*
- Learning to read a financial balance sheet and financial income statement, see any introductory book on business accounting
- Family banks, see chapter 4 of *Family Wealth*
- Investor allocation, see chapter 5 of *Family Wealth*; see also Charles Ellis's *Winning the Loser's Game* and Gregory Curtis's *Creative Capital*
- Vision and mission statements and their need for congruency with the vision and mission statements of the family's enterprises,

see chapter 2 of *Family Wealth*; see also Bert Nanus's *Visionary Leadership*
- Rules for family and family enterprise meetings, see chapter 2 of *Family Wealth*; see also David Bork and others, *Working With Family Businesses*
- Evaluation and assessment systems, see chapter 13 of *Family Wealth*
- Governance of trusts, see chapters 8, 14, and 15 of *Family Wealth*

These recommendations are the starting points that I use in developing educational curricula for family owners. Families should add to the list as their system of education evolves and they discover and create new tools for the family's governance.

Chapter Notes

1. Readers who wish to see a short list of the functions owners must learn should look at my "Reflection on the Roles and Responsibilities of Each Family Member as Owner of the Family Enterprise Within a Family Governance System" on my Web site, www.jamesehughes.com.

2. For an excellent exercise on the problem of boundaries in family enterprises and how to discover and manage them, see Ernest A. Doud and Lee Hausner's *Hats Off to You*.

3. As conservators they also develop excellent sell strategies to know when to take profits and, even more important, when to cut their losses. My view on this is more experiential and intuitive than certain. However, the greatest investors I've observed made their money on the sell side, even though almost all the investment books I've found emphasize the buy side.

4. Had they been considered transition plans, much harm might have been avoided. I wish I'd learned this forty years ago.

5. The term *per se* is Latin for "absolutely," and the term *surcharge* means the trustee must reimburse the trust for the loss it suffered due to the trustee's imprudence.

6. For families of great financial capital, I find that a private or limited-purpose trust company can reduce this tension measurably.

7. See "The Trustee as Mentor," "The Trustee as Regent within a Family Governance System," and "The Often Unexpected Consequences of the Creation of a Perpetual Trust" on my Web site, www.jamesehughes.com.

8. For readers seeking historical American examples, Generals William Tecumseh Sherman, Ulysses S. Grant, and George S. Patton were transactional leaders; President Abraham Lincoln and General George C. Marshall were transformational leaders.

Chapter 16 Sixteen

The Second Generation
Leadership's Critical Stage

The worst misfortune that can happen to an ordinary man is to have an extraordinary father.

—AUSTIN O'MALLEY
American physician and humorist

MUCH HAS BEEN written about the first and third generations of families but surprisingly little about the second. Perhaps that's because the first generation's exciting life of creativity and discovery often leads to articles in *Forbes* or *Fortune* and frequently to biographies. Tales of the third generation are more likely to fill books on dysfunction, as it dissipates its way to family oblivion. If books are being written about the second generation, I haven't found them. Yes, in books like *Titan*, about John D. Rockefeller Sr., there is much to learn about his son, John D. Rockefeller Jr., and in a book about Henry Ford, you'll learn about his son, Edsel. But by and large, books describing the journey and psyche of the second generation of a family don't exist. I find this deeply troubling because I'm convinced that a family's second generation and the complex developmental issues it must resolve are critical to the family's long-term success.

The Dual Mission

Indeed, the second generation's performance determines whether a family develops a system of joint decision making that will carry it to its fifth generation and beyond. In this generation, the leaders from behind are first discovered and developed, and their task is to develop a family system of governance that can be replicated in every generation thereafter, so that no generation ever becomes the proverbial third.

The second generation comes to life with the challenge to integrate successfully into its journey two interrelated but vastly different realities: its own individual dreams and its inherited responsibility to be steward-conservators of the founder's dream.[1] To visualize the challenge the second generation faces, it may be helpful to use the illustration in **FIGURE 16.1**.

In the yin-yang symbol, I see both sides of the dilemma of second-generation family members. The dilemma they face is essentially a dual mission, one chosen and one inherited, a mission in which both sides of the self—the yin and the yang—must simultaneously be both connected and separate. Only the psychic depth of the yin-yang symbol fully expresses the complexity of the second generation's mission.

Figure 16.1

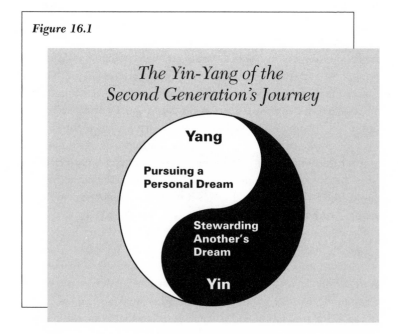

The Yin-Yang of the
Second Generation's Journey

Yang

Pursuing a
Personal Dream

Stewarding
Another's
Dream

Yin

Can the unity of two interconnected but separate consciousnesses be managed in a way that will enable a family member to achieve the highest degree of self-awareness, individual freedom, and happiness in life? Let's look more closely.

The Dream Not Shared

At the beginning of their adult lives, second-generation family members often face two seriously damaging psychological developmental dilemmas. First, their first-generation parents seek to have them study financial capital management to become steward-conservators of the dream the parents have tangibly created. The parents, believing financial capital management to be the most important skill their children need, expect the second generation to focus on that skill, to the exclusion of learning anything useful to further their own human and intellectual development or to realize their own dreams. Complicating this, the second generation often faces a second dilemma when they view their parents as larger-than-life

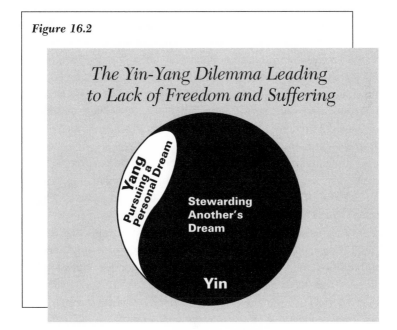

Figure 16.2

The Yin-Yang Dilemma Leading to Lack of Freedom and Suffering

Yang
Pursuing a Personal Dream

Stewarding
Another's
Dream

Yin

discoverers and creators and seek to live their parents' dreams to the exclusion of their own.

These psychic dilemmas, if accepted as destiny, almost always doom the lives of the second generation, because its members never individuate. Sadly, they never seek to bring their own dreams to life (see **FIGURE 16.2**). Such acceptance is a tragedy for the family as well, because it ushers in the plateauing and stasis that the proverb describes. The failed growth of human and intellectual capital in the second generation is the precursor to the entropy that fully emerges in the next. In my experience, if either of these dilemmas—or worse, both—dominates a family's life, the proverb always wins. The dilemma calls to mind Sigmund Freud's belief that the two greatest sources of a happy, integrated life are for an individual to learn to love and to work (with work defined as one's calling) and that the two greatest detractors are sex and money (with money the most difficult).

The Role of the Professional

This developmental problem is, unfortunately, aided and abetted by a great many financial professionals whose job is to help families, which is why it so often remains unremedied. These professionals look first to the desires of the first generation—their clients. And they almost universally define the second-generation family members only as steward-conservators. They forget that these are people of huge potential and pigeonhole them instead into the role of care-taking the dreams of another.

I've heard and read many platitudes offered by pundits on family well-being and on the need for every family member to have a dream and for the family system to be organized to support proactively the successful fulfillment of each such dream. I have rarely, however, witnessed any of these pundits actively setting up systems that accomplish that goal. All too often the systems they espouse promote only the development of the yin of the second generation's mission—as steward-conservators of another's dreams. The walk must follow the talk. A family's system must be constructed so that each second-generation member's dream has the chance to emerge.

Figure 16.3

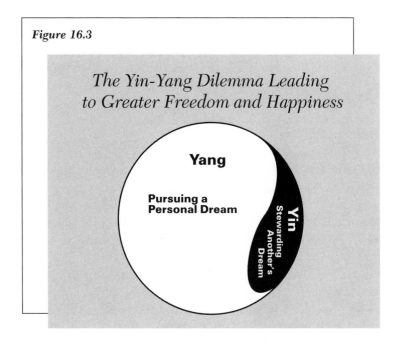

The Yin-Yang Dilemma Leading to Greater Freedom and Happiness

Yang

Pursuing a Personal Dream

Yin
Stewarding Another's Dream

If a second-generation family member does find a dream and, with the family's encouragement, apprentices himself to a master to bring that dream to life, that doesn't preclude development of his yin side. More likely, with mastery of that dream, and the mastery of self that flows from it, will come a natural opportunity later on in his life to initiate yin. Using the same apprenticing process, he can learn how to be a dynamic steward-conservator of another's dream, perhaps even the dreams of the next generation.[2] Having yin follow yang, so that the dream is not sacrificed, makes it more likely that he will achieve the healthy balance of the dual challenge of the second generation (see **FIGURE 16.3**).

If a family's second generation can be both dreamers and inheritors, the family will have effectuated the growth of that generation's human and intellectual capital. This is the growth second-generation members need the most to become dynamic generators of all forms of capital. If this process is learned and practiced in the second generation and then consistently applied in every generation thereafter, a family can avoid the curse of stasis in the second generation that the proverb predicts. Every succeeding generation faces the same yin-yang challenge. The families who do best will recognize it, embrace it, and actively manage it toward their individual members' highest potential.

In the Shadow of a Dream

Another syndrome of dysfunction in a family system that surfaces in the second generation develops when the business enterprise was created in the first generation by a male who treats it as if it were his eldest child. Imagine a family system in which the eldest, most-loved child is not real but virtual—a business enterprise. Clearly, a family of siblings dominated by a nonhuman eldest would make normal evolution and development of its children's adult personalities extremely difficult. More likely, it would be traumatic and emotionally chaotic for all. Although professional family advisers recognize and discuss this syndrome, it's surprising how few therapists I've talked with learned about this syndrome in academic settings. They've had to discover it, case by case, in their practices. Although I've yet to encounter a case of a problem like this where the founder was female, the growth of such individuals in the flourishing of the current women's social revolution is likely to produce one.

In his book *Succeeding Generations*, organizational psychologist Ivan Lansberg discusses how the first generation takes its dream to the idea stage and how an enterprise emerges as it lives its dream out. He explains that an enterprise that has a life force strong enough to cross the boundary from dream to idea and then to flourishing business enterprise begins to evolve organically on its own. It becomes a life form in itself that the second and third generations will have to integrate into their lives. Lansberg's idea of the founding dream can help solve the business-as-eldest-child syndrome.

When a family finds itself living out this syndrome, I've found it very useful for the family members to read Lansberg's book. In doing so, they can better understand the extraordinary energy, power, and force such a dream represents when it comes to life. One has only to note how few dreams ever reach the idea stage, and how few grow from there to materialize as enterprises that flourish, to recognize how unusually energetic such a dream must be. If members of the second generation of such a family can visualize and experience the nature of their parent's dream and the process by which it consumes him, they can often begin to achieve clarity on the nature of their position in their parent's hierarchy of offspring. This realization won't solve the problems the syndrome creates in their families or in their lives, but it will open a dialogue within the family on the reality of the business-as-eldest-child syndrome and how it works its will within the family system and in their lives.[3]

A Legacy of Trust

One of the seven paradoxes that lie at the heart of why many families succumb to the proverb's predicted outcome is integral to the role of the second generation. The second generation—and the model it offers—has a tremendous effect on the worldview of the third. The second-generation inheritors of a family fortune, in an attempt to caution the third generation to be skeptical of other people's interest in them—inadvertently teach them that no one is trustworthy. To understand this paradox, I ask families to try to imagine what a life journey would be like if the people a child trusts most—parents, aunts, and uncles—teach by their behaviors that no one is trustworthy. Would it be possible to form a relationship of any endurance? To ever be able to give oneself fully to another, with all the self-examination that engenders? In essence, one would never learn to love, and the consequence would be lasting unhappiness. The human suffering caused by this paradox cannot be measured.

Of course, learning to be skeptical of other people's motives is a necessary skill to becoming an adult, and I am in favor of teaching it. However, the slope from skepticism to complete lack of trust is a slippery one—one I have encountered all over the world in far too many families. Every family must be certain to understand such lack of trust and guard against fostering it. If one's own behavior in every aspect of life and in the life of the family renders one untrustworthy, all the preaching in the world about skepticism won't overcome it. We have to walk our talk.

Keeping Secrets

Communication between generations has always been difficult. What's even worse, however, is when they don't communicate. *The Paradox of Success*, a book by leadership expert John O'Neil, offers important insights into a family's systems and practices in this area. Although there are deep insights offered on every page, O'Neil's book presents one point that bears importantly on the set of skills about which family members need to be educated and in which they need to become proficient to guide their family enterprises.

In *Paradox of Success*, the chapter on secrets presents the idea that any organization whose leadership believes it has secrets to be kept from its membership is in entropy and running out of energy. O'Neil's point is that a secret unshared with the body of members of an organization asks the brightest members to spend their time trying to discover it instead of working productively on the work of the organization. How true. Although O'Neil writes principally to the business community, I have taken his insight into my work with families and their enterprises as a subject of huge importance to their successful functioning. Secrets are toxic when they lead to this form of entropic behavior.

Confidentiality, however, is a right that all family members, individually and as a whole, are entitled to expect from each other for the safekeeping of their most important information and privileged communications. To speak to outsiders or to other family members of things regarded by one's family members as confidential is to destroy their right to have confidence in you and leads to deep distrust. Confidentiality is a virtue in all human relationships and a deep honoring of one another's boundaries and sensitivities. Confidentiality is an appropriate place to repose trust in another, especially in our elders who in their roles as mediators of family relationships must be entitled to access to certain confidential matters to do their work. Families happily grant them the authority to do so because of the trust reposed in them. This privilege does not, however, create the atmosphere O'Neil describes of fear and entropy within a family or any other group created by secrets.

Although O'Neil doesn't make this point, I have applied his wisdom in seeing that all families have, as do all other organizations, white secrets and black secrets. White secrets are bits of information that the family believes are its special knowledge and which it calls "secrets." All family members know these bits of information and treasure them as part of the family's special lore. Families keep these bits of information as a part of their special mysteries. Families throughout history have celebrated such special knowledge in the rituals underlying their celebrations of their "differentness," often through special rites and oaths known only to their adherents. This form of secrecy is useful to the family's cohesion.

Black secrets, however, are bits of information that are thought to be known only to a special, self-anointed clique in a family. These are the kinds of secrets O'Neil defines as toxic to an organization; in families, they should be avoided like the plague. The ancient saying "Clarity to our friends and allies and confusion to the enemy" captures the wisdom underlying this admonition. Black secrets within families confuse the functioning of a family at best, and at worst they erode the fabric of a family's relationships: some family members deem other members to be outsiders by deciding who gets to know the secret and who doesn't. Such practices are the antithesis of family affinity. White secrets are transparent to all family members, but opaque to all outsiders, thus confuse only the enemy.

Transparency between the parties to a relationship has become a current byword for the behavior required for its highest functioning—whether familial or societal—and a synonym for trust. Perhaps transparency has always been the basis for the trust necessary for any relationship to flourish. Secrets are the opposite of transparency and have within them the possibility to lead to distrust, as O'Neil teaches. Family leaders depend on trust for their success. Indeed, don't all leaders worth their salt ultimately depend on the trust of their followers? Family leaders who decide they have secrets to keep from their family members are essentially saying I don't trust you. Why then should any family of affinity member follow them?

Regression to the Mean

In *Against the Gods: The Remarkable Story of Risk*, Peter L. Bernstein relates the history of the efforts to assess and mitigate risk. Bernstein tells the story of Francis Galton, who developed the theory of probability called "regression to the mean," a theory that predicts that over time, nature's laws cause all living things to become representative of what is average for their species. The theory is depicted using a bell curve. On the bell's left and right tails—that is, its extremities—are the most extreme forms of the type, and at the bell's top its average or norm. Galton discovered that over the many generations of a species' existence, its initial distribution into multiple variations gradually "reverts to the mean" as most of its members in form, intelligence, and all other characteristics cluster at the top of the bell.

The discovery is interesting, but what does it tell us about families in relation to the proverb? Here's how Bernstein describes it:

> Change and motion from the outer limits toward the center are constant, inevitable, foreseeable. Given the imperatives of this process, no outcome other than the normal distribution is conceivable. The driving force is always toward the average, toward the restoration of normality.
>
> Regression to the mean motivates almost every variety of risk taking and forecasting. It is at the root of homilies like "what goes up must come down," "pride goeth before a fall," and "from shirtsleeves to shirtsleeves in three generations."[4]

Bernstein is saying that nature's rule of regression to the mean, as explained by the probabilities graphed on the bell curve, makes the shirtsleeves proverb's prediction "constant, inevitable, and foreseeable." This is certainly not the outcome this book foresees. Even so, I've never suggested the proverb can be permanently overcome but rather that its prediction can be avoided for an extended period of time by adopting the philosophy and practices I've outlined. My beliefs don't defy the mathematical principle of regression to the mean.

Regression and the Second Generation

I want to highlight two very important aspects of Bernstein's observations because I believe them to be extremely important to long-term success. The first is the critical importance of the second generation. If we use the bell curve as a predictive indicator, how might the three generations of a family be plotted on it? By virtue of the first generation's extraordinary generativity (its capacity for discovery, creativity, and seeking), its two members, with their two names, would be plotted on the far right tail of the curve (see **FIGURE 16.4**). Almost all others born the same year would fall on all the other points of the curve, with the vast majority clustered around its topmost point, as representative of the average generativity such persons possess.

Next we plot the second generation. Giving its members the benefit of some generativity, they might fall halfway between the top of the bell, or average, of those born in their years of birth and the far

Figure 16.4

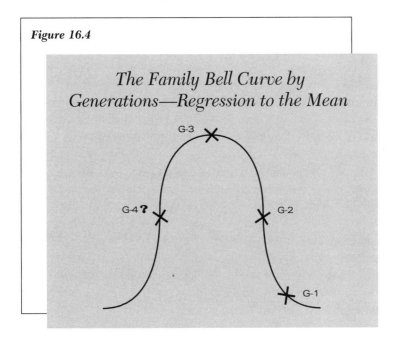

The Family Bell Curve by Generations—Regression to the Mean

right tail, where the most generative of their competitors would be found. Members of the third generation would almost all fall at the top of their bell and some on its left side.

Consider what's happening. The family's generative capacities are simply following the laws of probability, as its three generations become ever more representative of the average generativity of our species. Of course, compared with members on the far right tail, who represent all the people alive in their generations, they are just average. To constitute failure in competition with all other families, it isn't necessary that the third generation's members be disabled, as they would be if they were found on the far left tail, but rather just that they become *average*. This is disheartening, of course, but true.

The bell curve illustrates why I believe the development of the second generation is so critical: A family must help its members to keep functioning somewhere on the right side of the bell curve if it is to have a future. It does that first by consistently helping to bring each new generation's dreams to life and second by teaching its members to become dynamic steward-conservators of the earlier generation's dreams. A family that has the foresight to see the risks of becoming average and can help its second generation be generative by bringing its dreams to life—and, using that same process, keep every generation as generative as the second—will stay in the sweet spot on the middle of the right tail of the curve, the spot where I believe long-term success in avoiding the proverb's prediction is achievable.

If a family continually produced all members with the generativity of its first generation, the chaos of their competition would blow up the family as all dreams collided and none failed to be achieved. Equally, failing to achieve generativity would lead the family to fall into inertia, since the dreams of its members would be no more than average and would likely fail to come to life in competition with the great dreams of those outside the family who are on the right tail in their cohort. Thus the "Goldilocks" point for a family is to be in the middle of the right tail, with strong generative dreams of just the right temperature so that all may come true.

In-Laws: A Remedy for Regression

Another fascinating corollary to Bernstein's observation (one he doesn't make and may in fact disagree with) is that a family's "out-laws"—that is, those who married into it—may be the only family members who can change the outcome of Bernstein's prediction. Isn't it wonderful to realize that, as a matter of probabilities, it's likely that only those who marry into a family might possibly be on the far right tail of its bell curve, representing the highest level of generativity of their cohort? This assumes that genetic family members seek to marry well by "marrying up," choosing partners with exceptional human and intellectual capital.

Here is the wonderful paradox: Conventional thinking in most families, especially those with first-generation financial wealth creators leading them, is that "in-laws" and especially sons-in-law are the "outlaws." Ironically, the outlaws may be the family's only hope of having members with generativity high enough to keep the proverb at bay by keeping the family from regressing to the mean.

It is truly an example of affinity's wonderful gifts when a family is awake to see marriage as a blessing to the family's long-term successful journey. Marrying well is a merging of genetic lines of supreme importance to our capacity to remain competitive and generative.

Chapter Notes

1. Some may be surprised by this reality, perhaps never having considered the second-generation issue this way. But that may be because only a tiny percentage of the world's population inherits large financial capital, and so it is not an issue of large consequence to social scientists. It is, however, the critical issue for those of us who serve such individuals.

2. I'm coming to the view that dynamic stewarding-conserving of another's financial capital may well be work for the third stage of life—the stage when developmentally we are most concerned with legacy. This is not to suggest that financial literacy is not a crucial developmental task in the second stage of life. It is. Rather, concentrating on this task may simply be more natural in the third stage of life.

3. A paper by Dennis Jaffe and James Grubman deals with the complex issues of persons with their own dreams, the "inquirers," and those who steward others' dreams,

the "inheritors." I believe their definition and analysis of these types contains deep insights that carry forward Lansberg's work on dreams, as well as my work on the yin/yang issue.

4. Peter Bernstein, *Against the Gods*, p. 170.

Chapter Seventeen

Women and Ownership

Revolution is the festival of the oppressed.
— GERMAINE GREER, American author

ACCORDING TO THE United States Bureau of Labor Statistics, in 1998 wives earned more than their husbands in nearly 40 percent of married households in the United States. Many people who read the article in *Forbes* that popularized this statistic were astounded, but none doubted that the counting was accurate. I'm guessing that 2007 sees this financial statistic close in on 50 percent of such households. Many see this as a hopeful sign for gender issues in American society. Indeed, the statistic seems to reflect a fundamental change in the financial positions of women and men in America, growing out of the social revolution of women in the twentieth century.

A Time of Change

The question of whether the woman or the man in a long-term partnership household earns the greater share of income is an enormous new social phenomenon at all levels of American society. The integration of this reality into the psychology and dynamics of American families will, I believe, be the most important new issue of all for family counselors in the twenty-first century. Indeed, the same phenomenon is rapidly overtaking gender relations in families throughout Japan, China, and Western Europe as higher levels of female education, single-daughter families resulting from the reduction in birthrates to below two children per family, and new consciousness of human and gender rights affect those societies, just as they have affected America.

The social revolution of most importance to families of affinity is the redistribution of ownership and control of financial capital that occurred during the twentieth century in America—a revolution mirrored, although not quite so far advanced, in the societies mentioned above. This redistribution has transformed the ownership and control of financial capital within American society today.

A History of Less

In 1900, the distribution of financial capital through inheritance among daughters and sons in America followed the same basic pattern that had been in place throughout the world since biblical times: two shares to sons and one share to daughters.[1] Although on its face this seems unfair, the theory and practice behind it assumed—and in many cases the law required—that a wife receive half of her husband's estate if she survived him, which equalized assets. Because any family with financial capital assumed its daughters would marry, the system made some sense. What this system did not state, but which was grossly unfair to women, was that the daughter's share of her parents' estate frequently passed to the control of her brothers and then to the control of her husband when she married. Also, a study of the demographics tells us that until the twentieth century, a male's longevity generally exceeded a female's because so many women died in childbirth. Given the system of inheritance and the likelihood of males outliving women, financial capital was generally owned and controlled by men.

Skewing this unequal distribution even more in some societies was the principle of primogeniture, or the tradition that for generation after generation the eldest son inherited from his father all the lands and their incomes, which represented most of a family's wealth. In Japan, this principle is frequently practiced even today. To be sure, this form of distribution avoided the division of land into ever smaller and thus less financially productive parcels that would have resulted if all children inherited equally. The likely result would have been that all of their families would have failed financially. Regardless, this system led to greater and greater concentration of financial capital in the hands of men.

In America in 1900, another factor that contributed to men's domination of the ownership and control of wealth was the education men and women of families with financial capital might expect to receive. In 1900, very few Americans went to college, and most of the population did not even finish high school. In families with financial capital, however, most sons did finish high school and many of them made up the small percentage of Americans who went to college. Men from these families made up nearly 100 percent of the small group of postcollege graduate students achieving professional or academic degrees.

The daughters of these families often ended their educations at so-called finishing schools, where they learned deportment, hygiene, and home economics to prepare them for their expected lives as wives and mothers in affluent families. Very few fathers considered higher education useful for their daughters and, therefore, very few encouraged it. Consequently, only a very few daughters of these families went on to college. Next to none obtained advanced degrees. The idea of a daughter learning advanced financial investment skills was not just unthinkable; it was unimaginable. Given women's unequal educational opportunities, their reduced share of inheritance of financial capital, and the fact that men managed their assets, we can understand fully why women in America in 1900 held such a small percentage of financial wealth and controlled even less of it.

That Was Then, This Is Now

Let's follow women's financial progress through the twentieth century to the twenty-first century and see what has happened to the patterns of inheritance. I believe the changes constitute not only a revolution in women's rights but also a social revolution of historic proportion within America. A revolution, by definition, is a radical and total change to the core of something, whereas evolution is the gradual accretion of change over time. What is the pattern of inheritance today? Daughters inherit equal shares with their brothers, they attend and graduate from universities and postgraduate academic-degree programs in larger numbers than their brothers, and they own and control their shares of inherited financial capital, in addition to the capital they create as the fruits of their labors. This represents a revolutionary change in the ownership and control of financial capital.

Change of this magnitude is a social revolution of historic proportion, because the person who has the most money combined with the most education is likely to rule within a society. If we consider the demographics[2] and carry this new social reality of financial capital distribution within America forward fifty years, we are *likely* to see a society whose financial capital distribution has undergone a fundamental shift toward females, perhaps to a distribution close to or greater than the 60/40 current representation of women and men throughout higher education.

Why do I suggest this and how will it happen? Let's assume that education remains the foundation for upward social mobility and corresponding financial betterment in America's meritocracy, as well as in most of the developed world. Join that assumption to the reality that women now make up approximately 60 percent of the students of American colleges, approximately 50 percent (likely to rise to 55 percent) of the students in American law and medical schools, 50 percent of students in American business schools, and a significantly larger percentage of advanced academic-degree students. We can then project fifty years ahead that these very well-educated women are likely to succeed during their productive lifetimes while the males with whom they will be competing will be less equipped educationally. Add to this scenario women's equal inheritances, their clear ability and now-accepted right to control their earned and inherited financial capital, and their greater longevity and we have a remarkable revolutionary story unfolding within American society.

To imagine that in only four generations of families, this change in the pattern of inheritance has overturned millennia of social patterning is breathtaking. Imagine Great-Granny in 1900 inheriting a half share, having no higher education, and her brother as trustee controlling her financial capital. Next came Granny with some education, a half share, and her brother as trustee managing her financial capital. Following Granny came Mother, inheriting a full share, with a college education, but still likely to have her brother as trustee controlling her financial capital. Finally Daughter arrives with a PhD in astrophysics from Princeton, a full share, and in full control of her financial capital, with top grades in Samuelson's economics and Graham and Dodd's investment theory, and Abby Cohen as her mentor.

For couples and families living through this revolution, it has caused soul-searching and wreaked havoc on relationships. All revolutions require breaking some glass, so no one gets through one without facing, by definition, radical and total change. Twenty-first-century American society will be the first in which the full repercussions of this revolution will be felt and absorbed. It will be great fun to watch these wonderful, newly empowered women figure things out so that it works for them *and* for their partners.[3]

Chapter Notes

1. It remains the pattern today throughout most of the developing world, particularly the sharia-governed world of Islam, and some of the developed world.

2. I am not including in this discussion of demography's predictive power another variable, which is longevity. At present, women in America live five years longer than men. This suggests that wives are more likely to inherit from their husbands than husbands are from their wives. Should such a pattern persist, it will accelerate women's general control of wealth and accelerate the social revolution under discussion here.

3. The social revolution in America will be mirrored by similar revolutions in other societies, with this emerging pattern of education, wealth distribution and control, and longevity arising from the change in gender demographics. I anticipate that some societies, particularly in China and Japan, will for cultural and historical reasons find these changes extremely difficult to absorb. How they evolve to meet the challenges to their traditional masculine patterns of wealth control and distribution—when their

families will often produce only one child and 50 percent of the time it may be a daughter (I hedge here because of the horror of female infanticide)—will be a very significant question to be monitored closely by all professionals serving these communities. For more about this subject, particularly the relationship challenges it poses, see "Reflections on Fiscal Unequals," coauthored with me by Joanie Bronfman, a psychologist and author, and Jacqueline Merrill, founder of Centerpoint in Aspen, on my Web site, www.jamesehughes.com.

PART FIVE

Tools and Pathfinders

Chapter 18 Eighteen

The Essentials for Learning

All true educators since Socrates and Plato have agreed that the primary object of education is attainment of inner harmony, or the integration of personality. Without such integration, learning is no more than a collection of scraps.

—SIR ALFRED ZIMMERN, scholar and
international relations expert

As THE YOGIS taught 3,500 years ago, learning is a question of finding which of the many styles of learning best fits us and then developing a way of studying any body of knowledge in that style. The yogis believe that we are, in modern parlance, hardwired at birth to learn in one particular way. Today, Howard Gardner, a professor of education and of psychology at Harvard, offers—in Western scientific terms—this same philosophy of multiple paths to learning in *Frames of Mind* and in *The Disciplined Mind*. New academies and schools are being founded in America using Gardner's philosophy that everyone can learn provided they are taught in their individual learning style. He emphasizes that for any learning to be useful, the student must be able to integrate it into his life.

I believe that the only way a student can actually learn is to experience the information to be learned. That way it has the highest likelihood of being integrated into his long-term memory so that it can be used.[1] Socrates taught this centuries ago. The ways we learn, as described by the yogis and by Gardner, suggest that unless we learn in a style that suits us individually, we will be unable to experience the information and therefore unable to integrate it.

My own experience of learning has convinced me of the correctness of this view. I learn best through reading; I lack the ability to learn kinesthetically.[2] I do have visual or spatial ability, which helps me see synergies and syntheses as I read. The school I attended from first through eighth grades, the Far Brook School in Short Hills, New Jersey, teaches through the arts, and everything at the school is taught by having the student experience the subject. It was at Far Brook that I first understood how I learn and how to see both the fine arts and the performing arts as a way for me to experience information and to integrate it.

At Far Brook, every student from nursery school through eighth grade participates every day in either the fine arts or the performing arts. The annual curriculum for each grade provides links in all courses to the fine and performing arts, and the teachers make every effort to be sure the students are experiencing the information being taught. Although I later attended the Pingry School, Princeton University, and Columbia University Law School, I believe I was educated at Far Brook. The school understands the multiple learning styles of its children and sees to it that every child truly integrates the knowledge it offers by ensuring that he experiences that knowledge. It was at Far Brook that I found my calling as a historian, a cultural anthropologist, and a student of human behavior and of the groups people form to govern themselves. I was able to imagine what life was like in earlier times and, through the fine and performing arts of earlier cultural periods, to experience the lives of people throughout history. This was experiential learning.

I am convinced that experiencing information most deeply promotes learning, provided that the student is offered the data in the learning style that's most effective for him. Great teachers are all yogis when they seek to find the path that each of their students can best employ in absorbing knowledge. In the journey to know ourselves, knowing our learning style is critical to our ability to learn, experience, and integrate knowledge. When other members of the family discover their learning styles, it significantly increases all of the family's work together.

The Great Learning Traditions

The ancient arts and teachings of the Hindus, the Greeks, and the Zen masters all have ideas in common that can help us learn more deeply and perhaps achieve a modicum of wisdom. First, all of these groups offer, in their spiritual and mystic traditions, practices for their adherents to still and open their minds and hearts and to achieve higher states of awareness and wisdom. Each tradition's practices are different, but all recognize that we learn in multiple ways. Each states that experiential learning is the deepest form of learning. Each recognizes that clearing the clutter of one's mind through the cultivation of a beginner's mind and using the method of learning best for that individual opens the heart and mind to their greatest depths. Finally, each tells us that without great guides, in the form of tutors, gurus, and mentors, who will ask us the questions we need and seek at each stage of our growth, it is unlikely we will learn at all.

The Hindus

The Hindus, the oldest culture with written records, have a process of discovering a student's way to spiritual learning and then drawing from the student what he already knows. In *Autobiography of a Yogi*, Yogananda explains the age-old process by which a new swami is educated by his guru: "With wise discernment, the guru guides his followers into the paths of bhakti (devotion), karma (action), inana (wisdom), or raja (royal or complete) yoga, according to each man's natural tendencies...." The great guru taught his disciples to avoid theoretical discussion of the scriptures. "He only is wise who devotes himself to realizing, not reading only, the ancient revelations." On who we are and how we learn, Yogananda quotes the Indian poet Rabindranath Tagore: "True education is not pumped and crammed in from outward sources, but aids in bringing to the surface the infinite hoard of wisdom within." Finally for the Western mind, Yogananda cites Emerson's *Representative Men*: "The soul having been often born, or, as the Hindus say, 'traveling the path of existence through thousands of births'...there is nothing of which she has not gained the knowledge; no wonder that she is able to recollect…what formerly she knew…for inquiry and learning is reminiscence all."

Another great Indian spirit, Aurobindo, wrote: "The first principle of the teaching is that nothing can be taught. The teacher is not an instructor or task master; he is a helper and a guide. The second principle is that the mind has to be consulted in its growth. The idea of hammering the child into the shape desired by the parent or teacher is a barbarous and ignorant superstition. It is he himself who must be induced to expand in accordance with his own nature…. Everyone has in him something divine, something his own, a chance of perfection and strength in however small a sphere which God offers him to take or refuse. The task is to find it, develop it and use it. The chief aim of education should be to help the growing soul to draw out that in itself which is best and make it perfect for a noble use."[3]

India's Vedas and Upanishads represent the oldest set of written ideas we have on the nature of being human and of how we as human beings can learn to live our lives as consciously as possible. This ancient civilization realized and passed down to us the wisdom that no two human beings learn in exactly the same way. The Indian scribes determined that generally our way of learning falls into the four categories mentioned by Yogananda[4] and that the teacher's task before beginning instruction is to determine through deep study of that individual how he learns. The teacher is also required to pass the student on to another teacher if he determines that the way the student learns is not the way he is best able to teach.

Contained in the Hindu belief in reincarnation is the belief that each individual spirit comes into life knowing all it has learned in its past lives and, therefore, the teacher's task is to help the student draw out of himself what he already knows. The task is not to cram in information about what the teacher knows at the expense of drawing forth what the student knows.[5]

When a family begins the earliest education of its most valued assets, the members of the next generation, it would do well to begin developing its philosophy of how to educate them by studying the great truths of how children learn as they've come down from earlier cultures.

The Greeks

The Greeks also made important contributions to the study of educational theory. Among the most noteworthy is one I paraphrase here from Socrates: "No learning is meaningful and useful unless it can be experienced and then integrated into the mind and life of the student."

Socrates. How might Socrates' idea of experiential learning work? Daniel Garvey, a leader of the experiential learning community, brought Socrates' philosophy of education to life for me. Garvey teaches his students based on Socrates' philosophy. He continuously seeks to be sure every student actually experiences every bit of information he imparts. His students develop their curricula with him, so they can be experienced rather than simply memorized. Garvey's classes contain discussion and movement, leading not to short-term memorization of facts for successful test taking but to deep integration of the subject matter for lifelong learning and use. The result for the student is a qualitative difference between what he translates into knowledge and the data and information presented. What's learned is thus far more useful.

My work with families has demonstrated to me that when a teacher takes the time to create an experience, the depth of the family member's learning increases exponentially. Although teaching experientially means reducing, at least by half, the amount of information covered in every session, my experience and that of my colleagues is that far more of what we teach is absorbed, integrated, and put into practice by the family members.

I am convinced that as we seek to educate family members toward increasing the quality of their lives and toward increasing the family's human and intellectual capital, we must endeavor to provide them ways of experiencing what we want them to learn rather than just providing them with information. This will result in deeper integration of the knowledge and, therefore, greater usefulness to them.

The Buddhists

Another valuable ancient wisdom practice comes to us from the Zen Buddhists, as elucidated for us by the Zen master Shunryu Suzuki in his book *Zen Mind, Beginner's Mind*. Zen is an ancient set of practices devised in China and Japan to develop the minds of its practitioners so they will "awaken" and become enlightened. Perhaps the most famous example of these practices is the koan, or paradoxical statement, in which the student is asked to imagine one hand clapping.

From the Buddhists, we also have the proverb: "When the student is ready the teacher will appear," to which I add, "When the student is ready, the teacher will disappear."

Beginner's mind. The underlying practice in all of Zen is the cultivation of the beginner's mind. This is a mind empty of the illusions we create when we are either fearful or desirous. It is a clear, empty mind where ideas can enter and be welcomed for themselves and be considered with the absolute freedom of a newly born mind, a mind without clutter. The "work" of our lives is to find our callings, as expressions of our individual dreams and passions, and then to learn to use the tools that will bring those callings to life. If we are to succeed at this, we must adopt the mind-set of the apprentice, asking the master to teach us. The apprentice who seeks to learn by adopting a beginner's mind is a gift to the mentor as well as to himself, because the student will learn faster and more deeply than in any other mind-set.

Zen and my beloved master Shunryu Suzuki's works have been my deepest teachers as an adult in learning how to learn. Through the cultivation of a beginner's mind, I have found that every thought sharpens, and those that are most important deepen and ripen. My ability to experience and integrate ideas is greatly enhanced.

Readiness. The second injunction from the Buddhists is that the teacher will appear when the student is ready—and my addition that the teacher will disappear when the student is ready. These principles remind us of the nature of the teacher as mentor. In the context of this chapter, I want to equate the mentoring process to the tutorial practice used at Oxford and Cambridge Universities and to my experience of it at Princeton University.

Although in modern life it can be an extraordinary luxury to be tutored rather than taught in a group, still it is the deepest way we learn, since it incorporates two critical needs of the student. First, the tutor has time, as the Hindu sages observed, to find out how the student learns and then to teach in that way. Second, tutoring is about questioning, so the student finds out what he knows about the subject. It is not about imparting to the student what the tutor knows.

This second point lies at the heart of all mentoring relationships. Mentors are not coaches offering skills, elders offering wisdom, or best friends offering caring and love. A mentor is a person in unique relationship with a student. The student places such trust in the mentor that he empowers him to pose the questions he doesn't want to be asked. These are the questions for which he lacks knowledge or courage, the questions that, if asked, will cause him to show ignorance or fear. Yet, the student knows he cannot grow in any area of his life if he does not grant another this status called mentor. Equally, as the student grows, he finds that a mentor for one stage of life is often not the ideal person for the next.

Dante reminds us of this truth in *The Divine Comedy* when he brings Virgil to life as a mentor for two stages of his life. As he moves to the next and final stage of his spiritual development, he brings Beatrice to life to guide him. Tutors are our mentors for the particular subject matter that forms that teaching relationship. Great tutors are not "crammers" or "dumpers" of information; they are the gifted teachers who, as Tagore said, "aid in bringing to the surface the infinite hoard of wisdom within."

The Arts

To this synthesis of ancient knowledge of how human beings learn, I add another path: learning through the arts. I experienced this type of learning at the Far Brook School. Every day at this remarkable primary school, every student does some form of performing or fine art. The curriculum of each grade is designed to generate learning, using these tools to deepen the students' experience of the material. Graduation is celebrated with students performing either Shakespeare's *A Midsummer Night's Dream* or *The Tempest*. Thanksgiving and Christmas are celebrated with the rituals of those events and always accompanied by sacred music sung and played by the students. The beautiful campus celebrates nature, and when I was attending, the entire upper school decamped for a month to a spartan lodge in Vermont for skiing, with lessons continuing uninterrupted.

As I grew older, I came to know that it was at the Far Brook School that I was educated and prepared for life. Although my later education gave me much information, it added nothing to the person I am. It is perhaps a testament to the school's philosophy that among the awards given was one for citizenship. Unlike the academic awards, this award was given at graduation only in certain years and was the highest honor the school bestowed.[6]

Although so many experiences I had at Far Brook exemplify the depth of learning that comes to a student through learning through the arts, one is especially worth sharing. It's an example of experiential learning at its best, with an open heart and the cultivation of a beginner's mind. One day in the fall of my fifth-grade year, Mrs. Moore, the headmistress of the school, entered our classroom and called five or six of us out of class. Although this wasn't an everyday experience, it wasn't unusual at Far Brook that some higher purpose in one's education was found for you outside of the classroom. We trooped out, and Mrs. Moore informed us that for that week we would be going to the Metropolitan Museum of Art to study the medieval collections, especially the Unicorn Tapestries. It turned out that our class play that year was to be a romance de la rose called *Aucassin and Nicolette* from the thirteenth century. Mrs. Moore and Mrs. Ara Dodds (my favorite teacher, who inspired my love of the study of history) had decided that if we were to produce this play, we had to first immerse ourselves in the period during which the play was written and first performed.

So off we went to New York and sat in the Metropolitan Museum drawing all the flowers and animals we saw in the tapestries, imagining that we were wearing the clothing of the characters in the unicorn drama, and gradually becoming those people. We then returned to Far Brook. We built the stage sets to replicate the Unicorn Tapestries, and we helped make costumes like those we had seen. Finally, as we acted out the play, we were the people who were in the tapestry.

During the school year leading up to the production of the play, we had studied the minds and customs that formed the culture of the Middle Ages. We studied them not just in our history books but by singing the music, playing the instruments, dancing the dances, and reading and reciting the literature of the period. Each of us was required to build and decorate a medieval manor, with at least one building made out of wattle and daub.

It will probably not surprise the reader that this experience is as fresh for me today as it was when I was living it. Indeed, I still reread my copy of *Aucassin and Nicolette*. And I read with great enthusiasm histories of the Middle Ages. When I bike in France, it is the sites dating from the Middle Ages that I stop and visit.

—⁂—

As DID THE Vedic and Upanishadic scribes of 3,500 years ago, Socrates enlightened us 2,400 years ago on how our species learns. Losing sight of their wisdom on these matters means wasting the experience of great minds and spirits. It impoverishes our own experiences and opportunities today. Worse, it risks that our greatest treasure, our children's minds and spirits, will not reach their highest development. Families would do well, therefore, to reconnect with this wisdom in deciding how to educate their most-treasured assets.

Chapter Notes

1. I am indebted to the work of Daniel Garvey, president of Prescott College in Arizona, and the leading exponent of experiential learning, for his wisdom on what it takes to make something we learn useful to us.

2. When I was seven, my mother was advised by a guidance counselor that I was never to touch a tool because the world was not ready for the damage I could do.

3. *The Essential Aurobindo*, edited by Robert McDermott, pp. 225, 226

4. Huston Smith, in his book *The World's Religions*, pp. 29–50, explains each of the four patterns and how each of us will find one of these patterns to be our way of learning.

5. As I understand it, this is the same philosophy of learning that underlies Rudolph Steiner's work, which is taught and practiced in the Waldorf Schools, which he founded. To learn more about Rudolph Steiner and his philosophy, the book to start with is Robert McDermott's *The Essential Steiner*.

6. Unworthy as I was, I received this award along with another student, Sally Adams Chernoff, still a special friend some fifty years later. I consider the receipt of this award my finest moment. I have tried throughout my life to honor the Far Brook faculty's belief in me. Often I have failed, but with the healthy loving of the Far Brook experience, I have a deep reservoir of understanding of what is excellent in human beings to rely on, and it has given me the means to keep trying.

Chapter 19 Nineteen

Educational
Assessment Tools

*People should be free to find or make for themselves the kinds
of educational experiences they want their children to have.*
—JOHN HOLT, American educator

ONCE A FAMILY recognizes that it's composed of human and
intellectual capital and takes on as part of its mission the
responsibility to enhance the growth of these assets, I've found that
the family immediately wants to know how to evaluate the current
capital of its individual members. At this point in a family's work
together, tools for assessing the skills and potential of each family
member become necessary if it is to successfully benchmark its
enhancement process.

To do effective seventh-generation thinking together, family
members have to know each other well. Tribal members in earlier
times knew each other intimately because they were born, grew up,
and died together. The need to know each other's ways of learning,
professional calling, ways of working, and fundamental personality types was critical to the tribe's survival, whether while hunting
and gathering, when migrating, or in times of war or disease. As
extended families of affinity, members of such tribes had to know
each other in these key ways if they were to reach their fifth generations in good shape and go on from there.

In some ways, the journeys of these extended families of affinity were easier because their destinies as individuals were joined
for survival. Modern families of affinity lack this glue of risk; yet

they have the same ambition for long-term success. Today, family members can gain a great deal of the equivalent of tribal knowledge about each other if they will participate together in four key steps of assessment. In doing so, they can discover much of what tribespeople knew about each other through intimacy and thereby gain much of what they need to know about each other to manage the risks of our times.

Discovery in Four Steps

In starting the educational process underlying any long-term journey toward a family's higher functioning, it helps significantly to begin by discovering how each individual family member learns. In my practice, I use various assessment tools to help my client families and their individual members achieve higher orders of functioning, self-awareness, and happiness. These tools include:

• The Structure of Intellect (SOI) evaluation of intellectual styles—developed by Mary and Robert Meeker and brought to an extraordinary level of utility by Valerie Maxwell and David Garcia—and Maxwell and Garcia's system and process of remediation of learning capacities called the Learning Gym.[1]

• The Discovery™ process, pioneered by William O'Brien of the Uncommon Individual Foundation to discover one's "work as calling."[2]

• The 4MAT process, developed by Bernice McCarthy, an author and educational consultant for understanding our work styles and whether we are left- or right-brain dominant.[3]

• The enneagram for understanding our personality types, particularly as enunciated for the modern mind by organizational consultant Helen Palmer and Don Richard Riso, president of Enneagram Personality Types in New York.

Intellectual Style

If a family is journeying together to achieve greater happiness for its individual members, to promote the dynamic preservation of the family as a whole, it seems evident that the family must learn how each member learns. The most sensible approach is to use the SOI process as a first step. By so doing, all family members know how they learn. In this way, whether they're learning separately or together, they can help each other get to +1 on the calculus by insisting that anyone who seeks to educate them do so using the methods that work best for them. No family needs to accept teachers who can teach only a few members effectively. Not to know the dominant intelligence, when SOI can assess it precisely in four hours, is to start at –1 on the calculus.

Maxwell and Garcia have done SOI assessments for a number of the families I counsel, as well as for me and all members of the Merrill-Hughes family. In every case, the assessments revealed unexpected strengths and areas for improvement. In some cases, the experience for the family members—as they learned why school had been a misery and that, despite that misery their minds were absolutely first-rate—has been life transforming. Family members can finally offer their teachers faces that shine with enthusiasm in school, whereas earlier they presented frowns and tummy aches.

Every family that has undergone the SOI process has demanded changes in how information is presented to them by their employees and advisers. These changes have improved both the quality of their meetings and the quantity of information integrated by their participants. More family members find attendance at educational sessions useful and rewarding rather than equating it to being at a hated school. This is life-enhancing work that dramatically changes the quality of individual and family lives by making education fun and thereby rewarding a family with significantly increased human and intellectual capital.

Individual Calling

The next step in the assessment process is William O'Brien's Discovery process. Through a battery of self-administered assessments, which O'Brien compiles using the Discovery software, the Discovery tool seeks to answer for each individual journeyer one of life's deepest questions, "What work am I called to do?"

It is critical that each family member believe and accept as absolute and fundamental truth that each individual spirit has unique work to do in this lifetime and that each possesses unique gifts that will allow him to complete it. The most self-aware, free, and happy people I've met are those who have lived out their dreams by finding their work, the thing they were called to do, then apprenticing themselves to a master to learn it. These individuals became journeymen, practiced the skills the work required, and became masters of it within their individual competencies and capacities. Tragically, for members of many families, none of those who ostensibly love them seeks to help them find that work. Worse, those who supposedly love them most actively oppose that chosen work in favor of work they believe better suits the person, especially higher-paying work for wages. This happens all too often because of the parents' own egos and unfulfilled dreams.

To interfere with someone else's dreams and passions, provided their achievement would not harm the individual or anyone else, is to interfere with a human being's most basic drive toward a healthy mind and spirit—the drive to know oneself and with that knowledge bring the highest self to life. To block such a process is never an act of generosity; it is an act of ego that can only retard, if not terminate, the individual's healthy development. We must never forget that our most critical role in a relationship is to seek to help the other learn, from within, who he is and to help him emerge fully into the person he's meant to be. To frustrate this process is to act as an enemy, not an ally. This is the integrity of the enhancement process in a family, as it seeks to facilitate each individual family member's journey toward happiness. This is the practice through which family members' actions toward each other have the greatest potential for promoting individual and family growth or causing entropy.

Perhaps an example will clarify this point. In almost every family I've met, when we get to this discussion of a person's "calling," Mom or Dad will say, "Well, yes, Mr. Hughes, but suppose Johnny wants to be a surfer or Sally wants to be an actress?" These parents aren't really asking me a question. They're giving me their answer about what *they don't want*, regardless of what Johnny or Sally may be called to do. I answer by saying, "Well, suppose your child asked to be in such a role and you said, 'That's fine—provided you find the best coach possible and become excellent at it.' And suppose Johnny later won the gold medal at Waikiki and Sally played Portia on Broadway?" "Well," say Mom and Dad, "I see what you mean."

Finding the work a family member is called to do to achieve happiness should never be a question of how society or his parents value that work or, even less, what society pays for it. It should always be a question of finding the work that person is called to do.[4] Nothing I'm describing is necessarily easy to uncover, even with the techniques and guidance described earlier. Tragically, the vast majority of individuals never find their calling.

Discovery is the best assessment tool I know for revealing an individual's calling. Many people ask, "How can this process work, when the question of finding my calling seems such a mystery?" "Simple," I answer, "because as you answer the questions, you are telling you who you are." Why does this work? Because O'Brien's goal is to give you back what you told yourself in light of all the other answers you might have given to the questions. You are helped by how the questions were answered by all the other seekers of calling who've preceded you. Nevertheless, there is magic involved, because O'Brien, with his extraordinary gifts for serving others, finds the deepest truth in you. He draws it out of you by the gift you've given yourself by doing Discovery: the courage to look deep inside and know yourself.

Frequently, in my Q-and-A with Mom and Dad, they ask me and their children a question: "What about learning to manage financial capital? Our children are going to inherit a lot of money and surfing and acting don't seem to lead to learning about financial management." These fears are legitimate, and I tell them so. The children are going to inherit a great deal of money, so they will have to learn about managing financial capital, and therefore we will have to include that in their education. What Mom and Dad frequently miss, however, is how easy this kind of learning will turn out to be if their children first discover their callings and go through the apprentice-journeyman-master process of learning to become competent in practicing them. In my experience, if a person can attain excellence through the apprentice, journeyman, master process in the area of life to which he is called, especially when his dominant intelligence is fully engaged, that individual can use that process to learn *anything* else.

Work Style

The third step in the assessment process is Bernice McCarthy's 4MAT tool to determine individual work style and whether the person's left- or right-brain hemisphere is dominant. McCarthy's work, which she explains in her book *About Learning*, is founded on the extraordinary journey she undertook to learn everything she could about how the mind works and how we learn. McCarthy discovered that each of us is hardwired to want to start any work we do, solo or in groups, from the perspective of one of four questions—why, what, how, or if—and from either a left- or right-brain perspective, depending on which hemisphere of the brain is dominant.

McCarthy's system separates people into quadrants. Ultimately, the assessment reveals the most effective mode of working for each individual. The Quadrant 1 people ask *why* they're doing this task; they are the communicators. The Quadrant 2 people—the *what* group—ask what things and personnel they need to complete this task. They are the yellow-pad-list folks. The Quadrant 3 people—the *how* group—ask how they're going to get the task accomplished. They are the colonels, who want to go out and try it. Finally, the Quadrant 4 people—the *if* group—ask what outcomes can be imagined if this job is done well. They are the blue-sky visionaries. McCarthy further discovered that group work commencing with the Quadrant 1s—the why group—and moving through the other quadrants will provide results measurably better than group work done in a random fashion. Families seeking to reach their fifth generation will be doing a large amount of work together for a very long time, and any system that can accelerate the effectiveness of their work is greatly desired.

In 1999, when my partners Sara Hamilton, the founder of the Family Office Exchange; Lee Hausner, a psychologist and author; and Kathryn McCarthy, an attorney, educator, and adviser to wealthy families; and I created the Learning Academy to teach family members about human, intellectual, financial, and social capital, we required every teacher[5] to present material in all of the learning preferences Howard Gardner describes. As a dean and a teacher at the academy, I can attest that our faculty felt that our students experienced and integrated what we were offering them at a deeper level than in any other teaching situation we had ever participated in. Gardner's work isn't theoretical; it's practical.

During the life of the Learning Academy, the deans offered McCarthy's assessment tool to all students. We wanted to give them a view into the use of such tools so they would return home not only with useful new knowledge of themselves and their work styles but also a healthy view of such tools in general. Here's why we chose McCarthy's work as our examplar. When the deans of the Learning Academy were seeking an assessment tool for our students and we learned of McCarthy's work, we asked her to do an exploratory session with us so we could evaluate it. McCarthy came and spoke for about an hour and a half on the philosophy and practice, after which she said, "I assume you all remain skeptical." She was absolutely right.

She then asked each of us to take the assessment, consisting of many questions, all toward learning which of the four work styles we fit into and which of our brain hemispheres was dominant. Following the assessment, she asked us to divide ourselves into four groups according to whether our preferred question was why, what, how, or if. Our meeting room for this gathering was a large conference room in a downtown Chicago hotel arranged with two long rows of seats all facing forward toward a big white board and a podium—a room like thousands of conference rooms and school-rooms we've all been in. Sterility would describe it best. McCarthy gave us a question to work on, and we moved to join the others of our style so each group could discuss the question separately. Each group then went to work.

After about ten minutes, out of the blue, a voice began calling out, "Stop, stop." Finally and very reluctantly, my group gave in and looked up. Here is what the room looked like: Those in Quadrant 1 (the whys, or communitarians) had formed a circle with their chairs and were asking each other, "Do you understand why we're doing this? Are you ok with it?" Those in Quadrant 2 (the what-assets-do-we-have-to-work-with types) were still in their neat, tight row. All had yellow pads out and were eagerly making lists. Those in Quadrant 3 (the hows, or the devil-take-the-hindmost crowd) were all standing up, walking around asking, "How are we going to do this?" Those in Quadrant 4 (the ifs, or visionaries, including yours truly) were on the floor with a big sheet of white paper and crayons making a picture of what it would look like "if" such and such steps were taken. Get the picture?

We hired Bernice McCarthy on the spot.

McCarthy postulates that generally Quadrant 1s (whys) and 4s (ifs) make good owners and that Quadrant 2s (whats) and 3s (hows) make good managers. My experience corroborates this thinking. If the 1s and 4s are given the lead on the strategic decisions of owners and the 2s and 3s the lead on the tactical decisions of managers, final decisions in all areas of the family's work together turn out better. McCarthy explains that this is a horizontal system with no hierarchy. Everyone gets a turn in proper rotation for the best decision making.

I strongly recommend this assessment tool of our dominant work styles and brain hemispheres[6] for use by families in building a foundation of knowledge of itself. A family is destined in its journey to its fifth generation and beyond to do thousands of things together that link to form its transitions. If family members can learn to do each piece of work more competently, they will be adding strong foundation blocks to the heritage they leave future generations for how to succeed.

Personality Type

The fourth step in the assessment process is the use of the ancient Sufi—and possibly much earlier Chaldean—system of personality analysis called the enneagram. Happily, there are many wonderful teachers of this system. The one my family and I favor is Carolyn Schuham.[7] Many excellent psychotherapists and spiritual counselors are using this tool in their practices, so there are likely to be highly experienced people quite nearby.

The leading modern writers on the enneagram and its use for personality profiling and assessment are Helen Palmer and Don Richard Riso. Both of their foundation texts—*The Enneagram* by Palmer and *Discovering Your Personality Type* by Riso and Russ Hudson—are excellent places to begin. Families can also begin the assessment process by going on the Web at www.enneagram. com and, for a very modest fee, answering the questions set out there. Many of us, however, including me, start out assuming we're one personality type when, with the help of an expert (in my case, Carolyn), we find that we're another. Since family members are going to need to know their correct individual personality types for their long journeys together, I strongly recommend working with an expert.

The enneagram system is represented in a horizontal nine-pointed star, each point coinciding with one of the nine personality types. I am a 9, a peacemaker; Jacquie, my life partner, is a 1, a perfectionist, and our children are a 9, a 1, a 7, an 8, and maybe a 3. Our experience and understanding of each other's behavior has been enhanced by our knowledge of each other's basic enneagram personality types. Our experience of ourselves and each other has also been heightened through the enneagram's explanation of where on the star we'll go when we're happy and, even more important, the behaviors we'll revert to under stress. Having a gauge for measuring the behaviors we manifest and determining what's going on internally for each of us helps our relationships significantly.

I place the enneagram assessment last because it seems the logical order. We start by knowing how each of us learns, then determining what work we're each called to do, then understanding how each of us works best in a group, and finally assessing how our personality both makes us who we are and indicates how we're likely to interact with others. Correctly ordered, this succession of steps can tell a family a tremendous amount about itself and its members. Once completed, this four-step process can, I believe, lead to a family's highest functioning for many generations.

Further Discovery

There are two other areas of experiential education I recommend to families. The first is to do a values assessment toward deepening personal vision and understanding of self. The best tool I know for this is the Life Values Inventory, created by Dr. Kelly Crace of the College of William and Mary. The second is education about finance for children and young adults, based on the work of Joline Godfrey, the founder of Independent Means, who brilliantly explains the process and gives great practical ideas in her book *Raising Financially Fit Kids*.

Many readers may wonder which schools today embrace the wonders of the education discussed here and the ancient traditions that both underlie and illuminate the work of the ancients. Many of these ideas can be found in the Montessori and Waldorf systems, and other inspired new schools, like the Willow School in Bedminster, New Jersey, are now being established. These schools live out the dreams of their founders that children will receive an education that seeks to bring the spirit out from within, rather than "dumping" and "cramming" children with information they can neither experience nor integrate. These schools cultivate in their students a beginner's mind and—as does Far Brook—an open heart, so that their lives will be as rich in experience and as rewarding in happiness as their individual spirit can achieve.

A family of affinity seeking to reach its fifth generation and go on from there needs every individual in the family system to be a lifelong learner, with every tool at his command to accelerate life experiences and enhance his ability to integrate that learning so that he can use and express it. To achieve that, a family can adopt an education model that appreciates both our ancestors' wisdom about how we learn and their modern descendants' contributions to that wisdom and their marvelous new tools for helping us learn. Such a program leads to greater self-awareness and the freedom that comes with it, all toward the greater happiness of each family member, to the reduction of unnecessary human suffering, and to the dynamic preservation of the family.

Chapter Notes

1. For more information on the Meekers and SOI, see www.bridgeslearning.com. For more on Valerie Maxwell and David Garcia, see www.addsoi.com.

2. For more information on Mr. O'Brien, see www.uif.org.

3. For more information on Dr. McCarthy, see www.aboutlearning.com.

4. I am not naive about the need to make a living. Indeed, many of the most creative people I know subsist for most of their lives on small incomes by choice to ensure that the work they have to do to live does not interfere with the work they love.

5. We actually called them *facilitators* to reflect that they were facilitating the students' experience of the information rather than "pumping" and "cramming" it into them.

6. McCarthy's work also includes assessments to learn whether we are right- or left-brain dominant. Knowing this information helps us understand how we process information.

7. For more information on Ms. Schuham, see www.bepeoplesmart.com.

Chapter Twenty

The Personne de Confiance
Service Redefined

The best way to find yourself is to lose yourself in the service of others.

—MAHATMA GANDHI
Indian political and spiritual leader

IN EARLIER TIMES, ruling monarchs were advised by a group of professionals who formed a privy council. These privy councilors devoted their lives to service and were asked either to sleep in the monarch's bedchamber at the foot of his bed or to guard the door at night. Indeed, they demonstrated such loyalty and integrity that they were entrusted with their sovereign's life. For centuries, these devoted professionals sought to achieve the highest status the family could bestow: *the personne de confiance.*[1]

Do such professionals exist today? And if so, what defines them? The answer to the first question is simple: they do. The second is a little more complicated. But we can start by saying that these professionals are people who seek to grow a family's human and intellectual capital and for whom the call to service is life's highest purpose. They are serving professionals who seek to find families with whom to share their energy and who are in turn energized through that service. These families enhance the growth of their personnes de confiance in return.

Today's Legal Profession: A Failure to Serve

Let's begin our discussion of personnes de confiance with an example of an area of service that currently does not, sadly, foster the development of individuals—the law. The legal profession has hit such a low point of morale that the American Bar Association reports new disciplines in psychotherapy are being developed to help its members. The law is, and has historically been, a calling of service to help solve the problems of people who lack either the knowledge or the courage to solve a particular issue. But it is the call of financial reward, not the call of service, that motivates many members of the legal profession today.

In the field of private client work, I observe many professionals meeting their personal financial and ego goals by masquerading as family counselors. In fact, these are professionals conducting an adversarial practice feuding with the United States government about taxes and indirectly using the families they represent as the financial means to this end. This is doubly doubtful behavior, when these same families so badly need the counseling they seek to fight against their true enemy, the entropic effects of the proverb.

Complicating the difficulty for families of obtaining legal help are the ethical rules of the profession, which make it impossible for a counselor-at-law to represent an entire family. These rules in the United States and Canada require that a counselor-at-law have a single identified client with whom there is a letter of engagement. The rules strictly prohibit representing multiple clients unless each such client waives all sorts of issues of possible conflict between the imagined needs of the client and every other family member. Given that many law firms are, in my opinion, managed in part by their malpractice insurance underwriters, there is no practical way for a counselor-at-law to navigate this thicket of possible conflicts without risking the loss of insurance and therefore the ability to practice law.

As a practical matter, representation of a family as a personne de confiance very frequently requires that professional to cease practicing law completely. That's what I chose to do. Unfortunately, the only other option if you wish to serve the whole family is to go underground, taking great personal risk that the "uncertainty principle" may come to pass with dire personal consequences.[2] It seems tragic to me that insurance considerations that disregard the scope of the legal services the family needs should block those counselors-at-law who are capable of guiding an entire family's journey. When the rules of a profession make it impossible for a member of that profession to provide services needed by members of the society served by that professional, the fundamental social compact on which the special status granted to that profession by society is founded is irrevocably breached. How the profession I love will heal this breach I do not know, but for now it is failing the families in our society who need its services if they are to function and flourish.[3]

To bridge the disconnect between the needs of family clients and the profession's ethics rules, more and more in the profession are attempting to provide services to private clients via so-called boutique law firms that specialize only in the services such clients need. Many of these firms are founded by counselors-at-law who found no professional satisfaction in the large, general-practice firms where they started their careers. Sometimes their dissatisfaction arises because of their firm's lack of interest in serving private clients and sometimes because the firm decides to abandon this practice altogether. Indeed, the reality is that in all the major cities that serve as entrepôts of the global economy, nearly all the major law firms have abandoned the practice of serving private clients, believing that private client practice is an unimportant and frequently unprofitable sideline to their core litigation and commercial practices.

Regardless of how the boutique firms emerged, they are now, in my opinion, the centers of excellence for families seeking holistic services for all their family members. Although these boutique firms are subject to the same ethical conflicts as other law firms, they tend to be real partnerships of men and women committed to the well-being of the families they serve, rather than economic joint ventures of large law firms called partnerships committed to the economic well-being of their partners.

The boutiques have a greater capacity to find solutions to the conflict in providing legal services for families than do the few remaining large law firms with private client departments. Although the development of boutique firms has not resolved the difficulties families find when they seek legal services, their emergence does appear to be the means by which those difficulties will eventually be overcome, to the obvious benefit of families' ability to obtain the legal services they most need for their long-term success.

Ironically, counselors-at-law cannot meet the needs of the families they serve in a law firm because of the ethics issues discussed above, but they can serve exactly the same family by going "in-house" and leaving the practice of law. So some families hire counselors-at-law to run their family's private offices, and thereby obtain the legal services they require. This is an example of the world of Alice through the looking glass, where everything is backward.

How the legal profession will reconnect with its historical role as a critical intermediary in the healthy development of the individuals and societies it serves so the quality of the lives of both are enhanced, I do not know. I do know that this reconnection must occur if history is right about what individuals and societies need from their intermediaries to flourish. If families are to receive the help they need for their well-being, new economic models for the parts of the professions that serve them must come into being. Families can and must be instrumental in this process. They must encourage models that applaud service within those professions to individuals and families. They must honor those who choose such a serving professional's journey as a high calling.

Enter the Personne de Confiance

Personnes de confiance almost always begin their careers as personnes d'affaires.[4] These professionals serve the family and interact with them through the family's personnes de confiance. They're generally persons providing families with financial products, goods, and services, which the family needs for the dynamic stewardship and conservation of its financial capital. Generally, they are not in the business of seeking to grow the family's human and intellectual capital, nor are they personally energized by the family.

Personnes d'affaires most often begin their careers in one of the following fields: law, banking, accounting, investing, management consulting, medicine, psychotherapy, social work, or the ministry. Typically, individuals within these professions enter the field by serving the business enterprises of such families and the specific financial needs of the founders of these enterprises. Rarely do individuals start their service to families by serving the whole family or its nonfounding members.

Once they've had success in serving the family's financial needs, some personnes d'affaires begin to experience a strong conviction that they could be of more service to the family if they could help with the growth of its human and intellectual capital. They find within themselves a calling to this form of service, a longing to commit deeply to the people they're serving. Often these feelings result from a particular family asking questions of them that go beyond the products and services they've become expert at providing. Just as often, the motivation comes from the feeling that their current way of providing service is no longer fulfilling. They seek a different way of being a serving professional.[5] Regardless of what triggers the ambition, the wish to serve becomes an imperative in their lives. They come to understand that for their own well-being and highest awakening to their calling, they must shed the skin of the personne d'affaires and grow into the new skin of the personne de confiance.

Very often this period of transformation is highly painful emotionally, sometimes terrifying, and requires mentoring and the nurturance of psychotherapists—our modern world's spiritual intermediaries—to successfully complete. The transformation is a ritual. These practitioners break away from the familiar professional path of delivering financial or legal products and services and begin the learning required to integrate new information into their professional roles as nascent personnes de confiance.

In the process of this transformation, these evolving professionals often shift from being stars of their profession and become individuals noteworthy for being hard to manage. That's because they find that sitting on the employer's side of the table—whether it's a bank, a wealth-management firm, a law office, or an accounting firm—facing their clients and offering what their employer deems to be in the family's best interest is totally uncomfortable. Somehow, they now consistently find themselves more comfortable on the side of the table with the family they serve, aligned with their best interests. The products and services they once offered gladly, believing them to be sufficient for the family's needs, are evaluated with a more critical eye. They seek excellence in these products and services and often don't find it. They begin to demand something better—even greatness—of the institutions they represent. But the greatness they wish to deliver requires a kind of customization that would cut severely into the profit the institution builds into its products and services. The professional stars who had been ascending rapidly within the institution suddenly fall, often leaving the institution bewildered.

There are exceptions to this kind of evolution, but they are found only among those few institutions of greatness—greatness being defined as being entirely client-centric—that, in fact, seek out the professionals whom they believe will go through this transformation. They recognize that such practitioners make their institutions even greater by the stress they put on the firm to truly serve client families. The merely very good institutions will not tolerate such expensive client pampering and cannot afford the stress to the operating system such serving professionals impose. They quickly sever their connection to these budding personnes de confiance.

These institutions are satisfied to employ personnes d'affaires and can be well served by them, as are their clients—as long as both institution and client appreciate the differences in the roles and services each provides. The families must understand that the nature of the service provided by firms that employ personnes de confiance is very different from that of other firms.[6] Families need both types of professionals. What's most important to the integrity of a professional relationship is that professionals walk their talk. They must acknowledge which kind of service they truly provide. Above all, professionals should not offer marketing materials that claim they provide one kind of service and then offer another.

Service and Commitment

Well before I made my own "skin change," I was blessed by a learning experience early in my law practice that I hope illustrates the nature of a firm committed to the practice of being personnes de confiance to its clients. One day, probably in 1968, my first mentor in the law, George Farnham, a senior partner at Coudert Brothers, came into my office and advised me that we had been invited to lunch by a senior trust officer at the Morgan Guaranty Trust Company. At that time, New York State law gave a person with that title the authority to lend the entire capital of the bank, so this was a very important man. I was quite honored to be invited, and on the appointed day, George and I went to the Morgan.

In those days, the protocol for such lunches was carefully scripted. Each team consisted of a senior person and a rising junior whom the people from the other institution wanted to get to know better and introduce to one of its own up-and-comers. During lunch the seniors talked to each other and the juniors talked to each other. When the dessert was served, each junior was to ask a question of his opposite senior. It was very important in this choreography that the question be a good one. When my turn came, I asked the Morgan senior, "Morgan's policy sets the highest minimum account size for new clients of any institution in the business. Wouldn't it make good business sense for Morgan to reduce the minimum so it would get more clients?" The Morgan senior smiled and said, "Well, young man, that is a very good question, and here at Morgan our bright young men [sadly, there were very few women in either profession then] ask us that too from time to time. Whenever the question seems to be a particular concern to our young men, we seniors get together and discuss it. We then raise the minimum size account and go back to work."

I was nonplussed, until I remembered that the philosophy that led to Morgan's greatness and which it taught its juniors was this: "For your whole career, you'll have only this single family we're assigning you to serve; treat them accordingly." Although, of course, the officer would serve many families, the philosophy of client-centric service represented by this statement was what the junior understood was to be his creed.

The competing philosophy of "do the transaction today; there will always be another client" represents the polar opposite. Both models are profitable and both exist today. The Morgan model calls to the personne de confiance; the latter, to the personne d'affaires. I am most interested in professionals who seek to serve families most comprehensively, and I believe the Morgan model is the philosophy that relationship requires and expresses it well. Although I didn't immediately understand the depth of the message the Morgan banker was presenting, it has stayed with me my entire career.

Providing Courage

My father, James E. Hughes Sr., had a sound measure for testing the readiness of serving professionals who seek to earn their living as a personne de confiance. One day during my second year at Columbia University Law School, I was lunching with my father and it occurred to me to ask him what lawyers did. Given that our family had six generations of lawyers, he had many models from which to choose. To my surprise, after he thought about it for a while, he said, "Lawyers solve problems that their clients lack either the *knowledge* or the *courage* to solve themselves." He then added, "It is in the second category that we earn our bread."

In my father's explanation, there lies another clear way to distinguish between the personne d'affaires, the person offering advice or *knowledge*, from the personne de confiance, the person offering *courage*. The person offering knowledge fills a gap in a client's needs at a level that requires no ongoing lifelong relationship with the client. He can be comfortable that, with a delivery of knowledge, the client can complete the transaction that caused him to seek counsel. Frequently, this transaction will have to do with his financial capital; only rarely will it bear on the family's human and intellectual capital.

The person offering courage asks very different questions of the client, often bearing on a transition in the life of a family member or in the life of the family as a whole. These are family-system questions that seek to foster successful transitions. *Courage* is the defining word because the serving professional, as personne de confiance, will frequently be expected to provide the courage needed for the decision at hand, when the client knows the right answer but lacks the resolve to act on it. Yes, knowledge may and will be needed. But much more necessary to that client's well-being is the client's long experience of caring on the part of the professional, which will help the client to swallow the hard medicine. He will take the advice to do the right thing even when it's the step he fears most.

Yes, my father was right. Personnes de confiance earn their bread when they don't shrink from taking on the burden of their clients' most difficult decisions and supply the courage needed for them. Personnes d'affaires worry about being fired when courage is on the line; they prefer to find someone else to take the heat. Personnes de confiance worry about what will enable the families they serve to get to the next generation in healthy, flourishing condition. They stand ready to sacrifice themselves toward that end, should that be what courage calls for.

A Story of Courage

Perhaps a story will best illustrate the challenge of serving clients in this way. One day a very nice gentlemen and his wife were referred to me by a colleague. They explained to me that they had had a falling out with their in-laws. One partner's family was one of America's few great dynastic families. In the system governing family members' relationships, raising questions—and, worse, doubt about how the family did things—was seen as apostasy at best. They further explained that they had grave doubts about their family's well-being within that system and asked if I would represent them to the family to remedy their concerns. I agreed.

Soon I discovered, as in all such cases, that there were valid arguments and faults on both sides. I tried to help each side appreciate the other's position. Unfortunately, the family saw my client's views as lèse-majesté. In an act of hubris and mistaken judgment that I've found only the least-conscious people make—albeit often believing that their actions are for the well-being of the other—the family acted toward my clients in a way that could lead only to a permanent break. At this point, my clients saw me as their hero, the man who would lead them to the promised land of freedom and out of the bondage of their family of origin. I knew better.

Leaving one's family of origin is a breach of the heart that can never be fully repaired even if it's what we believe we most profoundly wish. The process of extrication would be the most difficult thing my clients were likely to face in their lives and it would leave deep scars. To this end, I counseled them to be very certain that they truly wanted a divorce, which is what this was. Again, they strongly averred that they did. I said I would help them, but I also told them that although they now saw me as their hero, at the end of this process, they would see me as a serious part of the problem and dismiss me. This would happen just as they were gaining what they now so adamantly sought. They said such a development was ridiculous and impossible to imagine.

I shared with them every bit of knowledge I possessed. I gave them the courage to go ahead and to succeed. In the end, their adversaries relented because the rest of the family saw the error of its ways and realized what a schism in the family would mean to all branches. But the die was cast. Sure enough, as I did my work, my relationship with my clients changed. They came to identify once again with the larger family and to see what they were losing. Still, they really did wish to be free. As the realization of that freedom approached, I became the scapegoat that let the entire family off the emotional hook of the breach in its relations. Just as I had predicted, I was relieved of my responsibilities and I never heard from them again.

This is the courage necessary to make a transition possible, even when the personne de confiance knows that providing that courage will lead to his dismissal. Although I had some bruises to my ego when I was relieved, my lasting feelings were of honesty and integrity to my calling. Providing courage does not always play out as a comedy, with everyone smiling at each other. It is sometimes a tragedy, a play that litters the stage with bodies at the end of the last act as the curtain falls. However, better for the personne de confiance to be the one who lies on the stage than the members of the family he served.

Many may be disheartened by the story of courage I've chosen to tell here. More predictable for illustrating the role of the personne de confiance would be one of triumph, in which the client attains the courage required to successfully negotiate a family transition. Indeed, my father and I have large numbers of very positive stories that prove his point on how and where we earn our keep. I selected this story to illustrate the reality that providing courage can be dangerous to one's career—if we measure success only by whether we retain clients following an act of our own courage. Rather, I believe the test of the success of a personne de confiance in offering courage is measured by the client's request for it and the integrity with which he responds. The real courage in this story was for me to consistently make the client family aware of what they were losing and the consequences—not merely to confirm their limited view of what they were gaining—despite what I knew the ultimate consequence to my practice would be.[7]

My Transition to Personne de Confiance

While making the transition from a personne d'affaires to a personne de confiance, I began to appreciate my father's wisdom regarding what clients need. I saw what my clients really wanted from me. Yet I lacked the courage to give it to them because it felt so frightening. To make this transition, I realized I needed a great deal of knowledge that I still lacked. I needed to be ready to ask my clients the questions that would signal to them that I was prepared for a deeper relationship.

With this reality, I left the dark wood of indecision and began to read the way Forrest Gump ran. I read anything and everything I could find that bore on the human condition and specifically on the system we call a family. I started with Dante and went backward and forward in time from him; going north, south, east, and west; reaching deep inside myself and wandering out into time and space. In my effort to keep going deeper, I used the bibliographies of the books I learned the most from as sources for in-depth study.

As time passed, I began to feel that my knowledge base was increasing. Finally, about three years into this process, I felt some confidence that I might truly serve a family by helping it on a deeper level than I had been able to do before. I decided to risk asking a client couple a more complex question. I selected the couple as a trial because I sensed that they were seeking to go much deeper in understanding how to truly grow their family. Whether I could help at all in what they seemed to want to learn, I could not know.

In the field of law, from which I am now retired, the typical first meeting with a client is about planning for the transfer of his financial capital, now or at death—so-called estate planning. Normally, the meeting is scheduled for an hour, with fifty minutes devoted to planning for avoidance of the U.S. federal estate tax, five minutes on who might serve as executor to execute the soon-to-be-prepared will and who might serve as trustee if the plan called for a trust, and the remaining five minutes on where and when to send the documents. If there was any discussion of the state of the family, it was cursory and designed to show empathy and smart politics and not normally a reflection of any real concern.

In the case of the meeting with my test couple, the first fifty-five minutes went, as I recall, according to formula. Just before the final pleasantries, however, I decided to go for it. My heart was racing, my gut was in a knot, and every signal from my ancient reptilian brain was saying, "Flee, flee, flee." I didn't. I said, "May I ask you a question?" They looked up and said, "Certainly. What is it?" I said, "Well, we've been talking about succession and we haven't discussed your children. I'm wondering how wealthy you'd like them to be?" There was total silence and after what felt like ten minutes but was probably more like thirty seconds they said together, "Thank you, that's the question we really wanted to talk about but didn't think you'd care about it."

We talked for an hour, each recognizing that there was no answer to this question. It isn't quantifiable. All that parents can do, we decided that day, is do their best to define the answer as empathetically as possible and to keep searching for a better answer. By the end of that meeting, I felt I had gained some courage. The couple felt it too, and they likewise felt more empowered to express their fears and desires. Over the months that ensued, as they searched for an answer, I found that my role was to continue to help them find the courage to keep the process going through iterative questions that shifted from knowledge-based questions to more courageous probing, depending on what step in their process the couple felt was needed next. In the end, they found *their* answer.

As the years have gone by, I thank that couple for being there for me and I continue to be there for them. My father was right: the gift of garnering courage defines the serving professional who is a personne de confiance.[8]

Chapter Notes

1. I use the French term because it expresses a higher level of client confidence than any equivalent English term, such as *counselor, most trusted adviser,* or the slang term *consigliere.*

2. The uncertainty principle in physics, according to Werner Heisenberg and Niels Bohr, expresses the reality that the same thing can be in two forms and in two places at the same time, thus we can never be certain exactly what and where it is. In the quantum world of infinitesimally small things, a photon of light can be a particle or a wave, depending on how we observe it, and it therefore is both at the same time. Thus, we can never be "certain" of what or where it is, especially as we, as observers, can only see it relatively.

3. For more on this subject, I recommend *The Betrayed Profession* by Sol M. Linowitz and Martin Mayer.

4. Again, I use the French term to define a group of professionals dealing with the financial affairs of a family, because I believe it better defines a different and second-ary order of service to a family than any English term, especially in stratifying the different levels of service discussed in this chapter.

5. At the point in my life when I found myself "in a dark wood with no place to go," I had both types of experiences. I encountered new questions from families and deep feelings about what I was called to do—all of which directed me into the dark wood because I had no way of responding to either. These same questions later became fundamental to how I found my way out of the wood.

6. If an institution still believes it can't do this because client families "won't pay" for this type of service, it should consider the spectacular growth of multiclient family offices and family advisory practices. Families are demanding and paying happily for them.

7. The 1959 movie *Warlock*, with Henry Fonda, illustrates this theme magnificently.

8. Professionals who read this will recognize that the current model of time billing makes a process like this very difficult financially. It changes a quick process—using forms—into an extended process, with no end in sight, no point at which to send a bill. True, the current model doesn't serve such a process, because it doesn't serve the client. The issue of form leading function is at the heart of much harm to families and is discussed at depth in chapter 3, "Obstacles to Affinity: The Seven Paradoxes."

Chapter Twenty-One

Roles and Characteristics of a Personne de Confiance

I dreamt and saw that life was joy. I awoke and saw that life was duty. I served and found that duty was joy.
— ELLEN STURGIS HOOPER, American poet

THE PERSONNE DE CONFIANCE is often the only member of the family system whose objectivity permits the 40,000-foot view needed to see what transitions the family and its members are undergoing and to guide the process from behind to the next stage of the journey. In this way, serving professionals perform the most critical role in maintaining the well-being of the family, whom they serve as intermediaries, as visionaries, and as leaders offering courage. Their calling and the journey of learning it inspired prepares them for this role, which they must be ready to perform with all the courage they can muster.

The Role of Number Two

History has told us much about the role of the great "number two"—the person whose mission is to make others great. Such men as Aristotle, Confucius, Cicero, Seneca, Boethius, Lao Tzu, Thomas à Becket, Thomas More, Machiavelli, Gracián, Richelieu, Metternich, Bismarck, Hamilton, Madison, Van Buren, George C. Marshall, Chou En-lai, Thomas Gates, John Gardner, and John O'Neil represent a partial list of men whose lives personified the role of personne de confiance in their journey to make another man or woman great.[1] Each in his own way served another, and none sought to displace the patron he served. Each saw in service to others a high calling, and none sullied the life of the person he served.

Seneca, Boethius, Cicero, Thomas à Becket, and Thomas More each died for his ideals at the hands of the man he served. Aristotle, Confucius, Cicero, Seneca, Machiavelli, and Gracián took what they learned in a life of service and chose to write it down to share with others. In each case, their wisdom remains with us today, as fresh and useful in our times to our understanding of human behavior as it was when they experienced the behaviors they cataloged. It would appear that human beings, while clearly shaped by their environments, have not changed much in the 2,600 years chronicled by these classic observers of the human condition. Reviewing the lives of the men listed above, we find some common characteristics that offer guidance to the twenty-first century personne de confiance.

An Interest in the Art of Governance. Often these advisers lived through times of great change in the governmental systems of the societies in which they lived. Many became students of this subject and some wrote on it. Each, in his time, offered to whomever he served a set of principles of government that, when practiced, brought success to the patron he served—sadly, all too often, until the patron's hubris caused him to abandon the adviser—and offered good principles of government to the civil society in which he lived. Each recognized that a society drifts into chaos unless all of its members share a clear understanding of their roles and responsibilities to each other in making the joint decisions necessary for their mutual well-being.

Aristotle lived in the Athenian democracy, served as mentor to Alexander the Great, king of Macedonia, in a tyranny becoming an aristocracy. In his book *The Politics*, he offered useful observations on the nature of the different forms of governance that human societies might choose, whether an aristocracy, oligarchy, republic, anarchy (pure democracy), or tyranny (dictatorship). Cicero lived in a time when Rome was passing from a republican form of government into tyranny, with the country in almost perpetual civil war—in effect, anarchy. Cicero attempted to explain this process and the risks it entailed, as well as seeking to maintain the Roman Republic. He ultimately died for his efforts. Thomas More, as Chancellor of England, offered Henry VIII advice on governance, which the king used to his benefit and to the benefit of England in the early years of his reign. Only when the king ceased to put the future of his country ahead of his own personal desires did that relationship break down. More lost his head, and England fell eventually into 150 years of civil war. More's *Utopia* is a wonderfully satiric book on the nature of human beings and their governance and remains fresh and useful today.

A Belief in Orderly Evolutionary Change. All of these men believed that government's highest purpose was the preservation of order and that change, as it occurred, should be evolutionary rather than revolutionary. Perhaps the person who described the entire group's overall views best was the Chinese philosopher Lao Tzu, who taught us the profound nature of leadership from behind.

Skepticism Without Contempt. Each man was skeptical of other men's behavior but did not look down on others. Rather, he assumed that natural self-interest directed every man's decisions.

Subordination of Ambition to a Higher Calling. Each of these men, while highly ambitious, accepted with complete equanimity the roles and responsibilities of being number two and subordinated his personal ambition to make his patron great. Each found a calling in service compatible with his highest ambition. This phenomenon of service to others in the role of a great number two has been underappreciated in modern times. We in the West have decided that leadership can come only from first achieving a position as "number one." All of these men's lives give the lie to that proposition, and it's fascinating that in many cases the number two is the man history remembers, while the man or woman he served is less well known. This is especially surprising, given that each of these men actively practiced the art of service and saw to it that his patron got the credit for the personne de confiance's successful acts. The intertwined lives of Cardinal Richelieu and his patron, Louis XIII, come immediately to mind.

The following characteristics, which link these personnes de confiance and were essential to their role as number two, are likely to continue to define successful personnes de confiance:

- An interest in the art of governance
- A belief in orderly evolutionary change
- A skeptical view of human behavior
- A willingness to subordinate ambition to the higher calling of service to another

The Role of Confidante

The best serving professionals willingly accept the isolation from their peers and communities, even from their own families, that comes with the confidentiality requirements their client families require for their security. These confidentiality requirements are not unlike those willingly assumed by the clergy.

As Paul Schervish, director of the Boston College Center on Wealth and Philanthropy, informs us, great financial wealth leads the individuals who own and control it to become "hyperagents" in all of their individual and community relationships.[2] Hyperagency, in turn, leads to heightened public interest in these people's lives and practices. It is a level of notoriety, which a few people of great financial wealth, like Donald Trump, actively encourage, but almost all others actively discourage. Who among us would seek to have every moment of our lives chronicled by paparazzi? The answer is very few. Princess Diana's frenzied effort to find privacy, which ultimately led to her death, is surely the worst outcome of the life of a hyperagent.

The life of a personne de confiance is rightly directed to maintaining, to the highest extent possible, the privacy of the lives of the families served and the utmost confidentiality of their financial affairs. The professional actively seeks to protect the families served from all risks to the quality of their lives and at the same time seeks to give them access to the people most able to enhance the quality of their lives. In this function as privy councilors, they bar the doors to the bedchambers. They are gatekeepers extraordinaire. In serving this way, personnes de confiance must remove themselves from certain normal social and professional interactions, so that they can be entirely committed to the requirements of the families they serve. Personnes de confiance willingly accept the constriction of their professional life and accept the privacy of a life committed entirely to the protection and improvement of the lives of those they serve. They do so for the benefits they perceive to the successful pursuit of their calling as a personne de confiance.

Necessary Choices

For many personnes de confiance, including me, there is frequently some sadness in this isolation, because they lose personal contact with many other professionals and friends whose relationships they might otherwise wish to deepen. I also know of many cases, including my own, where relationships with family are attenuated and in some cases broken by their commitments to the families they serve. These commitments are frequently so broad in scope that the physical and emotional demands cause them to take precedence over the commitment to their own families of affinity.

Key to understanding the characteristics of a personne de confiance is that this role is a chosen path of life and cannot be imposed and that what appears to be sacrifice to many outside of the profession is not necessarily so. The deep calling to be of service includes, at some level, the sacrifice of self in the service of another. Sometimes this sacrifice can be so severe that it causes a loss of self, followed unfortunately by all of the damage to ourselves and to the people we serve that inevitably arises from the chaos into which a lack of self-awareness leads. The ability to give oneself completely as a "number two," as a servitor, to the creation of a great "number one" and still retain full awareness of self is characteristic of a successful personne de confiance. To such an adviser, the commitment does not seem like a sacrifice at all. Rather, it seems fulfilling and fitting to the call to be of service that shapes the life of the personne de confiance in this role as a kind of secular priest.

In my role as a personne de confiance, there have been many times that I have listened, as an observer, to conversations about families I served. Sometimes these conversations made me wince, sometimes smile, but I never revealed that I knew any of these families, much less represented them. "Silence is golden" are words to live by for a privy councilor. On many evenings, as I traveled all over the world, I spent lonely solo dinners in hotel restaurants. (I was the man you saw alone reading a book.) Often, one or sometimes two of the families I was in that country to see dined at the same place on those nights. We never acknowledged each other and, of course, neither of the families had any idea that I represented the other. I had made it very clear to them at the beginning that our being seen in public together could jeopardize the privacy of our relationship and —because of the extremely privileged and confidential information they had entrusted to me—decrease their security. Yes, there were some long nights, but they were easy to accept in return for the depth of the relationship. I do, however, offer my apologies to my own family for the many times I put the needs of the families I served ahead of my responsibilities to them. I thank them for having forgiven me.

The Role of Intermediary

Many personnes de confiance seek to intermediate
- within the energetic sphere of the family members' internal relationships to improve them
- outside that sphere to improve the quality of the products and services provided by other professionals to the members of the family
- with the world's wisdom traditions and their current keepers to assure their wisdom is flowing gently and deeply into the family's energetic space[3]

Throughout history, societies have brought forth individuals who perform their mysteries, ceremonies, and rituals to ensure their survival. Most of the services these individuals performed focused on mediating relationships within the community to achieve the optimum performance of its social, political, and spiritual systems so that they would survive and thrive. At different times and in different cultures, these professionals were the shamans, magicians, medicine men and women, and priests and priestesses.[4] In modern secular societies, many of the practices of these critical intermediaries have been considered unnecessary or even nonsensical. The extraordinary growth of developmental psychotherapy, "life coaching," and all forms of skill building shows that the needs remain fully present. We prefer, however, to believe we're so strong psychologically that we don't need them. That pretense works until we get scared or "stressed"[5] and need someone to make the fear go away. In my view, this illusion of strength can only get us into trouble because it discounts our species' cultural and social histories. We have always needed intermediaries for an individual's and a community's safe passages through life's difficult moments. As with any illusion, its lack of validity and negative energy imperils our well-being with the risk of the loss of precious positive energy that always comes from ignoring the truth.

All of a family's relationships are generally open to intermediation toward higher orders of functioning by the serving professional as secular priest. But one relationship—that of a husband and wife—is sacrosanct and must never be mediated. My father once shared a story with me that illustrated the wisdom of this rule. One of his law partners took on the representation of a lady in a matrimonial dispute. In an effort to help the parties reconcile, he arranged a meeting between them. After a few minutes of talk, the parties became agitated and the lady took off her stiletto-heeled shoe to use as a weapon. As she lunged at her husband, my father's partner jumped in between them and she hit him on the soft spot on his head with the pointed heel of her shoe. Within a few weeks, he died from the injury. Yes, we must offer our clients our courage, but we can serve them best by living for another day.

The Intermediary as Secular Priest

What qualities should a family of affinity seek to find in their personnes de confiance as intermediaries? I suggest they look for those with the same qualities as a secular priest would have. After all, they perform critical intermediary functions but with no special costumes to announce their role. These serving professionals are most certainly *not* seeking to intermediate with any higher power. That is the province of the clerics who have been ordained and anointed to do so in the various religious congregations they serve. The serving professionals as secular priests are entirely secular in their orientation. Perhaps the best examples in modern society of the persons I'm describing are psychotherapists and social workers doing clinical practice and the increasing number of life coaches.[6]

These psychotherapists and clinical workers have chosen, often out of their own suffering, to take up the calling of intermediary to assist in the growth and development of their patients—especially their patients' relationships with their families of origin and of choice. They seek to help them find the proper boundaries of these relationships and to help them grow them within those boundaries.

Within psychotherapy, I've observed that there are two types of professionals. The first group's goal is to reduce human suffering by providing therapy; the second, much smaller group seeks to grow healthy individuals and families who are at the beginner's-mind stage of development. I observe, with great interest, that the callings of these two divisions within the field of therapeutic psychology are very different and I am seeking to learn more about this phenomenon. Equally, I am discovering that in all the professions that serve families, there are individuals who are performing the second of these services—fostering a beginner's mind—most often as leaders from behind, within the family systems with which they interact.[7] I am excited by the rapid growth of the profession of life coaching, which is another form of this service. People from many different professional backgrounds are called to offer this service for the improvement of the quality of life and the growth of the human and intellectual capital of their clients. I see the growth of this new profession as very positive for our society, because it makes possible in secular times a kind of professional mentoring that is deeply needed.

Every one of us will, at different crucial times in our lives, need someone to intermediate for us, as we break away from old habits, work to mend from failed relationships, and seek new information for new growth and help in integrating this new knowledge into our lives. The role of the secular priest—as a serving professional, as an intermediary—is to guide us through the space to safely complete these journeys.

The same role holds true for professionals serving whole families as together they go through their critical passages from one linked transition to the next. The serving professional, as intermediary, seeks to maintain the space for those transitions to take place as safely as possible so as to help the family increase the likelihood that each transition moves it closer to its long-term goal of greatness.

The Roles of Artist and Patron

In understanding the role of the personne de confiance as artist, consider that the professions are humane arts, not sciences, and therefore the personne de confiance is practicing an art and not a science. It is imperative that the personne de confiance's client, in a much higher calling of his own, appreciates that he will be this artist's *patron*. Wise patrons will understand such a role's importance to their own lifelong learning and that of their family. They understand that a family's prosperity lies in the health, both human and intellectual, that will grow from a positive relationship with such a person. Respect and honoring of the relationship between patron and personne de confiance, as in every relationship of patron and the individual whose art the patron seeks to bring to life, is fundamental to its success. If the patron knows that the serving professional's personal journey of service begins with a willingness to be subordinate to the patron, the gift of the art of the personne de confiance can be accepted by the patron without fearing loss of place or of competition. The essence of the relationship between the personne de confiance and the patron lies in the one giving his service and the other providing a means for doing so. Both parties benefit, feel gratitude, and grow.

My Journey of Service

It has been my privilege to act in the role of personne de confiance for a number of families, as it was for my father before me. To be in such a position of honored counselor has been for both of us a privilege deeply treasured. These positions have afforded us an opportunity to observe the evolution of families through the practice of our art—in the case of two families, we've served each for five generations. Our observations and the practices they generated have enabled us to assist these families in their growth while achieving our own ambitions and callings to be personnes de confiance. In this role, we found the offered wisdom and shared experiences of the personnes de confiance listed earlier to be our guide.

Teaching these families how to set up systems of governance to achieve excellent joint decision making over a long period of time has been enormously rewarding personally. More important, I've observed that successful family governance leads directly to the achievement of significantly higher orders of personal happiness among the individuals within these families—a result far more profound for me than any other.

Here is the process I use in helping families govern themselves and thus increase their individual members' personal pursuit of happiness.

Determine the Family's Personality. Every family is made up of the complex personalities of all its individual members. As a personne de confiance, I try through dialogue with each family member to determine how their individual personalities coalesce to create the personality of the family. I explore where the family's strengths lie, where its weaknesses are, and how its family system works. I learn where the individual journeys of each family member are leading.

When I feel that I understand a family's character, its processes, and its strengths and weaknesses, I attempt to mentor its leaders. Using the stories that grow out of my dialogue with the individual family members, I help the leaders appreciate how to offer guidance that will enhance the individual life journeys of each of their family members.

I also help them appreciate how the family's governance system can assist that process and thereby assist the family's positive evolution. In this mentoring role, I offer them, as objectively as possible, my observations on their character as a family, how their family system seems to work, any negative triangulations within their system, and what I perceive to be the individual goals of each of the family members.

Finally, I offer them suggestions on how to assist family members in achieving their personal happiness by finding the educators and mentors necessary for the growth of their individual human and intellectual capital. When I serve a family in the development, practice, and evaluation of a system of family governance that succeeds in *enhancing* the lives of the individuals who make up the family, I am practicing the first of the characteristics of a personne de confiance as a number two: assisting and coaching in the art and practice of excellent governance.

Encourage Orderly Change. In my experience with families, change is best achieved as an evolutionary process. Preservation of basic order and core values is a family virtue needed for long-term success. The good professional enables families to successfully evolve from one generation to the next. All too often today, I observe professionals who offer advice to their clients based not on what their clients need for orderly long-term change to meet new conditions but rather on a product that the professional has developed and wants to sell. This conduct is the antithesis of the behavior of a true personne de confiance.

A family is in the business of avoiding its own disappearance, as predicted by the culturally universal proverb "From shirtsleeves to shirtsleeves in three generations," and achieving greatness by doing so. Given current demographics, it will take one hundred years for three generations of a family to be born and die and two hundred for its fifth generation to be born and die. Thus it will be one hundred years before anyone can know whether the family has overcome the first hurdle in its perpetual war against the proverb and another hundred to know if it achieves greatness by achieving its fifth generation in thriving condition. A professional who wishes to be a personne de confiance has to face this truth. No product he can dream up can possibly meet the challenges of the world one hundred years or more from now. Only by living the life of a serving professional called to help families, with the help of the timeless wisdom that has come down to us from the great personnes de confiance of the past, can he truly help a family meet and overcome the challenges it will face over such a long time horizon.

Families will not achieve success in retarding the entropic effect of the proverb unless their serving professionals are willing to acknowledge that they can participate in only a small part of the cycle of a family's history and, more important, see their service as *requiring* consideration of the family's long-term goals. They must recognize that the families they serve seek the wisdom and understanding of the need for orderly change and the process of achieving it, not products whose shelf lives are much too short to be truly helpful.

Practice Healthy Skepticism. True counselors offer to those they serve a healthy and loving skepticism about all people's behavior. They always make clear to those they serve any self-interest they may have in advice they offer. After all, personnes de confiance are just as human as anyone else, with personal goals and ambitions that may, from time to time, overlap or even conflict with the goals of the families they serve. Skepticism about human behavior is not about viewing others through dark, anxious glasses or seeing human beings as fatally flawed. It is rather about viewing with compassion the truth of the human condition. It requires actively supporting, from a place of humility, each individual's struggle, as an evolving human being, to achieve deep spiritual happiness, despite doubts that anyone in this lifetime is likely to achieve it.

Personnes de confiance bring to the families they serve a deep awareness of human behavior and the truths, realities, and subtleties that such behaviors represent and exhibit. Often the financially privileged positions of the families I serve have isolated them from many human interactions.[8] And, all too frequently, members of the younger generations of these families have been abandoned emotionally by their parents and exhibit the behaviors associated with that loss in their interpersonal relations. These family members are ill prepared for normal human interaction and, in my experience, fall victim to actions on the part of others for which they are simply not prepared.[9] The most effective personne de confiance brings to these family members a worldly, wise view of human behavior and gentle mentoring in the arts of human interaction.

Subordinate Ambition to a Higher Calling. Perhaps of greatest importance to the calling of the true personne de confiance is the ability to naturally subordinate ambition to the service of another—in this case, a family and its individual members.

Serve as a Mentor. The most effective personnes de confiance frequently fulfill a number of substantive roles in the systems of the families they serve. Among these roles are mentor, trustee, steward, director of a family's foundation, teacher, and elder. In performing these tasks, they exemplify the most effective characteristics and, when leadership is required of them, gently lead from behind.

One salient characteristic of such professionals is that in every role, they seek to incorporate their skills as mentor.[10] In this capacity, they aim to assist each family member in performing more competently the functions assigned them in family governance. I've discussed the art of mentoring and the extent to which it can enable a family to flourish. Helping another by offering questions that empower that person's life and generally improve his relationships is to profoundly grow his human and intellectual capital. All the great serving professionals I have observed begin every interaction with each family member by seeking to ensure that every interaction offers the highest probability that it will move that person and the family system of which he is a part toward +1 on the calculus. Constant application of the mentoring art offers the greatest probability that serving professionals will actively improve the chances that the families they serve will achieve their fifth generation and go on from there to greatness.

The Responsibility of Personnes de Confiance as Professionals

Those called to be personnes de confiance have a duty to themselves to perform this work well if they are to achieve their own individual happiness. If they continue to lose their way by serving their personal profit goals rather than serving their deepest intuitions, then they will lose themselves. In losing themselves, they lose the cherished title so honored by history in the lives of the great men we've discussed—the title of personne de confiance.

I hope that in this stream of the legacies of the great personnes de confiance that have gone before, many will discover their true calling to professional service and in so doing complete what they're called to do.[11] As they do, here is my prayer for each of them: May those who elect, as Robert Frost suggests, to take the road less traveled that makes all the difference also honor all those in the past who sought to serve families and the societies of which they were a part. In their journey, may they be a light to all those who find the courage to begin journeys of their own. May they never hesitate to be the bard and tell their story and the stories of all those who went before. May they be secular priests for their colleagues by assisting those within their chosen profession on *their* journeys, asking only that they do the same for others. Above all, may they be the magicians who make what is truly hard seem easy.

Let the mystery flow. Bless those who show us the way, and blessings and good journeying to you if you are on or about to embark on this path. Should any of your lives intersect with mine, I promise you will find me ready to learn from and journey with you. We shall make our way together as pilgrims to all the other places of the heart where men and women of good will from time immemorial have gone for the refreshment of their spirits.

The Role of the Professional
in the Larger Community

What does the larger community seek and need from the professionals serving within it? For a society to offer a high quality of life to its members, its professionals must provide healing and humane preserving energy to that society. All historical and prehistorical societies have given professionals, including the clerics, the responsibility to preserve this life-generating space and to encourage the entry into society of this special energy. The essence of this energy is perhaps best understood through the metaphor of Vishnu—preserving energy. Vishnu's act of bringing the healing humane energy into life epitomizes the force that preserves life. When the professionals in a society cease to perform this Vishnu function, often because they begin to act only in their own self-interest, societies frequently break down and become grist for the historians. I believe Western society is at risk today because its professionals are no longer acting responsibly. The special healing energy they're responsible for in the societies in which they practice is ceasing to flow.

I hope that the twenty-first century will see a recommitment of professionals to their true calling: the calling of service to the deep human needs of the individuals and families they serve and to the societies of which they are a part. Without a rededication to the ideals of the great privy counselors, these individuals, families, and societies are in real danger. If professionals will rededicate themselves to their true calling to service, the chances of decline will diminish. In such service lies a part of the answer to the preservation of our global society and the happiness—in the Confucian, Aristotelian, and Jeffersonian senses—of its members.

Chapter Notes

1. It is a great disappointment to me that I am not yet able to list a woman in this roster. I know from experience that behind many a great man is a greater woman. Perhaps the best individual metaphor I know for the extraordinary role women played in the role of personne de confiance is that of the Chinese empress who ruled China

in the late nineteenth century from "behind the veil." In the Iroquois nation, the elder women of the tribe select the chiefs and can displace them. Through their accumulated wisdom, the tribe is preserved. Finally, the Greeks' most profound depiction of a mentor was Athena, goddess of wisdom.

2. Paul Schervish, in his writings on the wealthy and philanthropy, defines individuals who have significant financial capital as "hyperagents" in their social and professional relationships. He explains that great financial wealth creates in its owner a kind of powerful energy that radiates out for good and ill and significantly enhances the owner's impact on others. His acts have ramifications well beyond what similar acts by someone without such capital might have. Schervish believes that such individuals frequently have a much greater influence on other people's lives, positively or negatively, because of their financial capital. My experience is that Schervish is absolutely right. I have seen much good and much bad done by such individuals. I have come to see that their actions do often have very heightened effects. All of us who serve individuals and families with significant financial capital would do well to read Schervish's works on the concept of the wealthy as hyperagents, so that we can better understand and advise our clients about the likely heightened impact of their actions. Most of Schervish's work can be found at www.bc.edu/research/swri.

3. Frequently, personnes de confiance must withdraw from visibility. Here they are the families' visible representatives in the world. Balancing these two requirements is extremely complex, and often creates highly conflicting roles for them. There is no right answer to this dilemma of visibility, but normally the families' privacy concerns will determine a satisfactory resolution.

4. In this section, I discuss the personne de confiance as a healing intermediary. As with any practice that might do harm, individuals seeking to help another must have the professional training needed to ensure that they will do no harm in their attempt to do good.

5. I learned from His Holiness the Dalai Lama that there is no word for stress in Tibetan. The word that comes closest is *suffering*—a fascinating commentary on modernity and its idea of progress.

6. It is not surprising that most life coaches are women, given our cultural history of who most often performs these intermediary functions. Sadly, in modern times, most religions have not welcomed women into their clerical ranks, so they cannot follow that calling, even though many have felt drawn to it. Historically, however, and in the much longer prehistory of our species, priestesses were of equal rank with men. Their special roles as midwives and hospice workers continue today in the caregiving they offer at birth and death. Psychotherapy and its cognate professions are grow-

ing as the principal performers of the intermediary functions people need to relieve the stresses and sufferings in their lives. I believe that with women's open entry and predominance in these professions, we are once again, as a species, opening our hearts and welcoming into them the women we require for the critical functions of intermediation needed for our well-being.

7. I am excited about the rapid growth of divisions called family advisory services or family advisory practices within the financial institutions and multiclient family offices that serve families of financial wealth. In these embryonic and rapidly evolving groups lie the possibilities for service to families of this second kind and career paths for existing and would-be personnes de confiance. This development offers possibilities to the client families of these institutions and even more for their officers whose callings are to the high idea of service I describe here. I salute my mentor, dear friend, and fellow journeyer Peter White, vice chairman of the United States Trust Company, founder of this concept of advisory practices, and a force behind its development.

8. This is a negative result of their rightly perceived desire for privacy and the security it offers. However, anything that is carried to an extreme often proves harmful. Too much isolation breeds lack of understanding of the world and of the human relationships that are integral to it. Such a lack will always be entropic at some level and so must be balanced by sufficient experience of the world and its relationships to ensure that family members can successfully participate in it.

9. The movie *The Servant* (1963), starring Dirk Bogarde, illustrates what happens to wealthy individuals when their servants become their masters. I frequently recommend this movie to families so that they can appreciate the horror of one human being ostensibly helping another, while in fact destroying him.

10. I have discussed mentoring in many different forms in this book. For those who wish to know more, see chapter 17 of *Family Wealth*.

11. For more on the ethical question of work at its highest level of calling, see *Good Work*, by Howard Gardner, Mihaly Csikszentmihalyi, and William Damon; *Self-Renewal*, by John Gardner; *The Force of Character: And the Lasting Life*, by James Hillman; and *The Paradox of Success*, by John O'Neil.

Chapter Twenty-Two

A Father's Wisdom

Whosoever heareth these sayings of mine, and doeth them,
I will liken him unto a wise man, which built his house upon
a rock.

—MATTHEW 7:24

My FATHER, James Elliott Hughes Sr., practiced law the old-fashioned way, with his clients' interests paramount. "Your clients' interests come first," he would say. Putting your clients' interests ahead of your own and those of your law partners is difficult. In an age when malpractice insurance companies dominate law firms and "CYA" practices dominate professional systems, being a lawyer who puts his clients first is easier said than done.

True. But do it anyway. If you are honored by having another human being ask for your help (in my opinion there is no greater calling than to be able to provide that help) and you agree to do so, then committing yourself fully to meeting his needs is all you need to be concerned about. Once you reach that point, you need to focus on where your professional responsibilities lie.

Necessarily, clear canons of ethics govern lawyers' relationships with their clients and their fellow counsel. These rules clarify the limits of what constitutes proper representation and offer a code of conduct that permits adversaries to meet. My father's admonition assumes that every lawyer knows and lives within these rules. Still, his guidance isn't about rules; it's about honor, and the duties and obligations toward another that flow from that honoring.

As the son of James Elliott Hughes, I was privileged to experi-

JAMES ELLIOTT HUGHES SR.

JAMES ELLIOTT HUGHES SR. was born on May 6, 1913, in Clayton, Missouri, and lived in Chatham, New Jersey, and later in Stony Brook, New York. He graduated from the Lincoln School, from Horace Mann Academy at age 16, from Columbia College in 1933 at age 19, and from Columbia Law School in 1935 at age 22.

Upon his graduation from law school, my father entered the law firm of Coudert Brothers, where he practiced international commercial law for fifty years and from which he retired in 1985. He was the fifth generation in the Hughes family to practice law. During his tenure at Coudert Brothers, he served as a part of the leadership of the firm, taking it from a family practice into a general partnership and overseeing its growth from a single office with a small number of attorneys to a firm of 325 attorneys, with multiple American and international locations.

My father sat on the boards of directors of many international companies, including Thiokol, Coty, Michelin, Standard Products, and A. Zerega's Sons. He served as trustee for multiple families and as director for numerous not-for-profit foundations.

James E. Hughes Sr. passed away on November 21, 2004. I salute him—the last Roman—his work, his gifts, and his memory.

ence the unique deep wisdom of this plainspoken Missouri man, who spoke in short, pithy phrases. During my many years as his son, his law partner, and, most important, his mentee, I was often struck by the depth of his wisdom and have tried to practice the superb advice he gave me. I have also, in my practice with families, tried to share with them what he taught me.

I want to share his wisdom here. I hope that his words will be as inspiring to readers as they have been to me, to our family, and to his friends and clients.

A Lawyer's Practice and Role in Society

"A lawyer who creates capital from his law practice, rather than an excellent annual living, may well be stealing from his clients."

This is a very tough statement from a man with a Victorian (read "absolutely incorruptible") view of integrity and of the lawyer's role in society. In 1965, when I was in law school, my father and I had the first of many discussions about what lawyers do. He shared with me his view of a lawyer's proper role in society and what kind of living a lawyer should expect to make.

I often consider his words when I ponder the recent history of the legal profession: the historically highly respected role of lawyers in British and American history, the commercialization of the legal profession that occurred in the 1980s and '90s, followed by the depth to which morale fell in the profession, as lawyers became businessmen and -women and ceased to be members of a helping profession. As they ceased to be seen as members of a helping profession, they lost their raison d'être within society, which had earned them their previously high standing and respect. This sad history has been followed rightly by the general population's continuing deeply angry views of lawyers. For me, this history underscores my father's view of what is right about lawyers and what is wrong. Unfortunately, we have been living with the greed of the "wrong" during this period as well as the consequences that such sin engenders.

To my questions about what lawyers do, my father unusually offered a lengthy and truly impassioned answer. He believed that for any society to be one in which people want to live, there must be a few members who serve as helping professionals. In most societies, these are the clergy, the healers, those entrusted to do justice tempered with mercy, the statesmen and -women, the storytellers, the educators, the leaders from behind, and above all, the elders and the mentors. In earlier times, my father explained, these people formed a special class in society called the gentry or the "noblesse de robe." They were people of the mind whose educations enabled them to serve the other classes of society.

In return for such service, society accorded them the same kind of freedom and an annual living similar to that enjoyed by the landed upper classes. Society recognized that the extended period of education required for these people to become adept at their profession and the socially valuable professional services they rendered thereafter differentiated them from the general population. Their services needed to be compensated in such a way that encouraged them to offer them. Between society and the helping professions, there was, therefore, a kind of social compact recognizing their service to society and awarding appropriate compensation for that service.

My father's explanation of how that standard of living should be determined suggests that society assumes that the deferred economic gratification of extended study and putting that study to society's use should be compensated at a high annual rate. However, professionals do not venture or risk their financial capital in their practices unless they make a serious error. It is within the context of this economic reality that in compensating professionals for their contributions to the general economy, society recognizes they are unlike entrepreneurs who risk their financial capital every day in pursuit of profit. This distinction between the risking and nonrisking of financial capital is a crucial difference in the rewards available for different types of work.

My father believed, and I agree, that capital should accrue to those who risk their financial capital in endeavoring to gain more. I am, as he was, an enthusiastic capitalist, and we both advised people who are prepared to take such risks. Members of the helping professions are not risking their financial capital, nor do their clients expect them to do so. In fact, thoughtful clients discourage their professionals from participating financially in the risks they take because it creates a risk that the helping professional will lose objectivity. The history of the legal profession in the 1980s and 1990s demonstrates the risks lawyers run in losing objectivity as one law firm after another was sued for so doing and many were heavily penalized for their mistakes.

In my father's view, lawyers who create capital from their professional work, beyond saving regularly out of a decent annual income, must in some fashion be violating society's normal valuation of their services. He suspected that some part of the economic system is being bent out of alignment by these lawyers to serve their special interests. Otherwise, there is simply no way such capital can be created. "Creative billing," "premium billing," and "sales of lawyer's ideas with confidentiality agreements" are all euphemisms that, when carried to today's extremes, represent methods of transferring clients' capital to lawyers' firms. For such practices, my father's words prove true.

Those in the helping professions have been honored for centuries by the societies in which they work and compensated highly for it—not only with money but, more important, with respect. It should be no surprise to serving professionals that if they act toward society with greed and avarice, that respect will be lost.

—⁓—

> "Lawyers solve problems that their clients either can't solve because they don't have the knowledge or won't solve because they don't have the courage. In the second set of problems, the practice of a true lawyer is found."

This statement, which my father shared with me in 1966, needs very little explanation. My forty years of practice have shown me that he was correct. This is all practicing lawyers do. Whenever we're doing something else or something more, we're likely wandering in the fields of hubris, imagining that our brilliance and erudition give us a special license to tell others what to do and how to do it. When we can, with humility, acknowledge our weaknesses rather than our strengths, take a deep breath, and really look at a client's problem, we will readily see whether it is our knowledge or our courage the client is seeking.

As my father insisted, informational problems are normally relatively easy to solve. A good law-school education, with lots of time in the library, provides a lawyer with the skills needed to investigate such issues and find answers. The much more difficult problems a lawyer faces are those which the client lacks the courage to resolve. They are problems of a qualitative nature, whereas knowledge-based issues are quantitative. Solving qualitative problems often requires much more intuition than intellect—what educators call emotional intelligence. Great lawyers are those prepared to take the path less traveled, the intuitional, relational path where one takes risks.

What are these risks? First there's the risk of doing harm to your client in an effort to do good, which is always the risk of the serving professional who chooses to defend his client by putting himself in harm's way. Second there's the risk of failure when attempting to help another with a problem of courage, with all the injury to self-esteem that comes from that failure. But this kind of lawyering—helping clients solve a problem they lack the courage to solve—is where great lawyers are found.

—⁑—

> "The adoption of time billing will be the death knell of our profession. It will lead to the commoditization of our services and a loss of clients' view of us as trusted counselors."

In 1970, Coudert Brothers asked its attorneys to begin to keep track of their time. We were told it was not to be a part of our billing procedures but rather a helpful guide to make us more businesslike. My father opposed this decision and made the statement above. He was absolutely prescient. In my opinion, the adoption of time billing, the greed it represents, and the commoditization of legal services that ensued are the underlying reasons the profession he loved and I love has fallen to such a low level of esteem.

Working With Individuals

> "Eighty percent of the time, do nothing."

Many years ago, when I was first practicing law, I entered my father's office to ask him for advice on what one of my clients should do. I explained the facts of the case and suggested two very different paths the client might follow to resolve his issue. My father said, "I suggest for the time being you advise him to do nothing." I was quite perplexed. After all, he was my client and I was sure he wanted action. I also wondered how any lawyer worth his salt could actually tell his client, "Do nothing."

I asked my father what point he was making with this advice, and he explained that in his many years of experience, most seemingly intractable problems, whether of knowledge or of courage, ultimately solved themselves. Often they were resolved because time permitted a resolution that was coming anyway, but the client simply had not let things play out as they were clearly going to do. The passage of time also brought to light new information, which clients could use to solve the issue themselves. My father saw that forcing resolution by taking path A or B often didn't solve the problem anyway, but it certainly could exacerbate it.

As the years passed, I saw that great doctors, educators, and priests all seem to follow this rule. The doctor administers a placebo, knowing that the patient will get well on his own. The great teacher leaves students with the question to which they so ardently seek an answer, and the students find the answer on their own, gaining all the learning experience that such discovery engenders. Priests don't force dogma or ritual on the penitent. They let the parishioners find relief on their own out of the experience of daily life. Doing nothing 80 percent of the time requires the courage to let life work and the humility to know we don't have most of the answers. It is a wonderful way of hastening slowly.

―⁂―

"The role of courts is to resolve with finality issues that the parties lack the knowledge or the courage to resolve themselves."

My father's view of the courts follows from his view of the role of lawyers. When we, as practitioners, discover that no matter how hard we try we cannot resolve an issue, then and then only do we resort to the courts. In other words, if we truly cannot determine the answer to a legal issue on our own either because the issue is novel, such as with the developing field of gene therapy, or because two judges have looked at the same issue and resolved it in opposite ways, then we must resort to a judge to tell us what the law is. In cases of courage, we often find that two parties simply cannot bring themselves to take the emotional steps necessary to find a middle path. Settlements rarely satisfy either party. In such cases, only a court can render a decision with finality. Necessarily, the party who loses may bear the pain of the loss forever, but society's need for finality in resolving a dispute trumps what otherwise would be an endless argument.

—\~—

"Consider the law of tardy."

One day as a very young lawyer, I entered my father's office deeply upset. I explained to him that a client of his had directed me to do something, which I knew he would not want me to do if he had been clear-headed. I had tried to talk him out of it but to no avail. My father asked who the client was, and when I told him, he said, "Well, of course, you aren't going to do that." I said, "But I have no choice; I'm directed to do it." My father said, "No, you are not; you are going to be tardy and do nothing." When I protested, he explained the "law of tardy."

There are times when the most compassionate thing you can do for your client is to give him time to reconsider. If the client is right, act immediately; if he hasn't really got it right, be tardy and take the risk to your relationship with him that he'll figure it out. Since it was a Friday, and I was in for a terrible weekend of worry about my career, my senior partner was instructing me to do nothing. He also said he knew this client well and that come Monday morning, the client would be calling me, hoping I had not followed through on his instructions.

So I did nothing and had a worry-filled weekend. I arrived at the office Monday morning full of woe to find the phone ringing. It was the client. "You didn't do what I instructed you to do on Friday, did you?" he asked. "I am so sorry," I said. "I have been tardy with that." "Thank God!" he said.

—\~—

"The beginning of anything is often farther down
the road than we perceive."

Often, we think we are at the beginning of something, when, in fact, we are just starting to put the pieces together that might form a beginning. Evolutionary biology, as well as systems and complexity theories, teaches us that things begin only when a series of normally unconnected elements come together to form some new and apparently higher order of life or organization. Each of these elements often existed completely independently for long periods. Putting these elements together to form something new is when a beginning occurs.

Knowing whether we are at the beginning of something or only putting the pieces together that might form a beginning is crucial to our understanding of every part of our lives. It's crucial to comprehending the laws and systems of the organizations of which we are a part. Believing we're at the beginning of something when that something is still in disconnected pieces will cause us to expect life to exist in something that is in fact not yet born, and thus to profoundly misjudge its capabilities. To be able to see when something truly begins is, as my father explained, absolutely imperative for that something to achieve the potential we desire for it. As a corollary, how often is the beginning far back from the place where we perceive it to be?

—m—

"Beginnings and endings are what people remember;
middles are almost always forgotten. Endings, done well,
lead to new beginnings."

These sayings of my father have helped me greatly at points in my life when I endeavored to begin something new; they helped even more when something in my life was coming to an end. My father believed that if we can end things well, we leave open all possibilities for new beginnings. If we end things badly, we risk the permanent closing of many doors, some of which we will almost certainly wish—or worse, need—to open again in the future.

In a certain way, my father's view of endings exhibited his belief that orderly change leads to higher orders of complexity, rather than disorderly change growing out of chaos and leading to new forms of order that often serve no one well. Essentially, this wisdom reminds us that there are, in fact, no actual beginnings or endings; there are only transitions in our lives, which we incorrectly perceive as finite beginnings and endings. To appreciate how important it is to begin and end things well is to comprehend that these are transitions, not breaches, in the constant flow of our lives. The smoother we can make these flows in the rivers of our lives, the fewer rapids we will have to navigate. Rapids are fun and exciting, but they ultimately slow us down and put us at risk of overturning. Smooth-flowing rivers make our growth faster and entail fewer risks. In the flow of our lives, many see and participate in our beginnings and are affected by them and others see and participate in our endings and are affected by them.

Rarely, as my father pointed out do we remember others' participation in what we perceive as our middles. That's because they are the points in our lives when the river is often flowing so slowly that their actions toward us are rarely perceived. It is at the inflection points in the flow of the river that we and others perceive beginnings and endings. My father correctly saw that these are the points in our lives that we must manage well, because they are where people's memories of us will be defined, as those who are most affected by our actions see, feel, and relate them to others. Managing these points of inflection well carries us past the strategic bends in the river and on to the next long learning stretches of life. If we live this way, our endings become our friends, so that our futures—our beginnings—are not limited by them but rather are enhanced by them.

—∞—

"Think in long-term ways, use history to understand."

My father never invoked George Santayana's phrase "Those who fail to study history are condemned to repeat it," although he knew and practiced it every day. My father's view, unlike Santayana's, is simply positive. My father suggested that if we try to comprehend the times we live in and the spaces in the world we occupy without understanding the history of how things came to be as they are—that is, without *context*—then we cannot understand them. His saying, put another way, means that by studying the long term we can act in the short term.

My experience of life is that my father was quite right. I now understand why his antique Spanish bookshelf always had seven history tomes on it. I begin to see now what he saw clearly at age ninety: how to view the relatively short term in the context of nearly a century of linking together a series of life events in the larger context of the history that preceded and surrounds them. This kind of perception of context offers a highly informed way of living and being in the world. It offers a way of comprehending time and space that leads to a deeply appreciated daily existence, because we better understand the world we inhabit and the events occurring within it.

Working With Organizations

"Can I be your partner?"

During the second or third year of my law practice, I asked my father for a model partnership agreement because I had a client who wanted to create one. My father was, as usual, very busy and asked me to sit down and wait until he could respond. After he'd answered some phone calls and given instructions to his secretary, he turned to me and said, "Have you asked your client whether he can be the other party's partner?" I had *not* asked my client this question because the question hadn't even occurred to me.

I asked my father what he meant, and he explained that if clients want to create a partnership rather than a joint venture or some sort of profit-sharing arrangement, the issue they must consider isn't what benefit the other party will bring them but rather whether they can be that party's partner. Partnership is a term defining a relationship of intuition, not just the intellect, he explained, and it requires a commitment of one's heart to the other before it can be said to exist.

What has become clear to me over the years is not only how right my father was about the nature of the partnership relationship but how extremely right. I've come to realize that a true partnership is about the willingness of one party to commit 100 percent to the other. It involves a willingness to forgive the other over and over because the relationship is so powerful that it transcends the normal issues that rightly cause lesser relationships to be terminated. It is a commitment of the heart to the possibility that one party can grow by fostering another's well-being.

True partnerships should be very rare and should be entered into only with the greatest of care. Partnerships are our most important relationships and offer us the greatest learning about ourselves because they presume that anyone committing to be our partner is absolutely committed to our well-being and growth. They are relationships in which altruism is foremost and in which we're prepared to truly learn how to help another and be helped in return. They are the relationships in which we take on willingly the risk of having our hearts broken if our partners fail us or, more likely, if we fail them and must live with that truth ever after. Once again, my father was right. The only question clients need to be asked if they're considering creating a partnership is "Can you be the other person's partner?"

"Who is your successor?"

One day my father and I were discussing the transition about to take place in the accession of a new CEO in one of the companies on whose board he sat. We got around to the question of how happy the new CEO was going to feel about finally reaching the pinnacle of his career. "When a new CEO emerges in a company on whose board I sit," my father said, "after I congratulate him and allow him to express his delight in achieving this level of success, I immediately ask him, 'Who is your successor?'"

I was shocked. My father was a man of almost Victorian manners. I couldn't imagine him saying what then seemed to me such a discourteous thing, so I asked him why he would do that. He explained that he had two very important reasons: First, he believed that the only role CEOs have that matters during their time in that position is that of planning their succession. The CEO's role above all others, my father believed, is to ensure orderly transition in the organization's leadership should he disappear. My father would have argued that this was even more important in an organization where the CEO is also chairman of the board.

My father and I agreed that organizations that have the same person acting as both CEO and chairman of the board are probably not governing themselves very well. That's because the CEO's role is to manage the organization and represent the interests of the employees, customers, and communities where the company transacts business, whereas the chairman's role is to manage the board, which represents the stakeholder-owners' interests. It is a rare person who can fill both of these roles equally well, because they are often—and should be—in conflict, to ensure that the best answers for the organization surface before the board. Above all, the CEO's responsibility is to ensure for the stakeholder-owners the most orderly transition possible in the role of CEO, because without such transition the organization is unnecessarily put at risk.

My father also believed, and I do too, that hubris is perhaps the most dangerous of all human emotions to a person's well-being. As we discussed his question to CEOs, he reminded me about the Roman way of dealing with hubris. The Romans, at least during their days as a republic, were stern warriors, he explained, who had as their hero Cincinnatus. Cincinnatus, the farmer-turned-warrior, returned to his fields after his great victories rather than accept the community's desire that he become dictator or king.

The Romans prized such humility. When a general had a great success, the city granted him a triumph: the defeated and now enslaved people whom the general had overcome would be paraded through the streets of Rome, while the Roman population cheered the general's success. The general, meanwhile, would be in a chariot in the parade receiving the accolades of the city. In the chariot with the general would be one of the people he had recently defeated and who was now a slave. That person's duty was to stand behind the general and from time to time whisper into his ear, "Remember, tomorrow you may be standing in my place." Such wisdom. And such a strong message about the dangers of self-importance. Clearly, the Romans knew the dark side of hubris, and they sought to ensure that its curses were well known to their leaders. My father's reminder to new CEOs embodies his classical education and its teaching of the need to be ever vigilant against the risks that overwhelming ego poses to the good order of the organizations they are chosen to lead.

Indeed, "Who is your successor?" is the right question to ask every leader in every organization of which we are a part. It asks leaders to focus on the single most important issue to the long-term success of the organization, the orderly succession of its leadership. It brings leaders—who otherwise might risk that organization's future by their hubris in imagining that they'll last forever—back down to earth.

—m—

"Take small steps and succeed together before trying
to tackle the most difficult problems."

My father often reminded me of his view that a useful principle for all organizations to adopt is that incremental success breeds success, but quick failure almost always brings doom. In my view, this statement incorporates the wisdom of hastening slowly and the benefits to organizations of getting a taste of success before risking failure. My experience with organizational growth and development proves his wisdom. Families as organizations especially can benefit from that wisdom.

Family governance systems are notoriously complex because they are by nature voluntary, nonhierarchical, and constantly shifting as members with rights equal to all others' enter and leave the family system. I often say that leadership of families has to be from the rear; it's much like herding cats. Getting a family to act together over a long period of time is highly complex and challenging. Just to motivate it to start working together is often like getting cats to agree to march in order. Given these realities and given the reality that families often start to work together only as a result of some crisis, the likelihood of a family achieving a successful outcome is low. My father's wisdom to start joint decision making with small steps that lead to small, incremental successes is a useful way to change the odds of the outcome.

People who have made some joint decisions that worked out well are more likely to make more difficult decisions together successfully than those whose initial joint decisions failed. This is simple probability. The suggestion to start small and succeed is a way of managing the probabilities of family decision making or, for that matter, any organization's decision making, so that the probabilities of its long-term success are enhanced. Small steps together can grow to long treks, but one huge first leap without a lot of experience in jumping is likely to lead to a bad fall.

—◊—

> "Bring those who are complaining inside the group
> and give them important roles to play."

Often when my father and I were analyzing why particular organizations were limping along, we found that they were expending far too much of their energy trying to fend off the complaints of people outside of the organization. Instead of using its energy toward achieving its vision and goals, the organization was wasting it on combating negative personalities. My father's antidote for this problem wasn't to circle the organizational wagons and try to ward off these complainers but rather to welcome the critics into the organization and give them things to do.

I'm not sure if I understood all that his views on this problem encompassed, but I have found the strategy effective. Whether we approach this issue from the positive view that those who care enough to complain about us are really our best critics and friends or from the negative view reflected in the Middle Eastern saying "Keep your friends close but your enemies closer," it's clear that we have to deal with these folks effectively if we are to avoid wasting an organization's energy.

Any action in an organization that puts its energy into stasis puts it at risk of falling into entropy, since any blockage of energy is essentially entropic. Organizations need to use their energy as dynamically as possible toward their growth and positive evolution. Dealing with outside critics by bringing them inside and giving them important work to do won't always help to get an organization to dynamically preserve itself. However, on the scale of probabilities, my father's proposal offers a method of increasing the likelihood of a better outcome for an organization than circling the wagons or, worse, ignoring the problem. Anything that moves the organization toward a better long-term result is likely to increase the probability of its long-term prosperity.

—m—

"If you intend to kill the king, kill him on the first day;
otherwise, he will surely kill you on the second."

My father was a peaceful man, who spent his life conciliating difficult disputes. He was, however, a warrior for truth. He taught me early on that the world has evil people in it and that true leaders do not run away from this hard truth. I watched him act with extraordinary courage to bring down bullies and with a stab of words puncture the pompous. He often recommended patience when I wanted to act before thinking.

However, when real harm was occurring, he would remind me that if I chose to act, I must act decisively or my action would fail. Sun Tzu, in *The Art of War*, reminds us that the greatest general never needs to fight a battle because he brings his resources to bear so decisively on the enemy before the battle even begins that the enemy will capitulate before any fighting occurs. This is the essence of my father's insight about killing the king. If you have to make war on your enemy, then act decisively and completely to ensure his complete and immediate defeat, or else the next day will be your last. Prepare to the nth degree; leave no detail unattended. It is in preparation that you thrive, overcome, and live to tell the tale.

—∞—

THESE INSIGHTS OF my father have informed my life, personally and professionally. I am happily aware that he offered similar wisdom to other members of our family and to his many friends, and especially to the men and women who were blessed to be his partners and associates at Coudert Brothers.

My father's life, his integrity, and his well-chosen words were inspiring. I hope with the recitation and elucidation of his wisdom I have in some small way honored my best friend, my partner, my mentor, and above all, my dad. I thank him for his leadership and assistance on my journey.

EPILOGUE

When you have completed 95 percent of your journey, you're halfway there.

—PROVERB

MY GOAL IN writing this book was to recount my journey so that others called to the role of family stewardship or to the mission of a serving professional might have threads to pick up for the continuation of their journey—threads I picked up from those who went before me. I hope those who come after will write down their stories when the time comes, so that the journey will continue.

The human suffering inherent in the proverb "From shirtsleeves to shirtsleeves in three generations" can and must end, because its primary cause is the gloom of minds and spirits unaware. Together let us see what we can do to enlighten all human beings to the truths of our forebears on how to live a meaningful life and how to do so in community. Beginning with the virtues of love, joy, fusion, altruism, and beauty as harmony will surely help.

In these pages we've shared ideas from many arts and sciences that bear on the nature of a family and its journey to reach its fifth generation and to go on flourishing from there. Although the themes discussed in each chapter are far too many to list here, I will recap some that I believe are foundational. I hope these themes will offer threads for deeper journeys:

- Recognizing the shirtsleeves-to-shirtsleeves proverb as a never-ending principle and the risks to family it prophesies
- Adopting and practicing seventh-generation thinking
- Approaching every decision with a beginner's mind and with the willingness to be an apprentice
- Adopting *Homo ludens*—men and women curious and at play—as a model and encouraging all family members to be creators, discoverers, and seekers of the spirit

- Recognizing that the assets of a family are its individual members and that its financial capital is a useful tool to grow flourishing human beings
- Seeking, in everything a family does together, to enhance each individual member's journey to happiness in terms of the flourishing and the increased freedom and self-awareness that comes with it. This practice of enhancement is defined by the wisest of our philosophers and the wisdom-keepers through time in framing the question "How can we help you?" rather than the statement "First do this for us and we might do something to help you"
- Seeking to bring each individual family member's dream to life so that each can develop to his highest potential and competence and become more free and more self-aware and thereby thrive and flourish to the fullest
- Seeking to teach every family member to be a dynamic steward-conservator-stakeholder owner of every area of a family's financial capital; recognizing that it is ownership, not management, that is critical to the success of a family's enterprises
- Hastening slowly, so that evolution will be a friend and assist a family to move from its two founding members (with their two names always marking the family's evolving journey) to the clans of its third and fourth generations, then to a tribe, and continuing from there
- Recognizing that a family's multiple relationships create systems of extreme complexity, which must evolve to meet all the new challenges of a family's growth
- Recognizing that a successful family is a family of affinity, not a family of blood
- Recognizing and celebrating family "differentness" while not falling into the entropic trap of celebrating uniqueness
- Recognizing that all elements of a family's system must work to keep that system open to the new energy the family will need for its well-being
- Recognizing that great family leaders are those servant leaders, quiet leaders, leaders from behind, whose followers say, "We did it ourselves"
- Recognizing that the best form of governance for a family is a republic, a representative democracy, formed as a confederation of its clans, with three branches: legislative, executive, and elders/judicial
- Recognizing that a family's successful journey cannot be made without growing great elders and granting them the authority to mediate, to inter-

mediate, to tell the tribe's stories, and to lead its rituals

- Recognizing the developmental journey of human beings through the three primary stages of life and the nature of those stages
- Recognizing that every generation of a family as it rises to participate in family governance must make, as a generation, a horizontal social compact that reaffirms and readopts the family's system of joint decision making, that is, its system of governance
- Recognizing the difference between a gift of love and the increased freedom it offers and a transfer of wealth as a duty. The first enhances another life; the second brings the risk of victimization, loss of freedom, and depreciation
- Recognizing the critical role for a family's well-being filled by its personnes de confiance and the nature and journeys of such serving professionals
- Recognizing that a family in its journey to greatness will have multiple linked transitions to manage and that no single transaction will be meaningful to a successful result unless it integrates the changes naturally. Remembering and practicing the rule that form follows function can be useful in this process; form leading function violates a universal law
- Adopting the foundational virtues of love, joy, fusion, altruism, and beauty as harmony in all of its actions toward one another and toward all other sentient beings, as well as the earth itself, and to adopt as totems the copper beech tree and the tortoise as emblems of longevity

As each of us continues on our individual journey to Jerusalem, Canterbury, Santiago de Compostella, Rocamadour, Mecca, Lourdes, Benares, Pemako, and all the other sites to which humans have journeyed for their spiritual well-being, let's get up together, put on our round hats, take up our scallop shells, and all the other symbols that mark us as pilgrims. Let's pick up our staffs and walk a while together, telling each other our stories—the stories of how we seek to help grow all families and each of the individuals within them so that their journeys to greatness will be successful, bringing happiness that will help them thrive and flourish.

Namaste. And happy journeying.

APPENDIX

Recommended Reading

Abramson, Rudy. *Spanning the Century: The Life of W. Averell Harriman*, 1891–1986. New York: William Morrow, 1992.

Ackroyd, Peter. *The Life of Thomas More*. New York: Doubleday, 1998.

Akeret, Robert V. *Family Tales, Family Wisdom*. New York: William Morrow, 1991.

Aldrich, Nelson W., Jr. *Old Money*. New York: Allworth, 1996.

Allchin, Bridget, and Raymond Allchin. *The Rise of Civilization in India and Pakistan*. Cambridge: Cambridge University Press, 1996.

Aristotle. *Nicomachean Ethics*. Translated by J. A. K. Thomson. Revised by Hugh Tredennick. London: Penguin, 1953.

———. *The Politics*. Translated by T. A. Sinclair. Revised by T. J. Saunders. London: Penguin, 1992.

Armstrong, Diane G. *The Retirement Nightmare: How to Save Yourself From Your Heirs and Protectors*. Amherst, NY: Prometheus, 2002.

Armstrong, Karen. *Islam*. New York: Random House, 2002.

Arnett, Jeffrey Jensen. *Emerging Adulthood*. New York: Oxford University Press, 2004.

Aronoff, Craig E., and John L. Ward. *From Siblings to Cousins—Prospering in the Third Generation*. Marietta, GA: Family Enterprise Publishers, 2007.

Aurelius, Marcus. *Meditations*. Translated by Gregory Hays. New York: Modern Library, 2002.

Barzun, Jacques. *From Dawn to Decadence: 1500 to the Present*. New York: HarperCollins, 2000.

Beckett, Samuel. *Waiting for Godot*. New York: Grove, 1982.

Bee, Helen L. *The Journey of Adulthood*. New York: Simon & Schuster, 1996.

Bellah, Robert, R. Madsen, W. Sullivan, A. Swidler, and S. Tipton. *Habits of the Heart*. New York: HarperCollins, 1988.

Bennis, Warren G., and Burt Nanus. *Leaders: The Strategies for Taking Charge*. New York: Harper & Row, 1981.

Bergson, Henry. *The Two Sources of Morality and Religion*. South Bend, IN: University of Notre Dame Press, 1986.

Bernstein, Peter L. *Against the Gods: The Remarkable Story of Risk*. New York: John Wiley & Sons, Inc., 1998.

Blouin, Barbara, Katherine Gibson, and Margaret Kierstad. *The Legacy of Inherited Wealth*. Blacksburg, VA: Trio, 1995

Bly, Robert. *Iron John: A Book About Men*. Reading, MA: Addison-Wesley, 1990.

———. *Iron John: The Sibling Society*. Reading, MA: Addison-Wesley, 1996.

Boethius, Ancius. *The Consolation of Philosophy*. Translated by V. E. Watts. London: Penguin Books, 1969.

Boorstin, Daniel J. *The Creators*. New York: Vintage, 1993.

———. *The Discoverers*. New York: Vintage, 1985.

———. *The Seekers*. New York: Vintage, 1998.

Bork, David, Dennis T. Jaffe, Sam H. Lane, Leslie Dashew, and Quentin G. Heisler. *Working With Family Businesses*. San Francisco: Jossey-Bass, 1996.

Born, Max. *Einstein's Theory of Relativity*. New York: Dover, 1965.

Bowen, Murray. *Family Therapy in Clinical Practice*. Northvale, NJ: Jason Aronson, 1978.

Brands, H. W. *The First American: The Life and Times of Benjamin Franklin*. New York: Doubleday, 2000.

Braudel, Fernand. *A History of Civilizations*. Translated by Richard Mayne. New York: Penguin, 1993.

———. *The Mediterranean and the Mediterranean World in the Age of Philip II*. Translated by Sion Reynolds. 2 vols. Berkeley: University of California Press, 1995.

Briggs, John, and F. David Peat. *Seven Life Lessons of Chaos*. New York: HarperCollins, 2000.

Brinton, Crane. *The Anatomy of Revolution*. New York: Vintage, 1960.

Brizendine, Louann. *The Female Brain*. New York: Doubleday, 2006.

Bronfman, Joanie. *The Experience of Inherited Wealth: A Social-Psychological Perspective*. UMI Dissertation Service, 1987.

Brookhiser, Richard. *Gentleman Revolutionary: Gouverneur Morris, the Rake Who Wrote the Constitution*. New York: Free Press, 2003.

Brown, Bonnie M. *Unexpected Wealth*. Eugene, OR: Transition Dynamics, 2003.

Brunel, Jean L. P. *Integrated Wealth Management*. 2nd ed. London: Euromoney Institutional Investor, 2006.

Buber, Martin. *I and Thou*. Upper Saddle River, NJ: Prentice Hall, 1953. Reprint, New York: Charles Scribner & Sons, 1987.

Bunyan, John. *The Pilgrim's Progress*. New York: Signet Classic, 2002.

Burke, Edmund. *Reflections on the Revolution in France*. London: Penguin, 1986.

Burns, James MacGregor. *Leadership*. New York: Harper & Row, 1979.

Campbell, Joseph. *The Mythic Image*. New York: MJF Books, 1974.

Cannadine, David. *Mellon: An American Life*. New York: Alfred A. Knopf, 2006 .

Cantor, Norman F. *Civilization of the Middle Ages*. New York: HarperCollins, 1994.

Carlock, Randel S., and John L. Ward. *Strategic Planning for the Family Business*. Hampshire, England: Palgrave, 2001.

Cartledge, Paul. *Alexander the Great*. Woodstock, NY: Overlook, 2004.

Cavalli-Sforza, Luigi Luca. Genes, *Peoples and Languages*. Translated by Mark Sielstad. New York: Farrar, Straus and Giroux, 2000.

Cavalli-Sforza, Luigi Luca, and Francesco Cavalli-Sforza. *The Great Human Diasporas: The History of Diversity and Evolution*. Reading, MA: Addison-Wesley, 1995.

Ceram, C. W. *Gods, Graves and Scholars*. Translated by E. B. Barside and Sophie Wilkins. New York: Vintage, 1979.

Chaucer, Geoffrey. *The Canterbury Tales*. Oxford: Oxford University Press, 1998.

Chernow, Ron. *Alexander Hamilton*. New York: Penguin Press, 2004.

———. *The House of Morgan*. New York: Simon & Schuster, 1990.

———. *Titan: The Life of John S. Rockefeller, Sr.* New York: Random House, 1998.

Chevalier, Michael. *Society, Manners and Politics in the United States*.

Translated after the T. G. Bradford edition. Gloucester, MA: Peter Smith, 1967.

Childre, Doc, and Bruce Cryer. *From Chaos to Coherence*. Boston: Butterworth-Heinemann, 1999.

Chodren, Pema. *When Things Fall Apart*. Boston: Shambala, 1997.

Cicero. *On the Good Life*. Translated by Michael Grant. London: Penguin, 1971.

————. *On Government*. Translated by Michael Grant. London: Penguin, 1993.

Clark, Manning. *A Short History of Australia*. Victoria, Australia: Penguin, 1986.

Cohen, Joel E. *How Many People Can the Earth Support?* New York: W. W. Norton, 1996.

Coles, Robert. *Privileged Ones. Vol. 5 of Children of Crisis*. New York: Little, Brown, 1977.

Collier, Charles W. *Wealth in Families*. 2nd ed. Cambridge, MA: President and Fellows of Harvard College, 2006.

Collins, Jim. *Good to Great*. New York: HarperCollins, 2000.

Collins, Roger. *The Basques*. Cambridge, MA: Blackwell, 1990.

Comte-Sponville, Andre. *A Small Treatise on the Great Virtues*. New York: Metropolitan, 1996.

Confucius. *The Annalects*. Translated by D. C. Lao. Middlesex, England: Penguin, 1987.

Conniff, Richard. *The Natural History of the Rich*. New York: W. W. Norton, 2002.

Coontz, Stephanie. *The Way We Never Were*. New York: Basic, 1992.

————. *The Way We Really Are*. New York: Basic, 1997.

Cray, Ed. *General of the Army: George C. Marshall*. New York: Simon & Schuster, 1990.

Csikszentmihalyi, Mihaly. *Creativity. New York*: HarperCollins, 1996.

————. *Flow*. New York: Harper & Row, 1990.

Curtis, Gregory. *Creative Capital: Managing Private Wealth in a Complex World*. Lincoln, NE: Universe, 2004.

Dacher, Elliott S. *Integral Health*. Laguna Beach, CA: Basic Health Publications, 2006.

Damasio, Antonio R. *Descartes' Error: Emotion, Reason and the Human*

Brain. New York: HarperCollins, 2000.

Dangerfield, George. *Chancellor Robert R. Livingston of New York*. New York: Harcourt, Brace, 1960.

Dante, Alighieri. *The Divine Comedy: Hell, Purgatory, Paradise*. Translated by Dorothy L. Sayers. London: Penguin, 1949, 1955, 1962.

Danziger, Danny, and John Gillingham. *1215: The Year of Magna Carta*. New York: Touchstone, 2004.

Das, Lama Surya. *Awakening the Buddha Within*. New York: Bantam Doubleday, 1997.

Dawkins, Richard. *River Out of Eden*. New York: Basic, 1995.

Deutsch, David. *The Fabric of Reality*. London: Penguin, 1997.

Dhammapadha. *The Sayings of the Buddha*. Translated by Thomas Cleary. New York: Bantam, 1995.

Diamond, Jared. *Collapse*. New York: Viking, 2005.

———. *Guns, Germs and Steel*. New York: W. W. Norton, 1997.

Dickinson, G. Lowes. *A Modern Symposium*. New York: Barnes and Noble, 1962.

Dillehay, Thomas D. *The Settlement of the Americas: A New Prehistory*. New York: Basic, 2000.

Doud, Ernest A., Jr., and Lee Hausner. *Hats Off to You*. Los Angeles: Doud, Hausner Associates, 2000.

Drucker Foundation. *The Organization of the Future*. Edited by Frances Hesselbein, Marshall Goldsmith, and Richard Beckhurd. San Francisco: Jossey-Bass, 1997.

Earle, Timothy. *How Chiefs Come to Power*. Stanford, CA: Stanford University Press, 1997.

Ehrenreich, Barbara. *Blood Rites*. New York: Henry Holt, 1997.

———. *Fear of Falling*. New York: HarperCollins, 1990.

———. *Nickel and Dimed*. New York: Henry Holt, 2001.

Ehrlich, Paul R. *Human Natures*. Washington, DC: Island, 2000.

Eliade, Mircea. *The Sacred and the Profane*. Translated by Willard R. Trask. Orlando, FL: Harcourt Brace Jovanovich, 1987.

Elkind, Daniel. *The Hurried Child*. 3rd ed. Cambridge, MA: Perseus, 2001.

Elliott, J. H. *Richelieu and Olivares*. Cambridge: Cambridge University Press, 1989.

Ellis, Charles D. *Winning the Loser's Game*. Rev. ed. New York: McGraw-Hill, 1993.

Ellis, Joseph J. *American Sphinx: The Character of Thomas Jefferson*. New York: Vintage, 1998

———. *His Excellency, George Washington*. New York: Alfred A. Knopf, 2004.

Epictetus. *The Discourses*. Edited by Christopher Gill. Translated by Robin Hard. London: Everyman, J. M. Dent, 1995.

Erasmus. *The Education of a Christian Prince*. Translated by Neil M. Cheshire and Michael J. Heath. Cambridge: Cambridge University Press, 1997.

Erikson, Erik H. *Childhood and Society*. New York: W. W. Norton, 1993.

Erman, Adolf. *Life in Ancient Egypt*. Translated by H. M. Tiriard. New York: Dover, 1971.

Ernst, Carl W. *Sufism*. Boston: Shambhala, 1997

Ferguson, Niall. *The House of Rothschild: Money's Prophets, 1798–1848*. New York: Penguin, 1998.

———. *The World's Banker: The History of the House of Rothschild*. London: Weidenfeld and Nicolson, 1998.

Fischer, David Hackett. *Albion's Seed: Four British Folkways in America*. New York: Oxford University Press, 1989.

Flannery, Tim. *The Eternal Frontier: An Ecological History of North America and Its Peoples*. New York: Atlantic Monthly Press, 2001.

Flexner, James Thomas. *Washington, The Indispensable Man*. New York: Penguin, 1984.

Foner, Eric. *The Story of American Freedom*. New York: W. W. Norton, 1998.

Foster, Steven, and Meredith Little. *The Four Shields: The Initiatory Seasons of Human Nature*. Big Pine, CA: Lost Borders, 1998.

Frankl, Viktor E. *Man's Search for Meaning*. 3rd ed. New York: Simon & Schuster, 1984.

Freeman, Douglas Southall. *George Washington*. 4 vols. New York: Scribner's, 1948, 1951.

Friedman, Edwin H. *A Failure of Nerve: Leadership in the Age of the Quick Fix*. Manuscript. Edwin Friedman Estate Trust. Bethesda, MD, 1999.

Gabe, Grace and Jean Lipman-Blumen. *Step Wars*. New York: St. Martin's Press, 2004.

Gardner, Howard. *The Disciplined Mind*. New York: Simon & Schuster, 1999.

———. *Frames of Mind*. New York: Basic, 1983.

Gardner, Howard, Mihaly Csikszentmihalyi, and William Damon. *Good Work*. New York: Basic, 2001.

Gardner, John W. *Self-Renewal*. New York: Harper & Row, 1963.

Gebser, Jean. *The Ever-Present Origin*. Translated by Noel Barstad. Athens: Ohio University Press, 1983.

Gersick, Kelin E., John A. Davis, Marian McCollom Hampton, and Ivan Lansberg. *Generation to Generation*. Cambridge, MA: Harvard Business School Press, 1997.

Gibbon, Edward. *The Decline and Fall of the Roman Empire*. London: Penguin, 1988.

Gilligan, Carol. *In a Different Voice*. Cambridge, MA: Harvard University Press, 1982.

Gladwell, Malcolm. *The Tipping Point*. New York: Little, Brown, 2000.

Gleick, James. *Chaos*. New York: Penguin, 1987.

Godfrey, Joline. *Raising Financially Fit Kids*. Berkeley, CA: Ten Speed, 2003.

Goldberg, Steven. *The Inevitability of Patriarchy*. New York: William Morrow, 1973.

———. *Why Men Rule*. New York: Open Court, 1994.

Goldman, Eric F. *Rendezvous With Destiny: A History of Modern American Reform*. Chicago: Ivan R. Dee, 2001.

Goleman, Daniel. *Emotional Intelligence*. New York: Bantam, 1995.

Goodwin, Doris Kearns. *Team of Rivals: The Political Genius of Abraham Lincoln*. New York: Simon & Schuster, 2005.

Gould, Stephen Jay. *Wonderful Life*. New York: W. W. Norton, 1990.

Gracián, Baltazar. *The Art of Worldly Wisdom*. Translated by Christopher Maurer. New York: Doubleday, 1992

Grant, Ellsworth S. *Drop by Drop: The Loctite Story*. Hartford, CT: Loctite Corp. 1983.

Graves, Robert. *The Greek Myths*. London: Penguin, 1992.

Gray, Lisa. *Generational Wealth Management: A Guide for Fostering*

Global Family Wealth. London: Euromoney Books, 2007.

Greene, Brian. *The Elegant Universe*. New York: W. W. Norton, 1999.

Greenleaf, Robert K. *Servant Leadership*. Mahwah, NJ: Paulist, 1991.

Hahn, Herbert. *The Beginning of Wisdom: The History of the Pingry School, 1861–1961*. Pingry Trustees, 1961.

Halberstam, David. *The Reckoning*. New York: William Morrow, 1986.

Handy, Charles. *The Age of Paradox*. Boston: Harvard Business School Press, 1994.

Hardin, Garrett. *Living Within Limits*. New York: Oxford University Press, 1995.

Harris, Judith Rich. *The Nurture Assumption*. New York: Free Press, 1998.

Hart, Betty, and Todd R. Risley. *Meaningful Differences*. Baltimore: Paul H. Brooks, 1995.

Hatch, Elizabeth. *Initiation*. Gardenville, CA: Seed Center, 1965.

Hausner, Lee. *Children of Paradise*. 2nd ed. Irvine, CA: Plaza, 1998.

Hecht, Jennifer Michael. *Doubt: A History*. San Francisco: Harper San Francisco, 2003.

Hegel, Georg Wilhelm Friedrich. *The Philosophy of History*. Translated by J. Sigree. New York: Dover, 1956.

Heifetz, Ronald L. *Leadership Without Easy Answers*. Boston: Harvard University Press, Belknap, 1998.

Herman, Arthur. *The Idea of Decline in Western History*. New York: Simon & Schuster, 1994.

Herodotus. *The Histories*. Translated by Andre de Selincourt. London: Penguin Classics, 1996.

Herrnstein, Richard J., and Charles Murray. *The Bell Curve*. New York: Simon & Schuster, 1997.

Herz-Brown, Fredda. *Reweaving the Family Tapestry*. New York: W. W. Norton, 1991.

Hesiod. *Theogony, Works and Days*. Translated by M. L. West. Oxford: Oxford University Press, 1988.

Hillman, James. *The Force of Character*. New York: Random House, 1999.

———. *The Soul's Code*. New York: Random House, 1996.

Hoffman, Lynn. *Foundations of Family Therapy*. New York: Basic, 1981.

Hollis, James. *Creating a Life*. Toronto: Inner City Books, 2001

———. *Finding Meaning in the Second Half of Life*. Toronto: Inner City Books, 2005.

———. *The Middle Passage*. Toronto: Inner City Books, 1993

Holy Bible, New Revised Standard Edition. New York: Oxford University Press, 1989.

Homberger, Eric. *Mrs. Astor's New York*. New Haven, CT: Yale University Press, 2002.

Homer. *Iliad*. Translated by Robert Fagles. New York: Viking, 1990.

———. *Odyssey*. Translated by Robert Fagles. New York: Viking, 1996.

Hourani, Albert. *A History of the Arab Peoples*. Cambridge, MA: Harvard University Press, Belknap, 1991.

Hudson, Frederic M. *The Handbook of Coaching*. Unpublished manuscript. Santa Barbara, CA: Hudson Trust, 1998.

Hughes, James E., Jr. *Family Wealth: Keeping It in the Family*. New York: Bloomberg Press, 2004.

———. "A Study of the Conservative Reaction to the French Revolution of 1948: Through Its Leadership, the Union de la rue de Poitiers." Senior thesis, Princeton University, 1964.

Hughes, Robert. *The Fatal Shore*. London: Pan, 1988.

Hughes, Samuel Wheeler. *The Hughes Family History*. Privately published, 1948.

Huizinga, Johan. *Homo Ludens: A Study of the Play Element in Culture*. Boston: Beacon, 1955.

Huntington, Samuel. *The Clash of Civilizations*. New York: Simon & Schuster, 1996.

Isaacson, Walter. *Benjamin Franklin*. New York: Simon & Schuster, 2003.

Jacobs, Jane. *Cities and the Wealth of Nations*. New York: Random House, 1985.

———. *The Nature of Economies*. New York: Random House, 2000.

Jaffe, Dennis T. *Working With the Ones You Love*. Berkeley, CA: Concord, 1991.

Jaffe, Dennis T., and James A. Grubman. "Acquirer's and Inheritor's Dilemma." *Journal of Wealth Management* (2007) (forthcoming).

Jagannathan, Shakunthala. *Hinduism—An Introduction*. Bombay: Vakils, Feffer and Simons, 1984.

James, E. O. *The Worship of the Sky God*. London: Athlone, 1963.

James, William. *The Variations of Religious Experience*. New York: Vintage, 1990.

Jaworski, Joseph. *Synchronicity*. San Francisco: Barrett Koehler, 1996.

Jaynes, Julian. *The Origin of Consciousness in the Breakdown of the Bicameral Mind*. Boston: Houghton Mifflin, 1990.

Jennings, Francis. *The Creation of America: Through Revolution to Empire*. New York: Cambridge University Press, 2000.

Johnson, Allen W., and Timothy Earle. *The Evolution of Human Societies*. Stanford, CA: Stanford University Press, 1997.

Johnson, Paul. *A History of the Jews*. New York: HarperCollins, 1998.

Johnson, Robert A. *He: Understanding Masculine Psychology*. New York: HarperCollins, 1989.

———. *Inner Work*. New York: HarperCollins, 1989.

———. *Owning Your Own Shadow: Understanding the Dark Side of the Psyche*. New York: HarperCollins, 1991.

———. *She: Understanding Feminine Psychology*. New York: HarperCollins, 1989.

———. *Transformation*. New York: HarperCollins, 1991.

———. *We: Understanding the Psychology of Romantic Love*. New York: HarperCollins, 1983.

Johnson, Steven. *Emergence*. New York: Scribner, 2001.

Jones, Alan. *Soul's Journey*. San Francisco: HarperCollins, 1995.

Jones, Alan, and John O'Neil. *Seasons of Grace*. New York: John Wiley & Sons, 2003.

Jones, Gwyn. *A History of the Vikings*. Oxford: Oxford University Press, 1994.

Jung, C. G. *Memories, Dreams, Reflections*. Translated by Richard and Clara Winston, New York: Vintage, 1989.

———. *Psychology and the East*. Translated by R. F. C. Hull. Princeton, NJ: Princeton University Press, 1978.

———. *The Portable Jung*. Edited by Joseph Campbell. Translated by R. F. C. Hull. New York: Viking Press, 1987.

Kaplan, Justin. *When the Astors Owned New York*. New York: Viking, 2006.

Karoff, H. Peter, with Jane Maddox. *The World We Want. New Dimensions in Philanthropy and Social Change*. Lanham, MD: Altamira, 2006.

Kauffman, Stuart. *At Home in the Universe*. New York: Oxford University Press, 1995.

Kaye, Harvey J. *Thomas Paine*. New York: Farrar, Straus and Giroux, 2005.

Kaye, Kenneth. *Family Rules*. New York: Walker, 1981.

Keegan, John. *A History of Warfare*. New York: Vintage, 1984.

Keen, Sam. *Fire in the Belly: On Being a Man*. New York: Bantam, 1982.

Ketcham, Ralph. *James Madison*. Charlottesville, VA: University Press of Virginia, 1995.

Kindlon, Dan, and Michael Thompson. *Raising Cain*. New York: Ballantine, 1999.

The Koran. Translated by Marmaduke Pickthall. New York: Everyman's Library, Knopf, 1992.

Kramer, Samuel Noah. *The Sumerians*. Chicago: University of Chicago Press, 1971.

Krauze, Enrique. *Mexico, Biography of Power*. Translated by Hank Heifetz. New York: HarperCollins, 1997.

Krishnamurti, J. *To Be Human*. Boston: Shambhala, 2000.

Krishnamurti, J., and Dr. David Bohn. *The Ending of Time*. San Francisco: Harper & Row, 1985.

Kroeber, A. L. *Configurations of Culture Growth*. 3rd ed. Berkeley: University of California Press, 1969.

Kuhn, Thomas. *The Structure of Scientific Revolutions*. Chicago: University of Chicago Press, 1970.

Lamb, David. *The Africans*. New York: Random House, 1982.

Lansberg, Ivan. *Succeeding Generations*. Boston: Harvard Business School Press, 1999.

Lao Tzu. *Tao-Teh Ching*. Translated by John C. W. Wu. Boston: Shambhala, 2003.

Lasch, Christopher. *Haven in a Heartless World*. New York: Basic, 1995.

———. *The True and Only Heaven: Progress and Its Critics*. New York, W. W. Norton, 1991.

Leakey, Richard E. *Origins*. New York: E. P. Dutton, 1977.

Lefebvre, Georges. *The Coming of the French Revolution*. New York: Vintage, 1961.

Lehman, Robert. "The Heart of Philanthropy." Speech delivered at the Council of Foundations 12th Family Foundations Conference, February 23, 1998.

Le Van, Gerald. *Lawyer's Lives: Out of Control*. Alexander, NC: WorldComm, 1993.

Levine, Madeline. *The Price of Privilege*. New York: HarperCollins, 2006.

Levine, Mel. *A Mind at a Time*. New York: Simon & Schuster, 2002.

Levine, Peter A. *Waking the Tiger: Healing Trauma*. Berkeley, CA: North Atlantic, 1997.

Levinson, Daniel. *The Seasons of a Man's Life*. New York: Ballantine, 1997.

———. *The Seasons of a Woman's Life*. New York: Ballantine, 1997.

Lilla, Mark, and G. B. Vico. *The Making of an Anti-Modern*. Cambridge, MA: Harvard University Press, 1994.

Lillard, Angeline Stoll. *Montessori: The Scene Behind the Genius*. New York: Oxford University Press, 2005.

Linowitz, Sol M., with Martin Mayer. *The Betrayed Profession: Lawyering at the End of the Twentieth Century*. New York: Scribner, 1994.

Locke, John. *Two Treatises of Government*. Cambridge: Cambridge University Press, 1994.

Machiavelli, Niccolò. *The Prince*. Translated by George Bull. London: Penguin, 2003.

MacIntyre, Alasdair. *After Virtue: A Study in Moral Theory*. South Bend, IN: University of Notre Dame Press, 1984.

Madison, James, Alexander Hamilton, and John Jay. *The Federalist Papers*. New York: Penguin, 1987.

Mahdi, Louise Carus, Nancy Geyer Christopher, and Michael Meade. *Crossroads: The Quest for Contemporary Rites of Passage*. Chicago: Open Court, 1996.

Malinowski, Bronislow. *Magic, Science and Religion*. New York: Free Press, 1948.

Mallory, J. P. *In Search of the Indo-Europeans*. London: Thames and Hudson, 1989.

Mao, Tse-Tung. *Quotations From Chairman Mao Tse-Tung*. China Books and Periodicals, 1990.

Martell, Judy. *The Dilemmas of Family Wealth*. New York: Bloomberg

Press, 2006.

Martindale, Colin. *The Clockwork Muse: The Predictability of Artistic Change*. New York: HarperCollins, 1980.

Marx, Karl. *Das Capital*. Washington, DC: Gateway Editions, 1999.

Marx, Karl, and Friedrich Engels. *The Communist Manifesto*. New York: Signet Classics, 1998.

Maslow, Abraham H. *Toward a Psychology of Being*. New York: Van Nostrand Reinhold, 1982.

Mason, Marilyn. *Seven Mountains*. New York: Penguin, 1998.

Mazlish, Bruce. *The Uncertain Sciences*. New Haven, CT: Yale University Press, 1998.

McCarthy, Bernice. *About Learning*. Wauconda, IL: About Learning, 2000.

McClelland, David C. *The Achieving Society*. New York: D. Von Nostrand, 1961.

McCullough, David. *John Adams*. New York: Simon & Schuster, 2001.

McDermott, Robert A., ed. *The Essential Aurobindo: Writings of Sri Aurobindo*. Great Barrington, MA: Lindisfarne Books, 2001.

———. *The Essential Steiner: Basic Writings of Rudolph Steiner*. San Francisco: HarperCollins, 1984.

McDougal, Dennis. *Privileged Son: Otis Chandler and the Fall of the L.A. Times Dynasty*. Cambridge, MA: Perseus, 2001.

McEvilley, Thomas. *The Shape of Ancient Thought*. New York: Allworth, 2002.

McPhee, John. *Annals of the Former World*. New York: Farrar, Straus and Giroux, 2000.

McTaggart, Lynn. *The Field*. New York: HarperCollins, 2002.

Meade, Michael. *Men and the Water of Life*. San Francisco: HarperCollins, 1993.

Merton, Thomas. *The Way of Chuing Tzu*. Boston: Shambhala, 2004.

———. *Zen and the Birds of Appetite*. Boston: Shambhala, 2004.

Mill, John Stuart. *Utilitarianism, On Liberty, Essay on Bentham*. New York: Penguin, 1974.

Mogel, Wendy. *The Blessings of a Skinned Knee*. New York: Penguin, 2001.

Montaigne, Michel de. *The Complete Essays*. Translated by M. A. Screech.

New York: Penguin, 2003.

Montemerlo, Daniela, and John L. Ward. *The Family Constitution*. Marietta, GA: Family Enterprise, 2005.

Montesquieu, Charles de Secondat, Baron de. *The Spirit of the Laws*. Translated and edited by Anne M. Cohler, Basia Carolyn Miller, and Harold Samuel Stone. Cambridge: Cambridge University Press, 1994.

Moore, Christopher W. *The Mediation Process*. 2nd ed. San Francisco: Jossey-Bass, 1996.

Moore, Robert, and Douglas Gillette. *King, Warrior, Magician, Lover*. New York: HarperCollins, 1991.

More, Thomas. *Utopia*. Translated by Paul Turner. London: Penguin, 1995.

Morris, Simon Conway. *The Crucible of Creation*. Oxford: Oxford University Press, 1999.

Morton, W. Scott. *China, Its History and Culture*. New York: Lippincott and Crowell, 1980.

Moscati, Sabatino. *Ancient Sumerian Civilizations*. New York: G. P. Putnam's Sons, 1960.

———, ed. *The Phoenicians*. New York: Rizzoli, 1999.

Mosley, Leonard. *Blood Relations: The Rise and Fall of the du Ponts of Delaware*. New York: Atheneum, 1980.

Murray, Charles. *Human Accomplishments*. New York: HarperCollins, 2003.

Nanus, Burt. *The Leader's Edge*. Chicago: Contemporary Books, 1989.

———. *Visionary Leadership*. San Francisco: Jossey-Bass, 1992.

Nasaw, David. *Andrew Carnegie*. New York: Penguin, 2006.

Needham, Joseph. *The Shorter Science and Civilization in China*. Abridgement by Colin A. Ronan. Vols. 1 and 4. Cambridge: Cambridge University Press, 1997.

Neubauer, Fred, and Alden G. Lank. *The Family Business*. New York: Routledge, 1998.

Neumann, Erich. *Amor and Psyche: The Psychic Development of the Feminine*. Translated by Ralph Manheim. Princeton: Princeton University Press, 1973.

The New Encyclopedia Britannica. 15th ed. 29 vols. Chicago: Encyclopedia Britannica, 2002.

Nichols, Johanna. *Linguistic Diversity in Space and Time*. Chicago: University of Chicago Press, 1999.

Nisbett, Richard E. *The Geography of Thought: How Asians and Westerners Think Differently...and Why*. New York: Simon & Schuster, 2003.

O'Connell, Mark. *The Good Father*. New York: Scribner, 2005.

O'Hara, William T. *Centuries of Success: Lessons From the World's Most Enduring Family Businesses*. Avon, MA: Adams Media, 2003.

O'Neil, John R. *Leadership Aikido*. San Francisco: Crown-Harmony, 1997.

———. *The Paradox of Success*. 2nd ed. New York: McGraw-Hill, 2000.

O'Neill, Jesse H. *The Golden Ghetto*. Center City, MN: Hazelden, 1997.

O'Toole, James. *Leading Change*. San Francisco: Jossey-Bass, 1995.

The Oxford English Dictionary. 2nd ed. 22 vols. Oxford: Clarendon, 1999.

Palmer, Helen. *The Enneagram*. San Francisco: HarperCollins, 1991

Palmer, Parker J. *The Courage to Teach*. San Francisco: Jossey-Bass, 1998.

Pascale, Richard T., Mark Milleman, and Linda Gioja. *Surfing the Edge of Chaos*. New York: Crown, 2000.

Peck, M. Scott. *The Different Drum: Community Making and Peace*. New York: Simon & Schuster, 1987.

———. *People of the Lie: The Hope for Healing Human Evil*. New York: Simon & Schuster, 1983.

———. *The Road Less Traveled*. New York: Simon & Schuster, 1978.

Pellew, George. *John Jay*. New York: Chelsea House, 1980.

Peterson, Peter G. *Gray Dawn*. New York: Random House, 1999.

Pert, Candace. *Molecules of Emotion*. New York: Simon & Schuster, 1999.

Piaget, Jean, and Barbel Imhelder. *The Psychology of the Child*. Translated by Helen Weaver. New York: Basic, 2000.

Pine, B. Joseph, III, and James H. Gilmore. *The Experience Economy*. Boston: Harvard Business School Press, 1999.

Pipher, Mary. *Reviving Ophelia: Saving the Selves of Adolescent Girls*. New York: Ballantine, 1995.

Piver, Susan. *The Hard Questions: 100 Essential Questions to Ask Before I Say "I Do"*. San Francisco: Tarcher, 2000.

Plato. *The Republic*. Translated by Desmond Lee. London: Penguin, 1977.

————. *Timaeus and Critias*. Translated by Desmond Lee. London: Penguin, 1977.

Polybius. *The Rise of the Roman Empire*. Translated by Ian Scott-Kilvert. London: Penguin, 1979.

Pomeroy, Sarah B., Stanley M. Burstein, Walter Donlan, and Jennifer Tolbert Roberts. *Ancient Greece: A Political, Social, and Cultural History*. New York: Oxford University Press, 1999.

Pratt, Fletcher. *The Battles That Changed History*. Garden City, NY: Dover, 2000.

Pretat, Jane R. *Coming to Age: The Croning Years and Late-Life Transformation*. Toronto: Inner City, 1994

Prigogine, Ilya. *Order Out of Chaos: Man's New Dialogue With Nature*. New York: Bantam, 1984.

Puls, Mark. *Samuel Adams*. New York: Palgrave, 2006.

Putnam, Robert D. *Bowling Alone*. New York: Simon & Schuster, 2002.

Rawls, John. *Justice as Fairness: A Restatement*. Cambridge, MA: President and Fellows of Harvard College, 2001.

Real, Terrence. *I Don't Want to Talk About It: Overcoming the Secret Legacy of Male Depression*. New York: Fireside, 1997.

Rees, Alwyn, and Brinley Rees. *Celtic Heritage*. New York: Thames and Hudson, 1998.

Reischauer, Edwin O. *The Japanese*. Cambridge, MA: Harvard University Press, 1981.

Remini, Robert V. *Andrew Jackson*. 3 vols. Baltimore: Johns Hopkins University Press, 1988.

Renfrew, Colin, and Paul Bahn. *Archaeology*. 3rd ed. London: Thames and Hudson, 2000.

Reps, Paul, and Nyogen Senaski. *Zen Flesh, Zen Bones*. Boston, MA: Tuttle, 2003.

Ricard, Mathieu. *Happiness*. Translated by Jesse Browner. New York: Little, Brown, 2006.

Ridly, Mark. *Evolution, Third Edition*. Malden, MA: Blackwell Science, 2004.

Ridly, Matt. *Genome*. New York: HarperCollins, 1999.

The Rig Veda. London: Penguin, 1962.

Riso, Don Richard, and Russ Hudson. *Discovering Your Personality Type*.

New York: Houghton Mifflin, 2003.

Robbins, Alexandra, and Abby Wilner. *Quarterlife Crisis*. New York: Tarcher/Putnam, 2001.

Roszak, Theodore. *America the Wise*. New York: Houghton Mifflin, 1998.

Rotberg, Robert I. *The Founder: Cecil Rhodes and the Pursuit of Power*. New York: Oxford University Press, 1988.

Rudgley, Richard. *The Lost Civilizations of the Stone Age*. New York: Free Press, 1999.

Rue, Loyal. *By the Grace of Guile: The Role of Deception in Natural History and Human Affairs*. New York: Oxford University Press, 1994.

Russell, Bertrand. *A History of Western Philosophy*. New York: Simon & Schuster, 1972.

Ryder, Daniel W. *The Merrill Story*. San Francisco: Merrill Company, 1958.

Samuelson, Paul A., and William D. Nordhaus. *Economics*. 16th ed. New York: Irwin/McGraw-Hill, 1998.

Sandras, N. K. *Prehistoric Art in Europe*. New Haven, CT: Yale University Press, 1985.

Sandburg, Carl. *Abraham Lincoln: The Prairie Years*. 2 vols. New York: Harcourt, Brace, 1926.

———. *Abraham Lincoln: The War Years*. 4 vols. New York: Harcourt, Brace, 1939.

Santayana, George. *The Life of Reason (1905–1906)*. Vol. 1, *Reason in Common Sense*. Amherst, NY: Prometheus, 1998.

Schein, Edgar H. *Organizational Culture and Leadership*. 2nd ed. San Francisco: Jossey-Bass, 1997.

Schon, Donald A. *The Reflective Practitioner*. New York: Basic, 1983.

Schumacher, E. F. *Small Is Beautiful*. New York: Harper & Row, 1989.

Schumpeter, Joseph A. *Capitalism, Socialism, and Democracy*. New York: Harper Torchbooks, 1984.

Schwartz, Roger M. *The Skilled Facilitator*. San Francisco: Jossey-Bass, 1989.

Scurr, Ruth. *Fatal Purity: Robespierre and the French Revolution*. New York: Henry Holt, 2006.

Seligman, Martin E. P., *The Optimistic Child*. New York: HarperCollins, 1996.

Sen, Amartya. *Development as Freedom*. New York: Anchor, 2000.

———. *Identity and Violence: The Illusion of Destiny*. New York: W. W. Norton, 2006.

Senge, Peter M. *The Fifth Discipline*. New York: Doubleday, 1994.

Sennett, Richard. *The Corrosion of Character*. New York: W. W. Norton, 1998.

Sennett, Richard, and Jonathan Cobb. *The Hidden Injuries of Class*. New York: W. W. Norton, 1972.

Sheehy, Gail. *New Passages*. New York: Random House, 1995.

———. *Passages*. New York: E. P. Dutton, 1976.

Shepard, Paul, and Florence R. Shepard. *Coming Home to the Pleistocene*. Washington, DC: Island, 1998.

Short, Philip. *Mao, a Life*. New York: Henry Holt, 2000.

Silver, Lee M. *Challenging Nature: The Challenge of Science and Spirituality at the New Frontiers of Life*. New York: HarperCollins, 2006.

———. *Remaking Eden*. New York: Avon, 1997.

Simonton, Dean Keith. *Origins of Genius*. New York: Oxford University Press, 1996.

Smith, Adam. *The Wealth of Nations*. New York: Random House, 2000.

Smith, Huston. *The World's Religions*. New York: HarperCollins, 1991.

Smith, Jean Edward. *John Marshall*. New York: Henry Holt, 1996.

Snow, C. P. *The Two Cultures and the Scientific Revolution*. New York: Cambridge University Press, 1959 (based on his 1959 Rede lecture).

Sogyal, Rinpoche. *The Tibetan Book of Living and Dying*. San Francisco: HarperCollins, 1992.

Sonnenfeld, Jeffrey. *The Hero's Farewell: What Happens When CEOs Retire*. New York: Oxford University Press, 1991.

Sorokin, Pitirim. *Social and Cultural Dynamics*. New Brunswick, NJ: Transaction, 1991.

Sowell, Thomas. *Conquests and Culture*. New York: Basic, 1998.

———. *Migrations and Cultures*. New York: Basic, 1996.

———. *Race and Culture*. New York: Basic, 1994.

Spengler, Oswald. *The Decline of the West*. Abridged ed. by Helmut Werner. Translated by Charles Francis Atkinson. New York: Oxford University Press, 1991.

Spinoza, Baruch. *The Ethics of Spinoza*. New York: Carol Publishing

Group, 1991.

Staub, Robert E., II, *The Acts of Courage*. Greensboro, NC: Staub Leadership, 2002.

St. Aubin, Ed de, Dan P. McAdams, and Tae-Chang Kim, *The Generative Society*. Washington, DC: American Psychological Association, 2004.

Stevens, Susan Kenny. *Nonprofit Life Cycles*. Long Lake, MN: Stagewise Enterprises, 2001.

Stewart, Thomas A. *Intellectual Capital*. New York: Doubleday, 1999.

Strauss, William, and Neil Howe. *The Fourth Turning*. New York: Doubleday, 1997.

Sulloway, Frank J. *Born to Rebel: Birth Order, Family Dynamics, and Creative Lives*. New York: Pantheon Books, 1996.

Summer, William Graham. *Robert Morris, The Financier and the Finances of the American Revolution*. 2 vols. Washington, DC: Beard, 2000.

Sun Tzu. *The Art of War*. Translated by Thomas Cleary. Boston: Shambhala, 1998.

———. *The Lost Art of War*. Translated by Thomas Cleary. Boston: HarperCollins, 1996.

Surowiecki, James. *The Wisdom of Crows*. New York: Doubleday, 2004.

Suzuki, Shunryu, *Zen Mind, Beginner's Mind*. Boston: Weatherhill, 2005.

Sykes, Bryan. *The Seven Daughters of Eve: The Science That Reveals Our Genetic Ancestry*. New York: W. W. Norton, 2001.

Sykes, Charles J. *A Nation of Victims: The Decay of American Character*. New York: St. Martin's Griffin, 1993.

Talbot, Michael. *The Holographic Universe*. New York: HarperCollins, 1992.

Taleb, Nassim Nicholas. *Fooled by Randomness: The Hidden Role of Chance in the Markets and in Life*. New York: Texere, 2002.

Tarnas, Richard. *The Passion of the Western Mind*. New York: Ballantine, 1991.

Thucydides. *The History of the Peloponnesian War*. Translated by Rex Warner. London: Penguin, 1972.

Tift, Susan E., and Alex S. Jones. *The Trust: The Private and Powerful Family Behind the New York Times*. New York: Little, Brown, 1999.

Tocqueville, Alexis de. *Democracy in America*. Translated by George Lawrence. New York: Harper Perennial, 1988.

———. *The Old Regime and the French Revolution*. Translated by Stuart Gilbert. New York: Anchor, 1955.

Townsend, John. *What Women Want—What Men Want*. New York: Oxford University Press, 1999.

Toynbee, Arnold. *A Study of History*. 10 vols. Oxford: Oxford University Press, 1948.

Vaill, Peter B. *Learning as a Way of Being*. San Francisco: Jossey-Boss, 1996.

Vanderbilt, Arthur T., II. *Fortune's Children: The Fall of the House of Vanderbilt*. New York: William Morrow, 1989.

Van Gennep, Arnold. *The Rites of Passage*. Translated by Monica B. Vizedem and Gabrielle L. Caffee. Chicago: University of Chicago Press, 1960.

Vaughan, Frances. *Shadows of the Sacred*. Lincoln, NE: Universe, 2005.

Veenswijk, Virginia Kays. *Coudert Brothers, a Legacy at Law: The History of America's First International Law Firm*, 1853–1953. New York: Penguin, 1994.

Vidal, Gore. *Creation*. New York: Ballantine, 1990.

Voltaire [François-Marie Arouet]. *Candide*. Translated by John Butt. London: Penguin, 1987.

Waldrep, M. Mitchell. *Complexity: The Emerging Science at the Edge of Order and Chaos*. New York: Simon & Schuster, 1992.

Walker, Barbara G. *The Crone: Women of Age, Wisdom and Power*. San Francisco: HarperCollins, 1985.

Ward, John L. *Creating Effective Boards for Private Enterprises*. San Francisco: Jossey-Bass, 1991.

Weatherford, Jack. *Genghis Khan*. New York: Crown, 2004.

Weaver, Muriel Porter. *The Aztecs, Maya, and Their Predecessors: Archaeology of Meso-America*. 3rd ed. San Diego: Academic, 1993.

Weber, Max. *From Max Weber: Essays in Sociology*. Translated by H. H. Gerth and C. Wright Mills. New York: Oxford University Press, 1946.

———. *Protestant Ethic and the Spirit of Capitalism*. Translated by Talcott Parsons. London: Routledge, 1992.

Webster's Third New International Dictionary. Springfield, Mass: G & C Merriam, 1965.

Weiner, Jonathan. *The Beak of the Finch*. New York: Alfred A. Knopf, 1994.

Wells, Spencer. *The Journey of Man: A Genetic Odyssey*. Princeton, NJ: Princeton University Press, 2002.

White, Peter. *Ecology of Being*. Gambier, OH: All in All, 2006.

Wilbur, Ken. *Integral Spirituality*. Boston: Shambhala, 2006.

———. *Sex, Ecology, Spirituality*. Boston: Shambhala, 1995.

Williams, Roy, and Victor Preisser. *Preparing Heirs*. San Francisco: Robert D. Reed, 2003.

Willis, Thayer Cheatham. *Navigating the Dark Side of Wealth*. Portland, OR: New Concord, 2003.

Wilson, E. O. *Consilience, the Unity of Knowledge*. New York: Alfred A Knopf, 1998.

———. *The Creation*. New York: Norton, 2006.

Wolpert, Stanley. *A New History of India*. New York: Oxford University Press, 1977.

Wright, Robert. *The Moral Animal*. New York: Random House, 1994.

Yogananda, Paramahansa. *Autobiography of a Yogi*. Los Angeles: Self-Realization Fellowship, 1995.

Zakaria, Fareed. *The Future of Freedom*. New York: W. W. Norton, 2003.

Zander, Alvin. *Making Boards Effective*. San Francisco: Jossey-Boss, 1993.

Zimmer, Heinrich. *Myths and Symbols in Indian Art and Civilization*. Princeton, NJ: Princeton University Press, 1972.

INDEX

About Bloomberg

BLOOMBERG L.P., founded in 1981, is a global information services, news, and media company. Headquartered in New York, the company has sales and news operations worldwide.

Bloomberg, serving customers on six continents, holds a unique position within the financial services industry by providing an unparalleled range of features in a single package known as the BLOOMBERG PROFESSIONAL® service. By addressing the demand for investment performance and efficiency through an exceptional combination of information, analytic, electronic trading, and Straight Through Processing tools, Bloomberg has built a worldwide customer base of corporations, issuers, financial intermediaries, and institutional investors.

BLOOMBERG NEWS®, founded in 1990, provides stories and columns on business, general news, politics, and sports to leading newspapers and magazines throughout the world. BLOOMBERG TELEVISION®, a 24-hour business and financial news network, is produced and distributed globally in seven languages. BLOOMBERG RADIO℠ is an international radio network anchored by flagship station BLOOMBERG® 1130 (WBBR-AM) in New York.

In addition to the BLOOMBERG PRESS® line of books, Bloomberg publishes *BLOOMBERG MARKETS®* magazine. To learn more about Bloomberg, call a sales representative at:

London:	+44-20-7330-7500
New York:	+1-212-318-2000
Tokyo:	+81-3-3201-8900

FOR IN-DEPTH MARKET INFORMATION AND NEWS, visit the Bloomberg Web site at www.bloomberg.com, which draws from the news and power of the BLOOMBERG PROFESSIONAL® service and Bloomberg's host of media products to provide high-quality news and information in multiple languages on stocks, bonds, currencies, and commodities.

About the Author

JAMES E. "JAY" HUGHES JR., Esq., a sixth-generation counselor-at-law, was the founder of Hughes and Whitaker, a law partnership in New York, where he focused on the representation of private clients throughout the world. Now retired from active practice, he frequently facilitates multi-generational family meetings, with an emphasis on governance issues. He serves on the boards of various private trust companies and is an adviser to numerous investment institutions. Before starting his own practice, Mr. Hughes was a partner of the law firms of Coudert Brothers LLP and Jones, Day, Reavis & Pogue (now Jones Day), both in New York.

Mr. Hughes's articles on family governance and wealth preservation appear in professional journals, and his series of reflections on related issues are featured on his Web site. He is the author of *Family Wealth: Keeping It in the Family*, published by Bloomberg Press, and a member of the editorial boards of various professional journals. A widely recognized speaker, Mr. Hughes is frequently called on to address international and domestic symposia on helping families to avoid the fate of the shirtsleeves-to-shirtsleeves proverb and to instead flourish through the growth of their human, intellectual, and financial capital.

Mr. Hughes is an emeritus member of the Board of the Philanthropic Initiative, a counselor to the Family Office Exchange, an emeritus faculty member of the Institute for Private Investors, a retired member of the Board of the Albert and Mary Lasker Foundation, and former adviser to New Ventures in Philanthropy. He is also a member of the Friends of the Institute of Noetic Sciences, a member of the Roundtable of the Hastings Institute, a member of the board of the Spiritual Paths Foundation, and a member of the board of the Rocky Mountain Institute. Educated at the Far Brook School, Mr. Hughes is a graduate of the Pingry School, Princeton University, and the Columbia School of Law.

Readers may contact the author and learn more about his ideas at www.jamesehughes.com.